60 DAYS

A Spiritual Guide to the High Holidays

BY

SIMON JACOBSON

KIYUM PRESS

NEW YORK

FIRST EDITION

Designed by Batsheva Buchman
Edited by Uriela Sagiv

ISBN 1-886587-24-8
Library of Congress Control Number: 2003111191
Printed in the United States

KiYUM PRESS
An Imprint of VHH
788 Eastern Parkway, Suite 303
Brooklyn, NY 11213
(800) 3-MEANING

Publication of this book
was made possible through the generosity
of

GEORGE & PAMELA ROHR
שיחיו

and

is lovingly dedicated
to the memory
of his grandparents

YEHOSHUA ELIYAHU & PEREL ROHR

ר׳ יהושע אליהו בן ר׳ מנחם נחום ז״ל
פערל בת ר׳ מאיר הלוי לבית געלברד ע״ה

New York City
2003-5763

CONTENTS

Preface

THE PARADOX

The High Holiday season has always been a paradox for me.

On the one hand, these are awesome days, full of tradition and history. Days, we are told, that determine the destiny of our lives. Days when our prayers can reach the highest places. Days when our shofar sounding and heartfelt prayers pierce the very heavens. Even in our assimilated and secular society today, Yom Kippur evokes a sense of awe and sanctity.

On the other hand, how many of us experience the High Holiday season as awesome, holy or even memorable? How many of us are *truly* transformed on Rosh Hashana and Yom Kippur? Not just inspired for a moment, but actually transformed forever?

Speaking with thousands of people from vastly different backgrounds throughout my travels, I hear the same painful story—the High Holidays are a serious let down.

I cannot tell you how many men and women have shared with me the frustrated distance and irrelevance they experience on Rosh Hashana and Yom Kippur. People *want* to find some connection and meaning in the holidays and go to synagogue in desperate search for some insight, some inspiration—anything that will touch them. Instead, they are subjected to the same hollow sermons, long and unintelligible prayer services, and superficial social interactions—anything but warm, inviting spirituality.

If religion has in fact proven to be a huge disappointment in this generation, then it is in the High Holiday season that this disappointment is most keenly felt.

Even those who *have* had positive experiences relate that they cannot keep up with the pace of all the prayers or understand their significance, do not understand the meaning of many of the traditions, and above all, they do not find personal and spiritual relevance in the services and holiday customs.

Even traditional Jews who are fluent in the Hebrew prayers, who are well versed in all the holiday laws and customs and the meaning behind them, who have been praying for years and celebrating all the finer aspects of the holidays—even they are often challenged to experience each holiday anew, with freshness and vitality. We are taught that the Torah's commandments must be fulfilled "every day as a new experience." Mechanical Judaism is considered an insult to G-d.

EXCAVATING TREASURES
While these are legitimate complaints, truth be told, there are definitely individuals who immerse in the holiday experience and emerge as new people. These individuals know how to delve into the depths of the holidays and excavate its treasures. And there are others, who even though they relate to the High Holidays on a simplistic level, nevertheless demonstrate a beauty of character by their sheer persistence and dedication to the holiday traditions. As our Sages tell us, even if you don't always *feel* the benefit of your actions, just by making the effort, you open up doors in heaven.

Yet, these people are, unfortunately, the minority. The majority does not find much relevance in the holiday season. Thus, we see the inevitable drop in synagogue attendance and the ensuing alienation from one's roots. As one young woman once told me, "I find it more meaningful to stay home on Yom Kippur reading my favorite Zen poems."

My heart broke when I heard her words, because I realized what she was saying: when you don't find spiritual and psychological relevance in your own "backyard" of Jewish traditions, you will ultimately turn elsewhere for inspiration.

But the real tragedy is even greater, because the truth is that Judaism *does* offer us something we cannot find anyplace else—the most sophisticated, relevant blueprint for our lives. But many of us are simply unaware of it.

This is the greatest tragedy of all—that we have a treasure and we don't know it. We have wings to fly and we don't know how to use them.

Equally troubling is the complacency of many observant and traditional Jews, who don't find personal significance in the prayers and holiday traditions, except for the nostalgic component, and their commitment is often mechanical, driven primarily out of obligation, guilt or habit.

This is what compelled me to create this book for all the thousands of people looking to rejuvenate their High Holiday experience and discover transformative resonance in this most profound and sophisticated of psycho-spiritual systems called the Jewish High Holiday season.

This book, *60 Days*, is meant to provide a hands-on, companion guide to the powerful two Hebrew months of *Elul* and *Tishrei*. This is not a new prayer book, not a new *Siddur* or *Machzor*, but a day-by-day, item-by-item workbook that guides the reader along the most fascinating and beautiful journey of the High Holiday season.

The end goal is to revitalize and invigorate the holiday experience, both to those new to the experience and those who have become all-too familiar with it, for the non-affiliated and the affiliated, the initiated and the uninitiated.

For me, this book is a personal journey as well—a journey that has opened up my eyes to the endless wealth of knowledge and experience lying within the holiday season. As I researched the material explored here, I was astounded by the eloquent beauty and the complex infrastructure of literally every detail of the prayers, commandments, laws and customs. I have studied Judaism all my life, yet I have never appreciated the power of these months as I do today, and hopefully, will appreciate even more tomorrow.

For this I thank all my students and readers—you have taught me how to truly appreciate our rich tradition with all its spiritual power. I am forever grateful. In return I hope that I can convey some of what I have learned.

It is, therefore, with great satisfaction that I offer you this book as a guide that can perhaps open your eyes as well to a treasure that has been given to us all—a treasure that empowers us with the tools and the abilities to transform our lives for the better, forever.

(Rabbi) Simon Jacobson
New York
July 2003

Introduction
The ENERGY of TIME

The Hebrew calendar is like no calendar that exists in the world today.
It is not a highway that progresses from past to future in linear fashion as
does the Western calendar familiar to all. It is a spiral staircase that
winds around, cycling the events of history, drawing their energy ever
upwards.

As we travel through each year, we revisit the energy of ancient days—
energy of time and beyond time—energy of freedom, of destruction, of
mourning, of forgiveness, of empowerment, of joy. We use that energy to
uplift events from our lives that inevitably parallel the lives of those
that came before us.

In the spring—in the month of *Nissan*, the month of Passover—we gain
access to the energy that freed our ancestors from bondage in Egypt in
order to set ourselves free from whatever it is that enslaves us. In the
summer—in the month of *Av*, the month of destruction and mourning—

we come to terms with the ruins of broken homes, broken marriages, broken dreams, and learn to draw comfort and consolation from others and from G-d. In the winter—in the month of *Kislev*, the month of Chanukah—we use the light of victory and holiness to illuminate the darkness in our lives.

In this workbook we are concerned with two of the most powerful months of the Hebrew calendar—the month of *Elul* and the month of *Tishrei*. *Elul* precedes the High Holidays and is a month of preparation for them. *Tishrei*, which is the holiest month of the entire year, contains the monumental holidays of Rosh Hashana, Yom Kippur, Sukkot, Hoshana Rabba, Shemini Atzeret and Simchat Torah.

These two months embody the energy of renewal after destruction, rebirth after loss, the energy of love and forgiveness, of empowerment and joy. *Elul* and *Tishrei* capture the very story of life itself.

Before we explore how to use this workbook to maximize access to the energy of these two extraordinary months, we must understand the context within Jewish history from which the months of *Elul* and *Tishrei* draw their power.

— Some 3,300 years ago, in the month of *Nissan*, the Nation of Israel was born. Through a series of incredible miracles, the Jewish people were freed from slavery in Egypt by G-d Himself, leaving their state of bondage on the 15th of *Nissan*, a day which today we celebrate as Passover.

— Seven weeks, or 50 days later, on the 6th day of the month of *Sivan*—a day we celebrate as the holiday of Shavuot ("Weeks")—they encountered G-d at Mt. Sinai.

— Moses then went up the mountain for 40 days to receive the complete teachings of the Torah. Down below the people grew restless and built the Golden Calf.

— As Moses came down the mountain—on the 17th day of the month of *Tammuz*—he saw what the people had done. In response, he broke the tablets of the Ten Commandments. This date is now observed as a fast day; it is a date which begins the three saddest, most painful weeks of the Hebrew calendar that exude a negative energy. These three weeks, known as "Three Weeks of Affliction," culminate on the 9th of *Av*—*Tisha B'Av*—the most difficult day in Jewish history.

YEAR	TRAGIC EVENTS IN JEWISH HISTORY WHICH TOOK PLACE DURING THE THREE WEEKS BETWEEN 17TH OF TAMMUZ AND 9TH OF AV (partial list only)
1312 BCE	Israelites send 12 spies to scout out the Land of Israel and decide that entry is too dangerous. As a result of this decision, which showed a lack of trust in G-d, they are doomed to wander in the wilderness for 40 years.
422 BCE	Walls of Jerusalem breached by Babylonians and First Temple destroyed by Nebuchadnezzar.
70 CE	Jerusalem conquered by the Romans and the Second Temple destroyed by Titus. Some 2.5 million Jews are killed and another 1 million are exiled from the Land of Israel
133 CE	Jewish revolt against the Romans led by Bar Kochba mercilessly crushed at Betar.
1096	Crusades launched in which half the Jews of Europe (and all the Jews of Jerusalem) are brutally murdered.
1290	Jews expelled from England.
1492	Jews of Spain given an ultimatum by the Inquisition—leave, convert or die.
1914	World War I, the prelude to the Holocaust, begins.
1942	Deportations to Treblinka death camp ordered from the Warsaw Ghetto.
1994	Jewish community center bombed in Buenos Aires with 86 killed and 300 wounded.

- After he made order in the Israelite camp, destroyed the Golden Calf and punished the wrongdoers, Moses went back up the mountain for another 40 days to pray and ask G-d to pardon the people.

- During the time Moses was up on the mountain, we begin "Seven Weeks of Consolation"—starting with the Shabbat immediately following *Tisha B'Av*—seven weeks that include the rest of the month of *Av* and the entire month of *Elul*.

- At the end of *Av*, Moses returned to the people. Although G-d granted Moses permission to carve a second set of tablets of the Ten Commandments, He did not grant forgiveness.

- On the 1st day of *Elul*—Rosh Chodesh *Elul*, the birth of the new moon—Moses went up the mountain for the third time and remained there for yet another 40 days.

- While Moses was on the mountain came Rosh Hashana, the first day of *Tishrei* and anniversary of the creation of the world. Moses realized that G-d could not have created an imperfect world full of imperfect people (who were bound to show their imperfections now and then), without an escape mechanism. He knew that there had to be hope and he persisted in pleading with G-d for forgiveness.

- Moses remained on the mountain until he succeeded: 40 days after he ascended for the third time, 120 days after he first climbed the mountain, Moses prevailed. On the 10th of *Tishrei*—a day we know as Yom Kippur—G-d finally granted forgiveness.

- That does not end the cycle, however. Now comes the week-long celebration known as Sukkot ("Festival of Booths")—beginning on the 15th of *Tishrei*—when Jews dwell in huts covered only with palm leaves, indicating that they depend on G-d alone.

- The week of Sukkot concludes with the holidays of Shemini Atzeret ("Eighth Day of Assembly") and Simchat Torah ("Joy of Torah")—on the 22nd and 23rd of *Tishrei*—when the yearly cycle of reading portions from the Torah ends and begins anew.

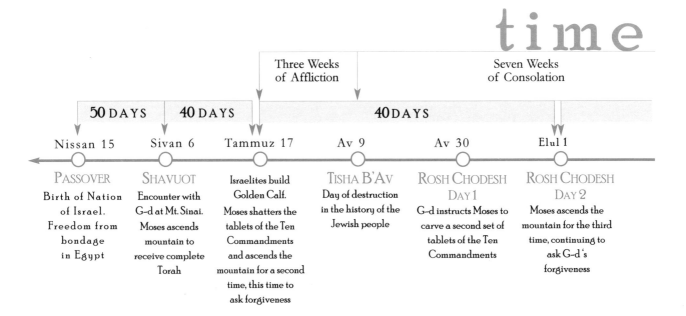

time

| Three Weeks of Affliction | | Seven Weeks of Consolation |

| 50 DAYS | 40 DAYS | 40 DAYS |

Nissan 15	Sivan 6	Tammuz 17	Av 9	Av 30	Elul 1
PASSOVER	SHAVUOT	Israelites build Golden Calf.	TISHA B'AV	ROSH CHODESH DAY 1	ROSH CHODESH DAY 2
Birth of Nation of Israel. Freedom from bondage in Egypt	Encounter with G-d at Mt. Sinai. Moses ascends mountain to receive complete Torah	Moses shatters the tablets of the Ten Commandments and ascends the mountain for a second time, this time to ask forgiveness	Day of destruction in the history of the Jewish people	G-d instructs Moses to carve a second set of tablets of the Ten Commandments	Moses ascends the mountain for the third time, continuing to ask G-d's forgiveness

This cycle encompasses half the year, and its energy repeats itself
every year at this time. We see it in the energy of destruction and loss in
the three weeks between the 17th of *Tammuz* and the 9th of *Av*; we see it
in the energy of consolation and love of the months of *Elul*; we see it in
the energy of renewal and forgiveness of Rosh Hashana and
Yom Kippur; we see it in the energy of joy and unity on Sukkot and
Simchat Torah.

line

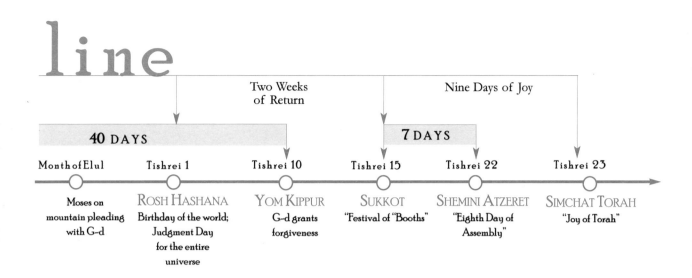

		Two Weeks of Return		Nine Days of Joy	

40 DAYS   **7** DAYS

Month of Elul	Tishrei 1	Tishrei 10	Tishrei 15	Tishrei 22	Tishrei 23
Moses on mountain pleading with G-d	ROSH HASHANA Birthday of the world; Judgment Day for the entire universe	YOM KIPPUR G-d grants forgiveness	SUKKOT "Festival of "Booths"	SHEMINI ATZERET "Eighth Day of Assembly"	SIMCHAT TORAH "Joy of Torah"

A STORY of LOVE

Essentially this cycle is the story of love, betrayal and reconciliation. The latter 60-day period of *Elul* and *Tishrei* is the final chapter of the story of love lost and love reclaimed. After the betrayal of the Golden Calf, Moses does everything possible to "woo" G-d back into a relationship with the people. In *Elul*, Moses succeeds to have G-d consider the proposition. On Rosh Hashana, G-d finally agrees to recommit. Yom Kippur is the *chupa*—the wedding ceremony. We then dance and sing in the wedding celebration on Sukkot. The union is consummated on Shemini Atzeret, followed by a final burst of ultimate unbridled joy on Simchat Torah.

In this 60-day workbook we concentrate on accessing the power of *Elul* and *Tishrei* to maximum spiritual benefit. We want to use it to remove whatever obstacles hamper our lives; we want to use it to get closer to G-d; we want to use it to improve our relationships, to start the New Year with renewed vigor, to make our lives better and to help build a better world.

Indeed, this 60-day period in time—as reflected in this book—is really the story of each one of our lives, as expressed in perhaps the biggest question of all: Is there hope after loss, can we rebuild after destruction? It's one thing to find happiness and life affirmation when we escape to a mountain; it's quite another to be able to experience it when we are immersed in a cruel, material life. Can we really find truth in a corrupt world? Can we reach the highest places from our limited place? Can we taste eternity as mortal creatures? Can we touch heaven even as we stand on earth? Can we, as people and as nations, ever discover true peace?

The 60-day story of *Elul* and *Tishrei* resolutely answers these questions with a resounding and unequivocal "Yes." Yes, there is hope. Yes, we can rebuild. Indeed, we can find an even greater love than the original one. Yes, we can marry heaven and earth. And yes, our entire world can unite in one magnificent symphony, each of us contributing our particular melody.

"60 DAYS" a WORKBOOK

The two Hebrew months of *Elul* and *Tishrei* have their own built in structure, with their specific obligations and customs. This workbook brings alive the 60-day *Elul-Tishrei* experience. It taps into the deeper meaning of each of these days—and their elegant sequence—illuminating the profound power contained in these months.

"Sixty Days" is thus structured like a sixty-day journey, paralleling the rich days of *Elul-Tishrei*. This is a journey toward finding hope, love, fulfillment, and the realization of your deepest aspirations and dreams—a journey to discover your calling and to make your peace with G-d.

Each day of this book is one leg of the journey. Yet, like every journey, each day has its own "life." You can, therefore, feel free to begin at any point and stay on any page for as long as you like. Optimally, it would be best to move along this journey from day to day, step after step. But this book is structured so that every day is both self-contained as well as part of a sequence.

Every day of *Elul* and *Tishrei* is rich with meaning, with history and tradition. Thus each day consists of two side-by-side pages. The page on the right is a daily calendar—it includes a daily quote, a listing of historical events that occurred on that day, and relevant laws and customs. The page on the left consists of an inspirational thought and a practical exercise for the day.

Though this season has universal themes and customs, the focus in this book is to personalize your experience. Each of the pages of *Elul* are meant to help you assess your life, to account for the past year and to prepare for the new year. The pages of *Tishrei* continue, at a heightened pace, the journey of *Elul*, with special focus on each holiday: Rosh Hashana, Yom Kippur, Sukkot, Hoshana Rabba, Shemini Atzeret and Simchat Torah. In effect the holidays are like milestones on the journey. Finally, the book ends with the post-holiday season, covering the last days of *Tishrei* and the beginning of the next month, *Cheshvan*, as we enter and integrate the holiday season into our daily lives during the entire year.

At the end of the book a special section has been included that deciphers and personalizes the powerful holiday prayer services. This is meant to be used as a companion guide to the holiday prayer book (a *Siddur* or *Machzor*).

Finally, the endnotes offer sources, additional details, and more complex applications of the material found in the actual days of the book.

(Though this book is filled with the laws and customs of *Elul* and *Tishrei*, by no means should this book be seen as replacing the *Shulchan Aruch*, the Code of Jewish Law that defines our obligations and customs. Any question of Jewish Law should be posed to a qualified rabbi.)

Start a journal for the work you will do in these 60 days. On the first page of your journal create a list of items you want to change in your life. To help you along, create three columns, labeled:

"Things I want to work on"
    Between me and G-d
    Between me and other people
    Between me and myself

Below these columns, list the areas you want to work on:

Intellectual—Torah   **Emotional** —Prayer **Action oriented** — *Mitzvot*
Other

Now divide the rest of your journal into 60 sections or pages, each page corresponding to its respective page in this workbook.

On each page of the workbook there are questions and an exercise for each day. As you move from day to day, write down in your journal the answer to each day's questions, and what you have done to implement the exercise.

You can also refer back to your first page, and connect your answers and exercises to the general areas in your life you want to change.

Continue this process day after day and you are guaranteed to be blessed with a transformative 60 days!

**May you have a sweet and happy year,
written and sealed for the most revealed blessings!**

Elul is the last month of the year

it encompasses the entire spectrum of existence—

the three pillars on which the world stands...

Torah

Prayer

Kindness

introspection

ELUL

aleph   lamed
lamed
vav

consolation

Introduction
END of the YEAR

The Hebrew month of *Elul* (which generally falls in August or September) is the last month of the Hebrew year—as opposed to the month of December, which is the last month of the year in the Christian/Western calendar. It is considered the month of self-examination and accounting in preparation for the new year and the High Holidays that come at that time—Rosh Hashana and Yom Kippur. In this regard, it is considered a month of *teshuvah*, of returning to G-d in repentance, with hope that it is never too late, that destiny can be changed by prayer, and that forgiveness is inevitable.

Elul is a month of Divine grace, because in this month Moses began his last 40 days on the mountain praying for G-d's compassion and forgiveness. On the mountain, Moses came the closest any human being ever came to knowing G-d, and G-d revealed and taught him the secret of His "Thirteen Attributes of Mercy" (Exodus 33:18-34:8). The days of *Elul* are therefore called "days of grace" or days of "compassion," because in this period G-d was open to listening to Moses—and Moses was successful in his appeal for forgiveness and renewal. Ever since, the month of *Elul* has served as the month of Divine mercy and forgiveness.

This is why *Elul* has such power—it is the month when the "King is in the field and receives all people pleasantly and with a smiling countenance"—the Thirteen Attributes of Compassion radiate to each one of us. *Elul* brings to the surface the intense love between G-d and His people. For this reason this month—and the entire 40-day period concluding with Yom Kippur—is dedicated to special prayers, shofar sounding, soul searching and *teshuvah*.[1]

The spiritual energy of *Elul* is hinted at by the many meanings of its name, each of which reflects an aspect of the spiritual work that is meant to take place at this time.

WHAT'S in a NAME

In the mystical terminology of the Kabbalah, a name is an intermediary between heaven and earth. It can be compared to film which has been threaded through a projector in order to give shape and color to the white light that shines through it. The light shines from the projector as it did before the film was threaded in; the light has not been compromised—it's still white light. But an intermediary has been introduced between the light and the screen which defines and shapes the light.

In this analogy, spiritual energy is the white light; the name is the film. The Hebrew letters of a name give shape and definition to the spiritual energy shining through it. This is why a name has a lot of power.

The name *Elul* is composed of four Hebrew letters:

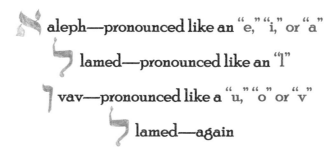

aleph—pronounced like an " e, " " i, " or " a "

lamed—pronounced like an " l "

vav—pronounced like a " u, " " o " or " v "

lamed—again

The name *Elul* is an acronym; each of its four letters stand for a separate word in five different verses from the Bible, each of which identifies a different aspect of *Elul's* spiritual energy.

THE FIVE ACRONYMS of ELUL

1)

Elul stands for a verse from King Solomon's moving and highly spiritual poem known as the *Song of Songs* (6:3):[2]

Ani l'dodi v'dodi li
"I am for my beloved, and my beloved is for me"

Elul is a month of love. In *Elul* we find our way back to G-d and seek to repair the spiritual destruction caused by mistakes and transgressions of the past year. We feel G-d's love for us as He responds to our initiative. We reach for Him from below, declaring "I am for my beloved" and He responds from above, showing us that "my beloved is for me." This is also the essence of **prayer**. Thus *Elul* defines our relationship with G-d as reciprocal— in other words, a loving partnership.

2)

Elul stands for a verse in the Book of Esther (9:22) which speaks of a month that turned from sorrow to joy; from mourning to feasting; and of sending delicacies to one another and gifts to the poor:[3]

ish lerei'eihu umatanot la'evyonim
"...(each) man to his fellow and gifts to the poor"

This verse expresses *Elul's* loving nature—especially at the bonding that takes place between people through **acts of kindness** and charity. It also hints at *Elul's* role as the month bridging the destruction of *Av* with the forgiveness of *Tishrei*. As such, it is a month of consolation and compassion.

3)

Elul stands for a verse from the Book of Exodus (21:13) which speaks of the "cities of refuge" established in Biblical times as places where a person who killed another unintentionally might find sanctuary from the wrath of his unintended victim's family:[4]

inah le'yado vesamti lach
"...deliver into his hand, I shall establish for you..."

Every transgression against G-d is a "killing." This is because like a killing, a transgression is a violation of the essence and purpose of life. It is "unintentional" because each of us is intrinsically good and all transgressions result from a lapse in the awareness of our true will.

This verse hints that *Elul* is a refuge in time established for us in the calendar—it returns every year, under all conditions. It also alludes to *Elul's* connection to Torah, as the sages teach us that the "words of Torah are a refuge."[5] *Elul* provides a haven, a sanctum for introspection, self-examination, atonement and rehabilitation. It is a month in which we resolve that, from now on, no accidental iniquity will mar the essential goodness of our soul.

4)

Elul stands for a verse from the Book of Deuteronomy (30:6) which speaks of the Jewish people returning in repentance to the Land of Israel after an exile, which had been a punishment for their transgression:[6]

et levavcha ve'et levav
"...your heart and the heart (of your children)."

This verse hints that *Elul* is a time of teshuvah—a time of regret, forgiveness and reconciliation; a time of return to pristine beginnings to rediscover our true self and the spark of G-dliness at the core of our soul.

5)

Elul stands for a verse (when read backwards) from the Book of Exodus (15:1) which speaks of the song the Israelites sang at the parting of the Red Sea, a song that alludes to the final redemption at the end of days:[7]

Hashem va-yamru leimor ashira
"(this song) to G-d and said, saying, 'I will sing...'"

Because *Elul* is the last month of year, it encompasses the entire spectrum of existence—the three pillars on which the world stands—Torah, prayer, and acts of kindness—and the two foundations—repentance and redemption—that anchor the pillars in vitality and purpose.[8] But above all, it is a month of hope—that forgiveness and redemption are inevitable because G-d could not have created an imperfect existence and expected from it perfection. For each one of us, forgiveness and redemption are possible—now, at this time. And this annual event carries with it a promise of the final redemption at the end of time, the realization of the purpose of our entire existence, which is dependent on our effort today, and which makes our work worth all the effort.

The Journey Begins

Imagine the scene:

A spouse has betrayed his or her partner in the worst possible way—defiled the very essence of their relationship. That fragile thing called trust has been broken.

The presenting challenge is this:

Can this damaged relationship be mended, can it be rebuilt after such profound betrayal? For 40 days, "a faithful shepherd" attempts to mediate. He cajoles, begs, prays, does everything he possibly can to reconcile between the partners. But to no avail.

Now the compelling question is this:

Should he give up or should he continue to persist in his attempts for reconciliation? No small question. Not only the relationship, but life itself hangs in the balance.

This is the essence of the month of *Elul*.

The Jewish people had betrayed G-d in the worst possible way: they built a Golden Calf a mere 39 days after an encounter with G-d at Mt. Sinai, which was the most momentous event in history! And after they had explicitly accepted G-d's commandment not to worship others gods!

Seeing what they had done, Moses shatters the tablets he received from G-d, and returns to the mountain for 40 days to pray for the people's forgiveness. But to no avail. G-d will not relent and forgive. These 40 days are called "Days of Wrath."

But Moses does not give up. After 40 days of tortuous pleading, unperturbed, he returns to the mountain for yet another 40 days.

From his unwavering faith in G-d's mercy comes the power of *Elul*. It is the power of hope. True hope—relentless, persistent, unwavering. Eternal hope—absolute belief in G-d and His infinite power of forgiveness and compassion, absolute faith in us, and absolute faith in the unconditional love between us and G-d. (Because after all, when we betray G-d we also betray ourselves—our soul, our essence, our Divine calling and ultimate mission in life.)

Finally, Moses does prevail—40 days later on Yom Kippur.

Elul is the story of Moses' journey. It is the story of building a true and enduring relationship, even after it has been challenged. Moses' *Elul* experience provides us with a special energy of love and compassion during this month, when the "King is in the field" and radiates the Thirteen Attributes of Compassion.

PERSONALIZING ELUL

In this month we have the ability to recreate Moses' experience on the mountain. Each of the 29 days of *Elul* (beginning with the first day of Rosh Chodesh, the 29th of *Av*, for a total of 30 days) we relive each step of Moses' journey—his prayers, his pleading, his hope. We work on breaking the "golden idols" that we worship and that fill our lives—the false idols that don't allow us to access our true selves. Each day, as we rebuild another aspect of our relationship, we grow as Moses did. After 30 days of preparation we are ready to enter into a renewed relationship with G-d—and a renewed relationship with our own souls—on Rosh Hashana. We continue to build the relationship for the first 10 days of *Tishrei*, concluding with Yom Kippur, when we finally are ready for complete reconciliation as we stand under the *chupa* with our Divine "spouse."

To help us along, *Elul*—and Moses' journey during these days—provides us with a specific day by day plan, that covers the entire spectrum of human experience and addresses the different areas of work necessary to reconcile and rebuild our relationship with our soul and with G-d.

Change breeds change. If you change an attitude—it will precipitate other changes in your life.

Would you like to change something in your life? Now is the time. *Elul* is a month when the doors are open. Special energy radiates in this month. And by our actions we create containers that channel this unique radiance into our lives.

Think of aspects of your life that you want to change. To make this manageable choose the most important things that you want to change. Perhaps you want change in a relationship—to make it better or get out of an unhealthy one. Or you want to change your single status and find your soul-mate.

Perhaps you want to change a psychological pattern that you seem to get stuck in time and again.

Perhaps you want to change your job, your place of residence, your status.

Whatever it is you want to change—Elul is the time for it. Unprecedented doors open up for you now, opportunities that do not come very often.

Act. Now is the time.

"I carved out two tablets like the first and I climbed UP the mountain with the two tablets in my hand... I remained on the mountain forty days and forty nights, just like the first time, and G-d listened to me this time, agreeing not to destroy you." (Deuteronomy 10:3;10. Exodus 34:1-4)

Preparing to Take Stock

Today is the first day (of two days) of Rosh Chodesh *Elul*, (which actually falls on the last day of the month of Av).

Elul is called *chodesh hacheshbon*, "a month of accounting," as it comes at the end of the spiritual fiscal year. It's also considered the month of preparation for the new spiritual year that begins with Rosh Hashana. The two themes of *Elul*—accounting and preparation—are interdependent, because how we account for the past is how we prepare for the future.

In *Elul* (the word in Aramaic means "searching"[1]) we examine the mistakes of the past year in order not to repeat them. In particular, this means taking an honest look at what is trapping us and preventing us from truly moving forward.

Obviously, fundamental changes do not happen instantly. But self-transformation is possible, and it is possible to the extent that we want it, that we examine ourselves and identify issues that need work, and that we invest ourselves in that goal.

In short, what will happen to each one of us on Rosh Hashana and Yom Kippur has a great deal to do with how we prepare for these great days.

We can be certain that if G-d created life, He gave us the power to change life. If G-d gave us the ability to get into patterns and habits, then He must also have given us the power of the soul to get out of the habit. Just like we got in, we can get out.

Any faith in G-d has to include faith in hope and faith in transformation—faith that we will be forgiven for past mistakes and faith that we can change.

Ask yourself: Do you believe that self-transformation is truly possible? Do you want to change? Are you prepared to resolve to do so?

Exercise for the day:

Open the journal you have prepared for the accounting work that you will do this month, and in it record your answers to the above questions.

Elul — Month of Accounting and Preparation

1st Day of Rosh Chodesh Elul

> "The *mazal* (sign) of the month of *Menachem Av* is the *Aryeh* (Leo), an acronym for *Elul*, Rosh Hashana, Yom Kippur, Hoshana Rabba[2]—four milestones in this time period,[3] all built from the pain and destruction of *Av*. This parallels Moses' efforts to rebuild our relationship after the sin of the Golden Calf."
> **(The Shaloh)**

Events

2448 (1313 BCE)—Moses carves the second set tablets of the Ten Commandments to replace the tablets which he had shattered upon witnessing Israel's worship of the Golden Calf.

Laws and Customs

Rosh Chodesh Observances.

Today is the first of the two days of Rosh Chodesh ("Head of the Month") of *Elul*. (When a month has 30 days, both the last day of the month and the first day of the following month serve as the following month's Rosh Chodesh). Special portions are added to the daily prayers:

Hallel (composed of Psalms 113—118) is recited following the *Shacharit* morning prayer.

The Yaaleh V'yavo prayer is added to the *Amidah* prayer and to Grace After Meals.

The additional **Musaf** prayer is said.

Tachnun (confession of sins) and similar prayers are omitted.

Many have the custom to mark Rosh Chodesh with a festive meal and reduced work activity. The latter custom is prevalent amongst women, who have a special affinity with Rosh Chodesh—the lunar month being the feminine aspect of the Jewish calendar.[4]

Some of the special *Elul* practices (see also *Elul* 1) begin on this day:

Psalm 27 is recited at the end of the morning and afternoon prayers (this special addition is recited throughout the month of *Elul* and the High Holiday season, until Hoshana Rabba—for a total of 50 days) (See *Elul* 2 and *Tishrei* 21)

Although the daily sounding of the **shofar** (ram's horn) officially begins on the second day of Rosh Chodesh *Elul*—announcing the opening of the gates of compassion—it is customary to practice sounding the shofar on the first Rosh Chodesh, introducing the *Elul* atmosphere of soul-searching and repentance.[5]

Breaking Damaging Patterns

Moses' *Elul* journey actually begins seven generations earlier, with Abraham's journey.

In the Book of Genesis (12:1), G-d speaks to Abraham and says: "Go from your land, your birthplace, the home of your parents, to the land that I will show you."

This is very strange because when you tell someone to travel, you specify the *destination* in detail, but you don't describe over and over again the point of departure. After all, the person knows where he/she is leaving from.

But here G-d tells Abraham to leave his land, his birthplace, and the home of his parents— three descriptions of his present location— and then, when it comes to the destination, He only tells him to go "to a land," without naming it or even hinting at where it is.

Chassidic thought, which gives voice to the inner dimension of the Torah, explains that in truth this verse is really a commandment issued by G-d to each of us: "Go on a journey of self-discovery. Leave behind anything that might hold you back. And then I will show you the landscape of your Divine soul—the true you."

If you want to discover your higher self, this is the secret.

Many people get inspired and motivated to go on such a journey; they actually pack their bags—literally or metaphorically—and set out on their way. But after a while, they end up coming right back where they started, repeating the same old patterns.

Good intentions are pure and real. When you decide to leave, you really want to get someplace. But you have so many things weighing you down, so many "golden idols." So the key to meaningful change is not so much knowing how to get to a new place, it's knowing how to unload the past, so that it shouldn't shape your future and bring you back to your old patterns.

Ask yourself: In what areas of your life are you repeating old patterns? In what ways are they damaging to you?

Exercise for the day:

Identify and describe one damaging pattern that you want to break in the coming year.

List one thing you must do in order to break that pattern.

> "In the *shtetl* of Lubavitch, on the Shabbat preceding the month of *Elul*, though summer still lingered and the day was bright and sunny, there was a change in the air; one already smelled the *Elul*-scent, a *teshuvah*-wind was blowing."
> **(The Rebbe Yosef Yitzchak)[1]**

Events

2448 (1313 BCE)—Moses ascends Mt. Sinai for the third time to pray and beseech G-d to forgive the people.[2] He will remain there for 40 days, descending on Yom Kippur, when he finally succeeds in his mission. The shofar was sounded when Moses ascended on Rosh Chodosh *Elul* and every day afterwards. This is why we sound the shofar every day of *Elul*.[3] We recreate these 40 days beginning from the first day of Rosh Chodesh *Elul*.[4] These 40 are hinted to in the 4 *yuds* (4x10) at the end of the words *ani l'dodi v'dodi li*.[5]

Laws and Customs

Every day of *Elul* the shofar is sounded as a wake-up call, reminding us that these are special days of compassion, open to receive all our prayers and *teshuvah*, as did Moses on Mt. Sinai. The shofar also elicits awe, like thunder before the rain, and prepares us for Rosh Hashana.[6]

We recite three additional chapters of Psalms each day, from the 1st of *Elul*[7] until Yom Kippur (on Yom Kippur the remaining 36 chapters are recited, thereby completing the entire Book of Psalms). This is a custom instituted by the Baal Shem Tov.

In the Sephardic tradition, *Selichot* (special prayers for forgiveness) are said beginning from the first day of *Elul*, through Yom Kippur. In the Ashkenazic tradition they begin in the week before Rosh Hashana. (See *Elul* 21.)

Today is Rosh Hashana of *Maaser Beheima*, tithing of the livestock (*Rosh Hashana* 2a).[8]

From Rosh Chodesh *Elul* until Yom Kippur it is customary, when corresponding, to wish one another a *Kesiva vechatima tova*, a happy and healthy new year.[9]

It is customary to increase charitable giving in the days of *Elul*.[10]

Identifying Personal Biases

By telling Abraham, "Leave your land, your birthplace, the home of your parents, and go to the land that I will show you," God instructed us, his descendants, that there are three forms of subjectivity we need to leave behind when we set out on the journey of self-discovery:

'Your land' represents the first level of subjectivity—the influence of society, community and peer pressure, which affect us in deep and profound ways. We all want to be liked and accepted by others, and we adjust our behavior accordingly.

The 'home of your parents' represents the second level of subjectivity—parental influence, which can be so subtle that we don't even recognize it. Often, we don't realize how deeply the attitudes of our parents permeate our own attitudes and behavior, for good and for bad.

'Your birthplace' represents the third level of subjectivity—inherent self-love. Each person is blinded by his or her selfish interests; no one is immune from that.

This does not mean that we must completely discard all good things that we have learned from our parents or our community, but it means that, first of all, we must become aware of how these influences affect our behavior, our opinions, and our thought patterns. Only then can we begin to know who it is that we are and what it is that we think, know and believe.

Similarly, personal bias or self-love—which isn't a crime in itself—becomes a crime when we don't acknowledge it, and when it begins to distort our vision.

Ask yourself: Are you able to identify where you blindly follow convention (or politically correct opinions) and where your path is truly your own, arrived at by you through careful consideration?

Exercise for the day:

Select one significant event of the past day and identify how your reactions and behaviors were shaped by each of the three levels of subjectivity named above.

Describe what role the damaging pattern you identified yesterday played in these reactions and behaviors.

Elul 2

16

"The entire work of *Elul* and *Tishrei* is comparable to cleaning, repairing and rebuilding a soiled or broken container. Rosh Chodesh *Elul* is the time for soul accounting. Through our tears during *Selichot* we wash out our 'containers.' On Rosh Hashana we repair the container, reaching the epitome with the sounding of the shofar."
(The Rebbe Yosef Yitzchak)[1]

Events

5315 (1555 CE)—The first printing of the *Shulchan Aruch* (the definitive Code of Jewish Law) by Rabbi Yosef Caro (1488-1575) is completed in the Holy Land.

Laws and Customs

During *Elul*, even those immersed full time in Torah study, take off some time from their study to increase their prayers and supplications.[2]

Facts ◉

The custom of reciting King David's Psalm 27 ("By David, G-d is my Light and my Salvation") each day of *Elul* until Hoshana Rabba[3] is based on the *Midrash*[4] which associates the "Light" of David and the "Light" of all human beings with Rosh Hashana, when by the light of the soul G-d searches out the deepest recesses of the human being. The *Midrash* associates the "Salvation" of David and of all human beings with Yom Kippur, the Day of Atonement, when everyone is redeemed. The theme of this psalm is also related to the revelation of the Thirteen Divine Attributes of Compassion which radiate during *Elul*.[5] Indeed, the psalm mentions G-d's name 13 times.[6]

Learning to be Free

Identifying damaging patterns and personal bias is an essential step on a journey to freedom from our personal bondage.

In one way or another, we're all enslaved—by our psychological demons, or by social standards, by our parents' words and attitudes, or by our responsibilities, by the consequences of the mistakes we've made, or by our careers, employers, or employees.

Learning how to be free is what is called in the Torah "leaving Egypt."

The Hebrew word for Egypt is *Mitzrayim*, which literally means "narrow" and which represents all forms of enslavement, be it dependency, conformity, subjectivity—whatever it may be in your life that sets up obstacles, limits or constraints.

To be free, you must leave your personal *Mitzrayim*. But freedom is not enough. You can be free for a while and then be enslaved again. This is why forty days after the Israelites left Egypt and tasted freedom for the first time, they received a guidebook—the Torah—on how to maintain freedom.

Look at your own life. There were undoubtedly many times you felt free, you felt inspired, you felt you could do anything, but then old patterns and biases took over. You couldn't maintain that inspiration. The resolve to change was there for a moment, but you couldn't sustain it.

This is where you need the guidance of the Divine Torah blueprint. It tells you how to access your soul, how to achieve freedom in every part of your life, from the moment you wake to the moment you go to sleep, and even while you're asleep.

Ask yourself: To what extent have you used the guidance of the Torah to access your soul? To what extent are you familiar with what the Torah teaches in this regard?

Exercise for the day:

Identify one area in your life where you badly need the objective guidance of Torah because you have not been able to make meaningful progress on your own.

"He made the letter *Yud* king over action, and He bound a crown to it, and He combined one with another, and with them he formed Virgo [*Betulah*] in the universe, *Elul* in the year, and the left hand[1] in the Soul, male and female."[2]
(Sefer Yetzirah 5:8)[3]

Facts ◉

Elul and Torah are intrinsically connected:

1) Moses spent all of *Elul* receiving the second set of Tablets of the Ten Commandments.

2) In the verse of the *Song of Songs*, "I am for my beloved and my beloved is for me; he feeds among roses;" 'feeds among roses' refers to Torah study.

3) The Thirteen Attributes of Compassion (the thirteen petals on the rose) parallel the Thirteen Rules of Biblical Interpretation.[4]

4) One of the acronyms of *Elul* is connected to refuge.[5] Torah provides refuge from our own subjective blind spots and other forces in our lives that tend to cloud our judgment.

Every hour in the month of *Elul* is considered like a day; it has the power to atone for a day of the year. Hence, all the days of *Elul* (each day x 12 daytime hours) is more than all the days of the year.[6]

The Truth Within

The *Ethics of the Fathers* teach, "No one is free except the one who is immersed in Torah study," in effect identifying the practice of religion—the study and observance of Torah—with freedom.

Yet many people don't think of religion as freeing. They think of it as limiting, dogmatic, oppressive.

This is because the religion they have been exposed to is an invention of human beings. The religion they know is not the religion of G-d; it is not the religion of the Torah.

If your experience of religion is not freeing, then you have fallen into a man-made trap.

Freedom is Divine; it cannot be human. As soon as it's human, then there's someone who's in control of it, someone who wants to sell it to you and own it. That is when religion becomes another form of slavery; it becomes oppressive because it has lost its Divine nature.

That's why the Torah was given—so that there would be a permanent record, a source that everyone could refer to. As a result, Judaism has remained a religion of uncommon strength, one that over and over again has defied being hijacked by people.

The Talmud teaches that every one of us is taught the Torah before we are born. Its meaning is ingrained in our psyches, and upon birth we're made to consciously forget. But the truth resonates. So when we hear it, we know. Great masters or teachers can't give us anything we don't already possess; they can help us in one thing only—to open our own pathway to the truth within.

Ask yourself: To what extent do you see religion as oppressive? To what extent is the religion in your life man-made or self-made? Have you gone to the source? Have you had the experience of hearing the truth resonate in your heart? Did you embrace it or reject it?

> *Exercise for the day:*
>
> Commit to regularly attend a Torah class that will help you in at least one area of your life (which you identified yesterday) where you have not been able to make meaningful progress on your own.

"And the tablets were the work of G-d, and the writing was G-d's writing engraved on the tablets."
(Exodus 32:16)

"Read not 'engraved' but 'freedom'—for there is no free person, except for one who occupies himself with Torah study." **(Ethics of the Fathers 6:2)**

The key to true freedom involves ensuring that the truth of the Divine letters is engraved in your spirit and not just superimposed like letters written on parchment.

Laws and Customs

During the month of *Elul* it is customary to have *tefillin* and *mezuzot* checked, as well as to review other *mitzvot* that require evaluation (*Mateh Efraim* 581:10).

Following the Shabbat *Mincha* afternoon service, some have the custom to continue studying *Pirkei Avot* ("Ethics of the Fathers") on each Shabbat of the summer (as we did on each Shabbat between Passover and Shavuot). The 1st Shabbat of *Elul* we read chapter 6; the 2nd Shabbat chapters 1-2; the 3rd Shabbat chapters 3-4; the 4th Shabbat, preceding Rosh Hashana, chapters 5-6.

Facts ◎

During the month of *Elul* we read the portions in the Torah: *Shoftim, Ki Teitzei, Ki Tavo, Nitzavim-Vayeilech* (when Rosh Hashana falls on Monday or Tuesday we divide *Netzavim* and *Vayeilech* into two separate weeks). We also read the last four Haftorahs of the "Seven Weeks of Consolation," which follow the "Three Weeks of Affliction." For seven weeks, beginning with the Shabbat after the Ninth of *Av* (*Tisha B'Av*), the Haftorah readings consist of prophecies describing G-d's consolation of His people and the rehabilitation of their relationship.

On the first Shabbat of *Elul* [1] we read *Shoftim*, which commands us to establish a judicial system. This is a major theme of *Elul*: preparing for the cosmic Day of Judgment. This is followed by the 4th Haftorah of the Seven Weeks of Consolation, in which G-d says: "It is I, I Myself come to comfort you." (See *Elul* 6.)

Developing Sensitivity

When the Rebbe Yosef Yitzchak was a child, he was walking in a garden one day and he ripped off a leaf and began rubbing it with his finger. His father rebuked him, "What right do you have to rip a leaf from a tree and mistreat it for no purpose at all?" When the Rebbe grew up he said that this incident had a deep impact on his life. It taught him to be sensitive to everything.

If a person is sensitive to a leaf on a tree, he will, without a doubt, be sensitive to all life forms—most of all to his fellow human beings. This is the essence of *tzedaka* ("charity"), the second of the three pillars upon which the world stands (Torah and prayer being the other two). *Tzedaka* is sensitivity in action.

Sensitivity to life is the goal of many of the practices of the Torah. Some of them appear deceptively simple—for example, take the act of making a blessing before eating.

On a basic level, a blessing on food is saying thank you to G-d. That makes sense—whenever anyone gives you something, you say thank you. And if you can thank the waiter who brought you the food, you can definitely thank the Creator who created it.

But on a deeper level, the blessing has a profound meaning. When you are hungry, you want to put that food in your mouth immediately. But the Torah says, "No, you can't." First, you must be sensitive to the environment, to every fiber of grass, every cell of life, because everything that God created has sanctity to it. You have no right to consume a part of creation unless you are sanctifying it.

It's true that many people just make blessings by rote, without sensitivity. That is mechanical Judaism. But if you understand and appreciate the concept of a blessing, you know that little daily acts like it can sensitize your life.

Ask yourself: How sensitive are you to the world around you? Do you have a plan for developing/increasing your sensitivity?

Exercise for the day:

Make a special effort to increase your charitable giving, beyond your natural tendency.

Place a charity box in your home, office and car. Teach your children to give of their money and time to others.

Before you eat focus on making a blessing, with added intention, thanking G-d and concentrating on the spiritual energy contained within the food that you are about to consume.

"*Tzedaka* is far more than charity. *Tzedaka* means 'righteousness' and 'justice.' When you contribute money, time or resources you are not just being benevolent and charitable. You are actually doing what is just and right—you are completing the give and take cycle that defines the structure of the universe. *Tzedaka* spiritualizes the material, unites diversity, and, above all, makes us G-d-like because we become givers and not just takers. Indeed, more than the giver gives to the recipient, the recipient gives to the giver."[1]

Events

5537 (1777)—The first Chassidic *aliyah* ("ascent" i.e. immigration to the Holy Land)—led by Rabbi Menachem Mendel of Vitebsk, Rabbi Abraham of Kalisk and Rabbi Yisroel of Polotzk—reached the Holy Land.[2]

Facts ◉

Elul and *tzedaka* are intrinsically connected:

1) It is customary to increase charitable giving in the days of *Elul*.

2) One of *Elul's* acronyms relates to giving charitable gifts.

3) The permutation of G-d's name that radiates in *Elul* is from the verse *Ve'tzedaka tihe'yeh lanu ki*,[3] meaning "It is our *tzedaka* to (safe-guard and keep this entire mandate)." (Deuteronomy 6:25).

To Console and be Consoled

This first week of *Elul* is the fourth week in the Seven Weeks of Consolation, which began immediately following the destruction of *Tisha B'Av*. G-d comforts and consoles us while we work on rebuilding our relationship with Him during *Elul* (as Moses did on Mt. Sinai), thereby showing us that a relationship with Him is a two-way street.

The *Midrash*[1] explains the progression of these seven weeks as a dialogue between us and G-d (which reflects our introspection in the month of *Elul*):

Week One: G-d sends His messengers, the prophets, to console the people after the destruction of the Temple.

Week Two: The Jewish people ask the messengers, "Why are you coming here? We want G-d to come."

Week Three: The messengers return and tell G-d, "The nation is not consoled."

Week Four (the first week of *Elul*): G-d agrees and begins consoling the people Himself.

Week Five: G-d's consolation intensifies.

Week Six: The consolation reaches a more profound and powerful level.[2]

Week Seven: (the week before Rosh Hashana): The Jewish people tell G-d, "We rejoice in Your consolation."[2]

Why doesn't G-d Himself console the people at the very beginning? Why does He send messengers and allow three whole weeks to pass by before He acts?

G-d teaches us here, that we have the power to bond with each other and to console each other. Though we are mortals and may be weak, G-d tells us that one vulnerable person can console another. It's a great gift that one person can give to another.

Ask yourself: Have you developed the sensitivity to console others in times of sorrow in their lives? Do you seek out opportunities to offer consolation or do you shirk away from such occasions? What has been your experience in being consoled by others?

Exercise for the day:

Console someone—visit a sick person in a hospital; or call a friend who is feeling down; or send a greeting to a person you know is lonely.

In the first week, we read a message from the prophet Isaiah: " 'Be comforted, be comforted, my people,' says your G~d." (Isaiah 40:1-26).

In the second week, we read the response of the nation: "And Zion said: 'G~d has forsaken me; my G~d has forgotten me.' " (Isaiah 49:14).

In the third week, we read, "O afflicted, storm-tossed, unconsoled one..." (Isaiah 54:11) The prophet informs G~d that the people are not consoled.

In the fourth week, we read, "It is I, I am He Who comforts you..." (Isaiah 51:12). G~d agrees to come to console the people Himself. This is the first week of *Elul*.

In the fifth week, G~d's personal consolation continues and we read, "Sing out, O barren one, who has not given birth, break out into glad song and be jubilant..." (Isaiah 54:1)

In the sixth week, the consolation intensifies, "Arise! Shine! For your light has arrived and the glory of G~d has shined upon you." (Isaiah 60:1)

And finally **in the seventh week,** we read, "I will rejoice intensely with G~d, my soul shall exult with my G~d ..." (Isaiah 61:10) The people signify that they are consoled, and now are ready for the renewal and rebirth of Rosh Hashana.

Facts

The Seven Weeks of Consolation correspond to the seven emotions[3] (which evolve from the seven Divine emotional attributes). These are: love, discipline, compassion, ambition, humility, bonding and sovereignty. These emotions comfort us, like the glow on a teacher's face as he prepares to "give birth" to a new revelation (which was conceived in the Three Weeks of Affliction). These "glowing" emotions motivate and prepare us for the work we must do to receive the new revelation and perspective on life. This work entails *teshuvah*: In order to grow and be receptive to a new perspective, we must suspend our former perspectives and free ourselves from old behavior patterns. *Teshuvah* consists of two steps (the Two Weeks of *Teshuvah* which follow the Seven of Consolation): "Lower" *teshuvah* which cleans up the past, and "higher" *teshuvah* which opens up the future. It is the latter that allows us to finally receive the new revelation of the Second Tablets on Yom Kippur. After all this work we are finally ready to celebrate our reception of the new "concept." And we celebrate this on Shemini Atzeret and Simchat Torah (Reb Hillel of Paritch).[4]

> **Netzach ("endurance" and "ambition") radiates in this first week of Elul (the 4th of the Seven Weeks of Consolation).**

The King is in the Field

In *Elul*, G-d comes to console us. During this month, G-d is very close nearby—all we have to do is reach out to meet Him.

What does this mean? It means that all year round there are many layers that shroud your own essence from yourself; there is a split between your inner self and your outer self— who you truly are and what you do, your spirit and your activities. In *Elul* many of these layers are stripped. You can access, if you wish, your true self, since it is part of the higher reality and the essence of all of existence called G-d.

In *Elul*, "the King is in the field," writes the Alter Rebbe.[1] He uses the analogy of a king who is returning home from his travels as a way of explaining the phenomenon of *Elul*.

The king had been traveling; he had left his palace and gone to a far off land outside his kingdom. And now he is on his way home. He is about to enter his palace and he stands outside in the field greeting his people. Then he goes back into the palace and again mounts his throne.

When the king is in the field, writes the Alter Rebbe, every person has the opportunity, without petitioning for an audience, to go over to him, say hello and ask for whatever he or she needs. The king is smiling, he is happy to be home, he is in his informal mode, and he is predisposed to grant all requests.

That's *Elul*. On Rosh Hashana and Yom Kippur, the King is back in his palace on his throne.

Rosh Hashana and Yom Kippur are holidays. *Elul* is amid workdays. We are in the field, we are still living our normal lives. Rosh Hashana and Yom Kippur have a very powerful energy, because on those days we petition the King in his inner sanctum. But in *Elul*, we petition the King on our turf.

It is a profound message of hope that we don't have to wait for Rosh Hashana and Yom Kippur to find G-d. We can go out to meet Him now.

Ask yourself: If you could literally go out to meet G-d in the field, how would you approach Him, what would you ask Him?

Exercise for the day:

Write a letter to G-d—say what you would if you were to meet Him in the field outside your home right now.

Sanctify one mundane ('field') item in your life, and use it for something that would make the "King" proud.

"During *Elul* 'the king is in the field' and everyone who so desires is permitted to meet him, and he receives them all with a cheerful countenance and shows a smiling face to them all." **(Rabbi Schneur Zalman)**[2]

Events

2367 (1394 BCE)—Moses' parents, Amram and Jocheved, remarry after having separated because of Pharaoh's decree that all male Jewish babies be killed. Their reunion was prompted by their six-year-old daughter Miriam's rebuke. Moses is born six months and one day later on Adar 7, 2368 (Talmud, *Sotah* 12b).

2449 (1312 BCE)—The Spies who slandered the Land of Israel die in the desert (Talmud, *Sotah* 35a; see Numbers 13-14).[3]

Facts ◎

The sin of the spies who died today was not in their actual scouting effort; indeed the word *Elul* means "to scout/search" in Aramaic—in context of the scouting of the spies (see *Av* 30). Search and discovery is healthy and necessary in the *Elul* accountability process. The sin of the Spies was that they did not merely scout out the land but they came to a decisive conclusion: "We cannot conquer this land that consumes its inhabitants. It is too powerful for us." But they and we have no right to question whether the mission can be accomplished; our job is to figure out *how* to do it, not *whether* we can or not. In the month of *Elul*, when we search and scout out our own lives, we repair the sin of the spies, which took place on *Tisha B'Av*, 40 days after they went out on their mission on *Sivan* 29. Yet again, we see how *Elul* repairs and transforms the broken pieces of *Av*.[4]

Taking Initiative

It takes initiative to go out to meet G-d, even when He is in the field, close and available. It takes initiative to extend yourself and it takes love.

G-d gave us the power to love each other—the power to unite the Divine image which was split at the time of creation of the world into male and female—because He wanted us to learn through that how to love Him.

We learn how to love through our interactions with one another, and we also, sadly, learn how not to love. We hurt each other sometimes. But in the healthiest sense, when we learn to love another person, it's the first step towards learning how to love G-d as well.

After the hurt and loss—which we remember in the month of *Av*—love must begin on our initiative. We have to show—down here below—that we are ready for G-d's love to shine on us from above.

Elul is the time in the Jewish calendar when we take the first step. One of the acronyms of *Elul* is: *Ani l'dodi v'dodi li*, meaning "I am for my beloved, and my beloved is for me." (*Song of Songs* 6:3)

In *Elul* "I" initiate and "my beloved" responds in kind.[1]

The Torah teaches that it is guaranteed—G-d will respond. That doesn't always mean that the results will be what we want. But something will happen, because there's nothing more powerful than taking initiative.

When the Jews reached the Red Sea and were despairing, one man named Nachshon took the risk and walked into the water. The water reached his nose and then the sea parted. When you take initiative, the seas part.

Ask yourself: How often do you take the initiative in your life? How often do you take the initiative in your relationship with your beloved? And with G-d?

Exercise for the day:

Find a new way today to express your love to your beloved.

Don't wait—initiate something beautiful.

Find a new way today to express your love for G-d by doing something that G-d wants of you.

 "Open up for me the eye of a needle and I will open for you the most expansive corridors of the Great Hall." G-d asks of us only one thing: "I don't ask you to change your entire life; I ask only that you open up for me the eye of a needle. Dedicate to Me, one moment, one space, one corner of your life. But this moment, this space, this corner should be only for Me…"[2]

Laws and Customs

Some synagogues have the custom to announce on each day of *Elul: Shuvu Bonim Shovivim* [3] "Return my children, return," echoing the daily heavenly call that summons everyone to *teshuvah.*[4] Though our ears may not hear the call, our souls do hear it.[5] It behooves us to cup our ears, absorb the call and act on it.

Facts ◎

The month of *Elul*, whose astral sign is *betulah* (Virgo) is the month of the bride, a month in which the love between the Divine groom and His bride Israel is at its height. "I am for me beloved and my beloved is for me." *Elul* is a time when the initiative comes from our side of the relationship, and the Divine response to our love is one that relates to us as finite material beings and embraces our natural self and personality. We, the "bride" purify and refine ourselves in preparation for the "wedding" with the Divine that occurs on Rosh Hashana and particularly on Yom Kippur.[6] This is also symbolized by the *yud* (the letter of this month), the purest and simplest of letters, and also the origin of all letters. *Yud* is also the first letter in the essential four-letter Name of G-d .

Seeing G-d

Perhaps the most dramatic experience that happens atop Mt. Sinai is when Moses asks to meet G-d face to face: "I beg you, show me your glory." (Exodus 33:18).

G-d responds, "You cannot see My face, for no man can see Me and live ... [but] I will put you in a cleft of the rock, and will cover you with My hand while I pass by, and I will take away My hand, and you shall see My back..."

This exchange is puzzling. How could Moses not have known that one can only come face-to-face with G-d in the next world? And why does the Torah document G-d's rejection of his request?

The answer is that Moses' request was not rejected. In the language of metaphor Moses asked to understand G-d. G-d responded by saying that it is impossible to see His essence in this world, but it is possible to see its reflection. In effect, G-d told Moses, "you'll see My face by not looking."

There are things we see in life by looking directly at them, and there are things we see with our eyes closed. There are things that we hold onto by grasping them, and things that we hold onto by letting go.

Creative people know that when they let go that is when the creativity starts flowing. When they try to control it or force it, it does not come—the channels of creativity are blocked. For creativity to emerge requires letting go. The same thing is true of "seeing G-d."

G-d said to Moses, in effect, "You will see Me when you stop looking. You will see Me when you get your self out of the way."

Ask yourself: How often can you get your self out of the way to achieve a higher goal? Do you "see" G-d in your life? Have you learned to see by not looking?

Exercise for the day:

Recall an event in your life when you were able to gain something by letting go. Examine the process—how did you get yourself out of the way in order to make it happen?

"G-d would speak to Moses face to face, just as a person speaks with a close friend."
(Exodus 33:11)

"No other prophet like Moses ever rose in Israel, who knew G-d face to face."
(Deuteronomy 34:10)

Events	Laws and Customs
Birth and passing of Dan.[1]	During *Elul* students should be focusing their studies on books and topics that discuss *teshuvah* and personal introspection and refinement.
5027 (1267)—Nachmanides (Rabbi Moshe ben Nachman, 1194-1270) arrived in Jerusalem (after being forced to flee his native Spain) and renewed the Jewish community there. The synagogue he established is functional today, having been restored following the liberation of the Old City during the Six-Day War in 1967.	*Elul* is at the beginning of the new school season. All efforts should be made to ensure that every Jewish child be enrolled in a proper Jewish school, where he/she will receive a healthy Jewish education and learn about Torah and *mitzvot* as a way of life.

Letting Go and Diving In

Elul requires letting go. This is what the verse from *Song of Songs* which gives it its name—*Ani l'dodi, v'dodi li* ("I am for my beloved")—teaches us:

The initiative begins with the self—**"I am"**

The self turns toward **"my beloved"** (I don't exist for me—for my self—I exist for my beloved)

And the beloved responds—**"my beloved is for me"** precisely because "I" let go of "me."

In Hebrew, "letting go" is called *bittul*, which really means "suspension of self."

Someone who knows how to suspend himself or herself has the ability to hear what another person has to say, has the ability to love, can "see" G-d . It is something we all want to master, so why is it so hard?

It is so hard because, metaphorically speaking, even when we know how to swim we are often afraid to dive. We find ourselves standing at the edge of the pool and counting to ten, then to twenty, then to fifty ... and never getting up the courage to just jump. Our fear is of letting go. We are terrified of the moment of suspension, when our feet leave the ground but do not yet hit the water.

Often, the only way we get past our suspension phobia is when somebody comes along and pushes us in. This is why we all need help from the outside—why we all need mentors.

In the moment when you must let go, talking yourself into it is not likely to work because a brilliant mind cannot speak to a vulnerable heart—they don't speak the same language. So you must invite someone to push you—someone you trust.

Ask yourself: Do you have a mentor who pushes you from time to time? If not, do you know someone who you could trust to do so with wisdom and care?

Exercise for the day:

Identify an area, from the work of *Elul* you have done so far, where you would benefit from the friendly push of a mentor.

"Only one thing I ask of G-d , this I seek: May I dwell in the house of G-d all the days of my life, to behold the pleasantness of G-d and to visit in His Sanctuary." **(Psalm 27)**

Powerful requests—the most powerful ones—are single and intimate in nature. We don't ask for many things, but the request we make is absolute, complete, all encompassing. The more intimate the request the more intense is its singularity and simplicity.

Events

1657 (2103 BCE)—After 40 days of the Great Flood waters subsiding and the mountaintops appearing (on *Av* 1), Noah opens the ark window and sends forth the raven.[1] Seven days later, on *Elul* 18 he sends the dove and it returns with an olive branch in its beak. Another 7 days pass, and on *Elul* 25 he sends the dove for the final time. This time it does not return. Finally, after another 7 days, on Rosh Hashana (*Tishrei* 1), the land begins to dry and Noah opens the ark to see the drying land. It would take another 57 days, on *Cheshvan* 27, for the land to dry completely and Noah and his family would leave the ark—an entire solar year after they had entered it.[2]

Facts ◉

The Divine compassion in *Elul*—the month of *teshuvah*—is also reflected in the fact that this month has the power to finally subdue the devastating effects of the Great Flood. This is similar to Moses repairing the damage of the Golden Calf and the Seven Weeks of Consolation bringing us comfort after the destruction of *Av*.

Yet, true *teshuvah* does not just escape or even repair the past; *teshuvah* transforms the past. It's not merely damage control, but a process that redeems and elevates past wrongdoings, turning them into enormously powerful assets. *Teshuvah* turns our past mistakes into fuel for growth.

By sending out the dove—symbol of peace and compassion—Noah was testing to see whether it was an *Elul* atmosphere, if the severities (*gevurot*) of the flood had ended, the world was cleansed of its corruption, and the time had come for reconciliation with G-d . And indeed, the time had arrived. With each passing day in *Elul*—in seven-day cycles—the raging waters subsided, until the world became ready for its rebirth and renewal on Rosh Hashana.

Focusing on your Destination

At times when you must let go and you ask someone to push you, you must know where you want to be pushed. You must know your destination.

Rabbi Mendel Futerfas, who spent many years in a Siberian *gulag*, tells how he learned a great lesson from a tightrope walker who was also imprisoned there.

The rabbi asked the tightrope walker about the secret to his art. "What does one need to master? Balance? Stamina? Concentration?"

The tightrope walker's answered surprised him: "The secret is always keeping your destination in focus. You have to keep your eyes on the other end of the rope. But do you know what the hardest part is?"

"When you get to the middle?" the rabbi ventured.

"No," said the tightrope walker. "It's when you make the turn. Because for a fraction of a second, you lose sight of your destination. When you don't have sight of your destination that is when you are most likely to fall."

Life is something like a tightrope. To navigate it successfully you must have your destination in focus. You must know where you are going. When the time comes to make a turn, and for a moment you cannot see where you are headed, you have to have your destination in your mind's eye.

The ultimate destination—the final goal of all human efforts throughout history—is called *geula* ("redemption"), when the world will realize its purpose and reach ultimate refinement. The Jewish people have always kept their eyes on this destination; it gave them the power and freedom to forge ahead, despite all difficulties.

Geula is not a destination you can see by looking in front of you, you can only see it by looking inside of you.

Real focus is not physical, it is transcendental. Real focus is your relationship with your Divine mission. If it is well developed, it can guide you past the moments of danger, and keep you moving with confidence even in moments of the greatest fear and darkness.

Ask yourself: Do you have a real focus in your life? Do you have a larger goal?

Exercise for the day:

Identify your personal mission in life. What do you believe is your calling in this world?

If you have difficulty with this, identify the steps you must take to discover your mission.

"Elul is called the Month of *Teshuvah. Teshuvah* means "return." We return to our Divine essence, and we return all of existence to its appropriate place. *Teshuvah* can be read as *toshuv heh.* The lower *heh* of G‑d's Divine name (the essential four-letter Name of God, the Tetragrammaton) is manifest in our world. Through *teshuvah* we elevate and return the *heh* and everything it energizes to its true source." **(Rabbi Schneur Zalman)**[1]

Facts ◉

Every successful journey needs a clear and defined destination. *Geulah* is the destination. If *teshuvah* illuminates all the three pillars with a deeper connection (see *Elul* 17), then *geulah* (alluded to by the fifth acronym of *Elul*) infuses them all with a sense of destiny. All our Torah study, prayers, *mitzvot* and acts of love and compassion, which are infused with the refined spirit of *teshuvah*, come to fruition when we keep our eye on the destination.

Moses on Mt. Sinai always kept sight of his goal and destination: complete and absolute reconciliation with G‑d under a *chuppa*. Every prayer he recited, every effort he made during the 40 days on the mountain was directed toward his goal, and his goal infused each day, each moment, each act with the power of the big objective.

Elul is not just about the details; it also includes the larger goal and objective. We recognize that every act, every effort, no matter how small or large, is a "building block" of a larger structure called Redemption.[2] We know that all our efforts are leading to something, and that destination in turn infuses each moment with eternal meaning and power.

Relating to G~d

The Kabbalah suggests that the biggest challenge for us human beings is to maintain our individuality and at the same time have a relationship with G~d.

G~d is an all-encompassing reality, and if we were consciously aware of G~d's reality, we would cease to exist. But we do exist, because G~d concealed His light in order to make space for another entity called us.

And yet transcendence—that is, crossing the line of the reality where G~d is concealed to the reality where G~d is revealed (but we continue to exist nevertheless)—is possible. Heaven and earth can be married, can unite, and we can become one with G~dliness. A defined existence like ours, with physical parameters, can become one with that which is completely undefined.

This can happen because we were created in the image of G~d—we have holiness within us. And we can connect to the G~d within us by getting our selfish selves out of the way so that the holiness can surface.

The only thing that is eternal is a thing that is not driven by its own self, its own fuel. Whatever is driven by its own fuel, though it can be very powerful, is limited. This is why we aim to get past the self in order to connect to the eternal so that we too can become eternal.

And we do so by acting like the holy beings that we are.

We are commanded in the Torah—our guidebook to life and our guidebook to freedom from slavery to the physical aspects of life—to be holy, like G~d. "You shall be holy, for I, the Lord your G~d, am holy." (Leviticus 19:2)

This means being compassionate, because G~d is compassionate. It means being patient, kind, just, loving, creative. When we become holy like G~d, we connect with G~d.

Ask yourself: Do you want to connect to the Divine image within you? Is being holy a goal in your life? How often do your actions approach holiness?

Exercise for the day:

Consider what it would take for you to connect with the part of you that is holy.

Do something holy today.

"Anochi Anochi hu menachem'chem.[1] Not messengers, but I Myself comfort you. Why? Because 'if a fire gets out of control…the one who started the fire must make restitution.'[2] Since G-d is the one who 'started the fire' that destroyed the Temple, G-d Himself comes to comfort the loss."[3]

The Ten Commandments open with only one *Anochi,* but here we have a double *Anochi,* because to build requires only one *Anochi,* but to rebuild after loss takes double the energy.

Events	Facts ◎
4954 (1194)—Birth of Nachmanides ("Ramban," Rabbi Moshe ben Nachman, 1194-1270)—Torah scholar, Kabbalist, philosopher, physician and Jewish leader—in Gerona, Spain.	*Elul* is an acronym of *Oy L'rasha V'Oy L'shechanoi,*[4] "Woe onto a wicked person and woe onto his neighbor."[5] The efforts and prayers of Moses infused *Elul* with the power of *teshuvah* to transform the negative energy of the "wicked" and also its "neighbor," the preceding month of *Av.* (See *Av* 30.) The *Zohar* explains[6] that three months were given to Jacob (*Nissan, Iyar* and *Sivan*); Esau should have also received three months (*Tammuz, Av*— when the Temples were destroyed by Esau's descendants—and *Elul*). In actuality, Esau only received *Tammuz* and part of *Av* (until the 9th). Moses turned the month of *Elul* and a large part of the sad month of *Av* into positive energy and thereby took it away from Esau's domain.[7]

Inner Holiness

The essence of each one of us is good and holy because it is a part of G-d. The challenge is to recognize this holy part of ourselves—which resides deep on the inside—and to allow it to shine on the outside.

Even when we recognize our own inner glow, it is hard to actualize it. It's not easy. Because we live in a world that doesn't respect goodness and holiness; it respects wealth, success and power, the acquisition of which often demands the abandonment of holiness and goodness.

But Torah teaches us that we have the ability to access the inner part of ourselves and actualize it in everyday life, without changing everything about ourselves and our work. We have to learn how to discover our own soul and bring it into the world that we're living in and working in.

Whether you work in the world of music, business or the sciences, whether you are a doctor or a lawyer, whatever sphere you're trained in, your mission is to reveal your soul in that environment. The soul is not meant to replace the body and not meant to replace your life; it's mission is to reveal your inner dimension and integrate it into your life in order to elevate it, and to bring out the best in both your body and soul.

If you are on a spiritual journey and it's completely annihilating your life, there's something wrong. A sign of a healthy spiritual path is integration and transformation, not annihilation.

Ask yourself: Are you able to recognize your inner holiness? Is your spiritual path helping you or hindering you? Are you able to balance your spiritual and your social life? Do you live/work in an environment which respects holiness? Are you able to your reveal the things you hold sacred in this environment?

Exercise for the day:

Choose a simple act of holiness and demonstrate it in an environment which is usually oblivious to holiness. (This simple act could take the form of expressing gratitude, demonstrating patience/graciousness in a stressful situation, saying a blessing when eating, consoling a sick person, or giving charity.)

Resolve to make this a regular practice throughout *Elul*.

"I don't want your Paradise, I don't want your World to Come, I want only You—You alone"
(Rabbi Schneur Zalman)[1]

In the Haftorah of week five, G-d continues his consolation, which progressively grows more powerful[2]: "Sing barren one, you who have not given birth. Break into a song and cry aloud... for the children of the abandoned are more numerous than the children of the married... Enlarge the place of your habitat...for you will expand abroad to the right and to the left, until your descendants possess the nations and populate the desolate cities.

"Do not fear, for you will not be ashamed... You will forget the shame of your youth and the reproach of your widowhood... For your Creator is your husband... The Holy of Israel is your Redeemer. He will be called the G-d of the whole earth. For G-d called you as a wife abandoned and grieved in spirit. Can a wife of youth be rejected? says your G-d. For a brief moment I forsook you, but I will gather you with great compassion. In an outburst of wrath, for a moment I hid my face from you; but with everlasting kindness I will have compassion on you." (Isaiah, chapter 54)

Hod ("humility") radiates in this second week of Elul (fifth week of the Seven Weeks of Consolation). See Elul 6.
Do something today with deep humility.
Be humble in one area of your life today. In an area where you are usually aggressive, act humbly today.

Events

5669 (1909)—*Yahrzeit* of Rabbi Yosef Chaim of Baghdad (1835-1909), the renowned Sephardic Halachic authority and Kabbalist, known as *Ben Ish Chai* after his work by that name.

Facts ◎

On the second Shabbat of *Elul* (which falls on either *Elul* 9, 11, 13 or 14) we read the Torah portion *Ki Teitzei*, which opens with the theme of waging war against any adversary. "When you will go out to wage war above your enemy..." The Divine compassion of *Elul* teaches and empowers us to "go out to wage war" because all our battles are *outside* of our true selves, and we always remain *above* our enemies.[3]

Unmasking the Soul

We tend to think of the English word "face" as describing the outer layer of a person. However, in Hebrew, the word for face— *panim*—comes from the same root as *pnim* meaning "interior."

In the Hebrew language—the holy language of creation—things are named for their essence. And here Hebrew teaches us that the essence of a face is the opposite of what we think of ordinarily.

For many of us, our face has become a mask for our feelings rather than an expression of our higher self, our inner holiness. We have learned how to put on a smile while feeling terrible inside, or how to shed tears as a manipulation or pretense when we are not truly sad. In this instance, Hebrew is telling us what the face is supposed to convey, not what we do with it.

A mark of a holy person is that the inside is the same as the outside. And we recognize this. It is common, when we meet such a person to say that he or she has an aura—a special glow. Ecclesiastes (8:1) states: "The wisdom of the person shines in the face." We see this as a light of a holy person's face, because the face reflects that person's soul.

We're told that the great 15th century Kabbalist, the Ari, could read people's faces. And many people, when they would pass him on the street, would cover their faces because they felt that he saw past the mask and they were ashamed.

Ask yourself: If the Ari was walking the earth today, would you want him to see your face? Would you be ashamed to? To what extent is your face a mask for feelings you want to hide? To what extent does it reveal your inner core of holiness?

Exercise for the day:

As you interact with people today be conscious of what your face projects and to what extent it is an expression of your inner self.

At least once during the day try to feel a connection to the holiness inside and let it shine on your face.

Make a special attempt to smile to people today. Remember that everything is projection and reflection—your smile elicits a smile, etc.

"My heart says to you, seek out my countenance, Your countenance, G-d, I seek." (Psalm 27:8, recited twice daily during *Elul*)

"As water reflects a face, one heart reflects another." (Proverbs 27:19)

Laws and Customs

Today marks two weeks before Rosh Hashana and thirty days before the festival of Sukkot. Moses taught that we should begin preparing for a holiday thirty days earlier by studying its laws.[1] This is especially important in preparation for the upcoming month of *Tishrei*, which is filled with many holidays: Rosh Hashana, Yom Kippur, Sukkot, Shemini Atzeret and Simchat Torah.

It is also appropriate to prepare for the holiday by doing everything possible to provide for the needy, enabling them to properly celebrate the holiday and fulfill the *mitzvah* on Rosh Hashana to "eat delights and drink sweets and send gifts to others in need." (*Nechemia* 8:10).

Facts ◉

Elul acronym (word ends): *Lo yachail divoroi k'chol* (*hayotzei m'piv yaaseh*), "If a man makes a vow to G-d or makes an oath to obligate himself, he must not break his word, all (that he expressed verbally he must fulfill)." (Numbers 30:3). We derive from this that in the month of Elul we absolve ourselves of our vows.[2] [See also *Elul* 29.]

A vow reflects our respect for the inherent sanctity of the universe. We absolve our vows because we don't have the power to detach ourselves from the universe, but through our *teshuvah* in *Elul* we receive the power to transform the universe. This is because in these 40 days Moses was able to prevail on G-d to forgive the people for the sin of the Golden Calf and empowered them to transform their immersion in the material world into an even deeper spirituality.

Facing Yourself

The Baal Shem Tov[1] taught that everything we see, whether good or bad, is really a reflection of ourselves. If it was not, we'd simply not see it.

This phenomenon is part of a merciful way that G-d has of teaching us lessons in life. Most of us have a difficult time hearing from others that we have a flaw which we ourselves don't recognize. Therefore, G-d sets us up to have a confrontation with a person who exhibits that same flaw in some form. We see it and we say "how terrible." But then it dawns on us that we exhibit the same behavior, though perhaps in different form.

The same is true for positive things. We recognize a positive characteristic in others because we have it in ourselves. If we didn't have any element of it, we wouldn't recognize it.

In other words: You are what you see. And you see what you are.

Many Jews living in Germany in the 1930s didn't recognize the evil of the German people because they had none of it in themselves. They couldn't fathom that anyone could murder them in cold blood. If you are incapable of a crime, it's impossible to imagine that someone else is capable of it.

There are atrocities that we can't even relate to because we're not capable of doing such a thing ourselves.

The same is true for goodness or holiness.

Many of us are cynical because we never met anyone truly holy or truly pure. So we don't believe that it's possible to be that way because it's not part of our own experience.

Ask yourself: Are you cynical about the holiness of others? Do you see the goodness around you? When confronted with a behavior that you dislike are you able to see the same flaw, in some form, in yourself?

Exercise for the day:

Of the events of the past day, select a positive experience and identify how the goodness you encountered is embodied in you.

Of the events of the past day, select a negative experience and identify how this reflects a negative characteristic that you possess.

Elul 15

"Elul's unique power (even over *Tishrei*) is that the Thirteen Attributes of Divine Compassion radiate even when we are immersed in the mundane activities of the weekday."
(Rabbi Schneur Zalman of Liadi)[2]

Full moon.

This fulfills the ultimate purpose of life, but it requires the most powerful energy of all: to integrate the Divine into our material lives.

Facts ◉

Today is the full moon of *Elul*, which symbolizes fullness in all our activities of the month, in our case: fullness in our soul-searching work. What makes the moon full? When the moon is aligned with the sun and earth in the exact angle that allows its entire body to reflect the light of the sun to us on earth. The moon is the embodiment and epitome of *bittul* (suspension of self): Having no light of its own it reflects the light of the sun. *Bittul* is the primary ingredient in our *teshuvah* work in *Elul*. According to Jewish mysticism the full moon represents the fullness of *malchut* ("sovereignty" and "dignity"). As we prepare in *Elul* to rebuild *malchut* on Rosh Hashana, the full moon of *Elul* gives us special power to intensify our work.

A Time of Refuge

אצל

Whatever shortcomings you may find in yourself as you undertake the process of facing yourself in the month of *Elul*, know that within G-d's compassion that radiates this month everyone can find refuge.

In the introduction to the month of *Elul*, we noted that it is an acronym for a verse from the Book of Exodus (21:13) which speaks of the "cities of refuge" where those who committed an accidental crime could flee and make a new home: *inah le'yado vesamti lach* ("...deliver into his hand, I shall establish for you...").

By the Torah's command, nine cities of refuge were to be established in the Land of Israel, but not all in the same territory:

three in Israel proper—the Holy Land

three east of the River Jordan—the Wild East where manslaughter was common

three in the Time to Come, when G-d will enlarge the borders of Israel—the Holy Land of the future

This teaches us that G-d provides a refuge for everyone—from the relatively lawless to the holy.

At every stage of our spiritual/religious life there is the possibility of some "crime" (relative to our unique potential) and there is a safe place where we can take refuge to safely undergo self-examination and endeavor to make atonement.[1]

G-d gives us the month of *Elul* as that special time of refuge in the Hebrew calendar.

It is the way of the Western world to make Elul—which typically falls in high summer—a time for vacation. But there is another dimension to this: While you take vacation from your material work, you are freed to do serious spiritual work—accounting for the past and returning to your true self and to your mission from G-d.

Ask yourself: Have you made *Elul* a time of introspection in the past? How is this *Elul* different for you?

Exercise for the day:

Dedicate some of your vacation time for spiritual introspection, making the most of the opportunity that this *Elul* offers.

Sincerely express to G-d your desire to return to your Divine mission.

Intensify your intention when reciting Psalm 27 during this month.

"The sounding of shofar in the month of *Elul* is compared to the trumpet blasts preceding the arrival of a king. Because in this month we prepare ourselves for Rosh Hashana, the day when we coronate G-d as King of the universe."

Laws and Customs

In this month of compassion and love—the *mazal* of *betulah* and the month of the bride—it is customary to perform weddings all month long[2] (unlike other months when weddings are scheduled only during the first half of the month when the moon is waxing).

Facts ◉

From this day of *Elul* onward the moon continues to wane, until it will take its final "curtain call" and disappear on the last day of *Elul*, only to be reborn with an entirely new face on Rosh Hashana. We count the lunar cycle and emulate its rhythms, by using the next 14 days to clean up and remove any of our old baggage, and thus prepare ourselves for rebirth on Rosh Hashana.

Returning to Our Divine Essence

In our process of returning to our true selves—our Divine essence—we have much to learn from the way Moses reconciled with G-d after the sin of the Golden Calf.

Moses did not just plead. First of all, he took action. After he broke the tablets, he punished those responsible for making the idol, he made order in the Israelite camp, and he motivated the people to repentance. After that, he demonstrated to G-d that he was willing to sacrifice even that which was most precious to him in order to save the relationship between G-d and the Jewish people.

Moses told G-d, "If you don't forgive their sin, then, erase me, I beg you, from the book which You have written" (Exodus 32:32). Moses broke the Divine tablets—G-d's sacred word. He put himself—and his very connection to G-d and Torah—on the line in order to protect the people.

For this reason he is called the Shepherd of Israel—not a scholar, warrior, orator, or anything that generally distinguishes a leader, but a mild-mannered shepherd who cares about every lamb that might have strayed from the flock.

Following the sin of the Golden Calf, Moses knew the stakes were high. Moses wanted G-d to return to the people, and in so doing demonstrate to the human race that nothing is irreversible, that there is always hope. If you make a mistake, if you err and break something, it is always possible to repair it. Resignation or fatalism is never an option. If you turn away from G-d and betray your true self, it is always possible to return through a process called *teshuvah*.

Moses won this for us, and today we can always prevail even when things seem irreversibly broken.

Ask yourself: Can you recall a time when you were willing to sacrifice something precious in order to win forgiveness for a wrong you had committed? Can you recall a time when you felt this strongly about reconciling with someone you love?

Exercise for the day:

Describe how far you would be willing to go to win total forgiveness from your beloved.

Find an area in your life which you gave up on and make a move to repair the situation with absolute determination. Do something, do anything—never resign yourself.

"Of all the great things Moses accomplished, the greatest was breaking the tablets 'before the eyes of all of Israel,' to which G-d said 'thank you for breaking them.' This single act demonstrated Moses' absolute and total *ahavat Yisroel* ("love for the people") even at the expense of breaking G-d's tablets! The sign of a true leader."

Facts ◎

The five letters of the word *teshuvah* stand for the five paths of *teshuvah*:

T (tav) - *Tomim*, "Be sincere with your G-d"—Sincerity

Sh (shin) - *Shiviti*, "I have set G-d before me always"—Humble Awareness of the Divine

U (vav) - *V'ahavta*, "Love your fellow as yourself"—Love

V (bet) - *B'chol*, "In all your ways know Him"—Recognizing Divine Providence

H (heh) - *Hatzne Lechet*, "Walk discreetly with your G-d"—Discretion and modesty[1]

The Meaning of Teshuvah

The Hebrew word for "repentance"—*teshuvah* —actually implies the opposite. When you repent, the implication is that you're leaving the wrong path, regretting that you ever took that turn in your life. But *teshuvah* literally means "return," which implies that you are not leaving something, you are coming back to something.

This is not to suggest that there is anything inappropriate in repentance. Before you can embrace the right path you *must* leave the wrong path, you *must* regret having taken it, you *must* go away from it.

But return is much more profound. It's not just going away from bad behavior, it is going back to your true self, your Divine soul. It's not just damage control, it is returning to the essence that was always pure—it is returning to G-d.

We can understand this better through the following analogy of two teachers disciplining a student. One teacher reprimands, demanding that the student acknowledge he did wrong and agree to make amends. The other teacher tells the student, "You know, I want to tell you I am very disappointed that you didn't live up to who you really can be. Your soul is much greater than that."

Which teacher is correct? Both are.

You can't just wax eloquent about the soul, you have to acknowledge the error and make good on the damages. There is no way around that. But then you have see that this is not the real you—the real you is greater than that.

These are the two levels of *teshuvah*. The first level involves cleaning up the mess in your room, so to speak, because your room has to be clean before you can bring something new or fresh in there. This is step one—making order and repairing that which was broken. But step two, the critical step, is connecting to your essence.

Ask yourself: How much about you is an expression of your essence, and how much is added baggage? Can you distinguish between the two?

Exercise for the day:

Identify a few areas that need to be cleaned up in your life.

Identify a few areas that reflect your essence, your higher self.

Listen to music or read something that resonates and helps you recognize what you are really about, what you really want.

"Chai (18th day of) *Elul* infuses *chai* (life) into the month and work of *Elul*, and into our efforts toward achieving 'I am to my beloved and my beloved is to me.'"

(The Rebbe Yosef Yitzchak)[1]

Countdown

Twelve days left to Rosh Hashana. Today is the day of accounting for last year's Rosh Hashana and last *Tishrei*—the High Holiday season.

Events

Noah sends out the dove from the ark for the first time. (See *Elul* 10.)

1609—*Yahrzeit* of Rabbi Yehudah Loewe, the Maharal of Prague (1525-1609), outstanding Torah scholar, philosopher, Kabbalist and Jewish leader. Popularly known for creating a *golem* (clay man) to protect the Jewish community of Prague from the frequent threat of blood libels.

5468 (1698)—Birthday of Rabbi Israel Baal Shem Tov (1698-1760), founder of the Chassidic movement. After many years as a member of the society of "hidden *tzadikim*," living under the guise of an ignorant clay-digger, Rabbi Israel Baal Shem Tov

was instructed by his masters to reveal himself and begin to publicly disseminate his teachings. This he did on his 36th birthday, *Elul* 18, 5494 (1734).

5505 (1745)—Birthday of Rabbi Schneur Zalman of Liadi (1745-1812), founder of the "Chabad" branch of Chassidism. He was born on the same day as the 47th birthday of his "spiritual grandfather," Rabbi Israel Baal Shem Tov (Rabbi Schneur Zalman was the disciple of the Baal Shem Tov's disciple and successor, Rabbi DovBer of Mezeritch). This day is thus called the "birthday of the two great luminaries."

Laws and Customs

The last twelve days of *Elul* correspond to the twelve months of the year. On each of these twelve days we have the ability to reflect on and amend any of our shortcomings in the corresponding month of the past year. *Elul* 18 corresponds to the first month of the year (*Tishrei*); *Elul* 19 corresponds to the second month of the year (*Cheshvan*) and so on.

The Gate of Tears

Judaism teaches that a soul is never damaged. The body perhaps, the psyche perhaps, but the inner core of goodness that is the soul, never. The essence always remains intact.

Although that is true, the damage that we do in our physical lives can create a ruin so big, so high, and so wide that it completely obscures the pure essence underneath.

And yet, Moses taught us that there is never a ruin so big that it can't be rebuilt; there is nothing that breaks that can't be mended.

After the sin of the Golden Calf, in his plea for forgiveness, Moses told G-d, "You created human beings as a flawed race who are bound to make mistakes. You must create a way for them to repair these mistakes. You must tell me that there is a way out, that there is hope."

In response, G-d told Moses, "I created the world in accordance with the laws of cause and effect. For every action there is a reaction. And sometimes the reaction is such that it can't be reversed. You're asking Me to change the natural laws that I Myself created."

But Moses argued, "I'm not asking you to change the laws. I'm asking you to crack open just one door."

And G-d did.

This one door is called the "gate of tears."

Tears are like the spout on a kettle that allows internal pressure out. They have the power to pry open any door.

Moreover our Sages say that "tears bathe the soul." When we cry out to G-d with genuine sincerity, we wash away the muck that obscures our pure essence.

Ask yourself: Have you ever made a mistake so big that you thought there was no way to repair it? What must you repair that was broken in the past year? Do you believe that it can be repaired? Do you believe that G-d will help you in the process?

Exercise for the day:

Identify what is broken in your life.

Take the first step to mend one thing that is broken—either in your relationship with a friend, or a loved one, or G-d.

Allow yourself to cry.

Countdown
Eleven days left to Rosh Hashana.
Today is the day of accounting for last
Cheshvan—the beginning of the
"regular" year.

" 'She weeps for her father and mother an entire month'[1]
refers to the month of _Elul_, a time of _teshuvah_; a time of
healthy tears."
(The Ari)[2]

"I firmly rely on the thirteen words [Divine Attributes],
and on the gates of tears which are never closed; therefore
I have poured out my prayer before the Searcher of hearts;
in these I trust, and in the merit of the three Patriarchs.
May it be Your will, You who hears the voice of weeping,
to store our tears in Your flask, and save us from all cruel
decrees, for to You alone are our eyes turned."
(Yom Kippur Neilah prayer)

Facts ◉

Yet another acronym for _Elul_ is _Aron Luchot U'shivrei Luchot_,[3] meaning "Ark
(of) tablets and broken tablets." Inside the Ark lay both the second set of
Tablets that Moses received on Yom Kippur, and the first set of Tablets that
Moses shattered after seeing the Jews worship the Golden Calf. This
teaches us that _Elul_ has the power to not only achieve renewal (a new set of
tablets), but also to transform the broken tablets through _teshuvah_.[4] This is
because true _teshuvah_ not only repairs but transforms the past. When our
hearts feel like "broken tablets," then the break itself is redeemed and elevated; this awareness of feeling broken brings us to a new and deeper connection to G-d.

The Secret of a Broken Heart

We all make mistakes and break things in our life, but life also breaks us. We've all been broken in one way or another. We have all experienced broken promises or broken relationships; we have experienced the loss of a job or the loss of a loved one.

Different people react in a different manner to the hurt that inevitably accompanies breakage. Some people are devastated. Others grow because of it.

Some people have strength, some don't. And there is a reason why. A tree that doesn't fall over in a storm is a tree that was strong before the storm. The storm just revealed the strength of the tree. But a tree with no roots may be able to stand up in normal weather, but it breaks when a storm strikes.

And yet, the miracle of creation is that, paradoxically, the more broken you are now, the more whole you have the chance to become.

The Rebbes teach that there is nothing as complete as a broken heart. When your heart is broken, you are in a place that is real.

Why is a broken wall the holiest place for Jews? Why do Jews stand and pray at a broken wall when there are such beautiful edifices around? Because, Jews know that this isn't a perfect world. As long as the world is not perfect, Jews cannot stand in a beautiful edifice. Jews can only stand and cry at a broken wall.

The illusion of perfect edifices in an imperfect world makes us feel good. But it is an illusion nevertheless—good for Hollywood and Broadway, but it's not reality.

The reality is that the world is a broken place —it's a broken place full of broken people whose job is to mend what is broken.

Ask yourself: When is the last time you felt that your heart was broken? Did you feel more alone or closer to G-d when you acknowledge that to yourself?

Exercise of the day:

In your prayers today, describe to G-d your broken heart and explain why it is broken.

The Seven Weeks of Consolation continue and accelerate. In this sixth week the Prophet Isaiah (chapter 60) tells of G-d's even greater consolation and of the vision of the world's Redemption:

> "Arise, shine for your light has come, and G-d's glory has risen upon you. For, behold, darkness will cover the earth and thick clouds the peoples, but G-d will arise over you and His glory will be seen upon you. Nations will come to your light, and kings to the brightness of your rising...
>
> "Aliens will build up your walls...The sons of your oppressors will come bending to you, and all who despised you will bow down at your feet. They will call you, 'The city of G-d, the Zion of the Holy one of Israel.' Though you were forsaken and hated with no one passing through you, I will make you an eternal majesty...
>
> "Violence will no longer be heard in your land, neither desolation nor destruction within your borders...Your sun will no longer set, not will your moon wane. For G-d will be your everlasting light, and your days of mourning will be ended. Your people will all be righteous; they will possess the land forever; the branch of My planting, the work of My hands... The smallest will become a thousand, and the least a mighty nation; I, G-d, will hasten in its time."

Yesod ("bonding") radiates in this third week of Elul (the sixth week of the Seven Weeks of Consolation).

Countdown
Ten days left to Rosh Hashana. Today is the day of accounting for last *Kislev* —the month of Chanukah.

Facts ◉

On the third Shabbat of *Elul*[1] we read the Torah portion of *Ki Tavo*, which opens with the commandment to enter the Promised Land and bring *bikkurim*, the first-fruit offering—appropriate as we prepare to enter the new year by offering of our own "first" and best fruit toward G-dly ends. This is followed by the sixth Haftorah of the Seven Weeks of Consolation.

Ezra decreed that *Ki Tavo* be always read before Rosh Hashana (with a break of Parshat *Netzavim-Vayeilech*) in order to emphasize that before the new year all the curses (discussed in this Torah portion) come to an end.[2] The Rebbe Dovber once fainted upon hearing the curses read in this portion. Later he explained why he had never fainted before. "When my father reads, I only hear blessings..." The year he fainted, his father did not read the portion.

Faith in G-d's Mercy

Moses had faith. Although he knew that the Jews had sinned and that there was no excuse for it, he had faith in G-d's mercy. And his faith gave birth to hope.

As a result, we human beings have the faith inside of us that we can achieve the impossible —build a machine that can fly; find the cure for any disease; walk on the moon. And Moses was the first one who brought this absolute faith into the cosmic consciousness.

Faith in G-d's mercy gives us the courage to fight for forgiveness when we have transgressed and are sincerely sorry. Faith means that we bring all our broken pieces and our broken heart to the table and we challenge G-d just as Moses did.

Our faith also gives us the right to challenge G-d when we are suffering. It is actually a lack of faith not to challenge G-d, because it's not being sensitive to the way G-d created us. G-d created us so that when we experience pain or witness suffering, we cry. And our tears give us a right to challenge.

But faith also means that even if we don't get what we want, we still move forward. We don't become bitter and we don't give up.

In October of 1994, the Wachsman family— whose son Nachshon, an Israeli soldier, was kidnapped by Hamas terrorists—mobilized Israel to pray for his rescue. In the end, however, Nachshon was murdered.

Fearing that some who had prayed for their son might have a crisis in faith, Yehuda and Esther Wachsman issued a statement at his funeral: "G-d had answered all the prayers for Nachshon. But G-d's answer was 'no.'"

That is unwavering faith. That is real faith.

Real faith of an intelligent person is a tool that's beyond logic and beyond reason. It's super-rational. Reason can only reach so high, faith can reach heaven.

Ask yourself: How strong is your faith? Have you ever challenged G-d to forgive you when you were sincerely sorry?

Exercise for the day:

Examine your faith and identify its strengths and its weaknesses.

Cultivate your faith by looking for examples of things you absolutely believe in that don't have a rational basis—like love, for example.

"G-d is my light and my salvation, whom shall I fear? The L-rd is the strength of my life, whom shall I dread?... [They would have crushed me] had I not[1] believed that I would see the goodness of the L-rd in the land of the living.

Hope in the L-rd, be strong and let your heart be valiant, and hope in the L-rd." **(Psalm 27)**

Countdown
Nine days left to Rosh Hashana. Today is the day of accounting for the month of *Tevet*— in the dead of cold winter.

Laws and Customs

During *Elul*, we recite special prayers of forgiveness called **Selichot**. Sephardic Jews recite these prayers from the 1st day of *Elul*; Ashkenazic Jews begin reciting these prayers on the Saturday night before Rosh Hashana, after midnight (when the severities of night begin to wane).[2]

When Rosh Hashana falls on a Monday or Tuesday, we begin saying *Selichot* on the Saturday night of the preceding week (*Elul* 22 or *Elul* 21), thus there are seven or eight days of *Selichot*. When Rosh Hashana falls on Shabbat there are six days of *Selichot* (beginning on *Elul* 24). When it falls on Thursday there are four days of *Selichot* (beginning on Elul 26).

Selichot are begun at a time that would provide at least ten opportunities for their recitation before and including Yom Kippur. This is based on the custom, once prevalent, to fast for ten days (eating at night, of course) before and including Yom Kippur. During the period from and including Rosh Hashana through Yom Kippur, there are four occasions when fasting is inappropriate (the two days of Rosh Hashana, the Shabbat between Rosh Hashana and Yom Kippur, and *Erev* Yom Kippur).

Since in the Ashkenazic tradition, *Selichot* always commences Saturday night, the first prayer begins "At the end of the Day of Rest, we approached You first." *Selichot* begin in and is generated by the spirit of Shabbat—not with sadness, but with joy and pleasure.[3] On subsequent days, the custom is to recite the *Selichot* in the early morning hours, before the morning prayers, because this time is considered a specially favorable time, in terms of G-d's presence and closeness to us.[4]

Facts ◉

The awe of Rosh Hashana and Yom Kippur can begin being felt on the first night of *Selichot*. An hour after midnight we solemnly gather to recite these special prayers, which include the Thirteen Divine Attributes of Compassion. The *Selichot* prayers are recited with the same serious hushed tone as the prayers of the Days of Awe. In effect, the *teshuvah* of *Elul* intensifies with *Selichot* as we get closer to Rosh Hashana.

The Strength of Giants

אלול

As we approach the final week of *Elul*, when we begin to recite *Selichot*, the special prayers for forgiveness, we have the confidence that, as weak as we may feel, we have tremendous strength nevertheless.

The cumulative *mitzvot* of the past generations gives us that strength. The good that our parents, grandparents, and great-grandparents did lives on forever and accumulates, and is our inheritance.

We might be midgets, but we stand on the shoulders of giants. Although we are puny, we can see even farther than the giants, because we are standing on the shoulders of past generations.

Nine generations ago, the Baal Shem Tov would go to a special place on Rosh Hashana, he would light a fire in a special way, say a special prayer, and as a result the entire world would be blessed.

In the next generation, his successors knew the location of the special place and they knew how to light the fire but they forgot the prayers. So instead, they would pray, "Whatever the Baal Shem Tov achieved here with the fire, we should achieve."

The next generation knew the location but they forgot the rest. So they just stood in the location and said, "Whatever the Baal Shem Tov achieved here, we should achieve."

Today, we have forgotten even the location. So what do we do? We tell the story...

We are asked to do only that which we are capable of. We do not have to be like the giants of the past. We just have to do what is in our power—stand on their shoulders. When we do so we lay claim to everything they achieved plus we add our own small part—and that small part, added to the good deeds of our ancestors, might just be enough to tip the scales and bring redemption.

Ask yourself: Do you know what your small part in this world is? What can you add to the cumulative accomplishments of the giants of the past?

Exercise for the day:

Do one small *mitzvah* you have not done before.

Identify something positive that your parent or grandparent did and take it one step further.

"G-d will answer you on the day of distress." (Psalms 20:2) David knew that the Holy Temple was to be destroyed and that the offerings were to cease. He was aggrieved for the sake of Israel and asked: "How will they attain atonement for their iniquities?" G-d answered: "David, do not be distressed, for I already disclosed to Moses the *sidrei selichah* [the orders of prayers for forgiveness] and I said to him: When troubles come upon Israel because of their iniquities, let them stand before Me as one band and utter the *seder selichah*, and I will respond to them."
(The Midrash)[1]

Countdown

Eight days left to Rosh Hashana. Today is the day of accounting for the month of *Shevat*—when we celebrate *Tu B'Shevat*, the "New Year for the Trees."

Facts ◉

"But if we had not waited so long, we could have returned there and back twice by now." (*Shavnu zeh paa'mayim*)—Judah's words to his father Jacob urging him to allow Benjamin to be brought before Joseph (Genesis 43:10). *Shavnu paa'mayim*—"return twice"—refers to two types of *teshuvah*: a) The general *teshuvah* of Rosh Hashana, and b) The specific *teshuvah* of Yom Kippur, in which we specify our iniquities. Both these types of *teshuvah* are dependent on the accounting of *Elul*. *Elul* is the same letters as the word *lule* ("but if we had not"). In *Elul* we "wait" and reflect on our actions and behavior, and that prepares and enables us to "return twice," in the two types of *teshuvah* on Rosh Hashana and Yom Kippur. *Elul* however, is a general preparation; the more specific preparation for Rosh Hashana is in the days of *Selichot*; and the specific preparation for Yom Kippur is in the Ten Days of *Teshuvah* that begin on Rosh Hashana. (Baal Shem Tov)[2]

Praying for Forgiveness

In our prayers before and during the High Holiday we repeatedly ask G-d to forgive us in three different ways:

selach lanu

mechal lanu

kapper lanu

While these Hebrew words are virtually synonymous—all meaning "forgive us"—they have different implications which shed light on the process of seeking forgiveness from G-d as well as from other human beings.

Selach lanu comes from *selichah* meaning "pardon." To ask for pardon is to say to the one we have injured: "I am sorry for what I did; I sincerely regret having done it, and I will never do it again." According to Jewish law, the appropriate response to this request is for the one we've injured to believe we are sincere and to respond positively. One who refuses to do this is considered a cruel person.

Mechal lanu comes from *mechilah*, meaning "wiping away." Here, we are asking the one we've injured to wipe away the transgression as if it never happened, and restore the relationship to the former level of warmth and intimacy. For the one who has been injured a positive response to this is naturally difficult.

But it is within each person's G-d-given powers to forgive to this extent. Hence, one must, according to Jewish law.

Kapper lanu comes from *kapparah*, meaning "atonement" (as in Yom Kippur, the Day of Atonement). When we request from the one we've injured to grant us atonement, we are saying, in effect, "My conscience will not let me live with myself, because of what I did to you and to our relationship. Please forgive me and take away the guilt and hurt that I feel." To respond positively to this is beyond human capacity. It is only G-d who can reach inside our hearts and say, "Be consoled."

Ask yourself: How have you responded when someone has come to you asking forgiveness? Have you forgiven others as completely as you want to be forgiven by G-d?

Exercise for the day:

Make a list of people you have hurt in some way.

Describe what you must do to ask their forgiveness.

Begin.

"Pray like a pauper[1]—suspend all your sophistication, literacy, and intelligence. Stand vulnerable, with no layers, with your essence exposed before G-d's essence. Stand innocent like a child. Then you will reach and see G-d's face—G-d's essence." **(Baal Shem Tov)**[2]

Countdown
Seven days left to Rosh Hashana. Today is a day of accounting for the month of *Adar*—the joyful month in which Purim is celebrated.

Facts ◉

Teshuvah infuses all your activities (Torah and *mitzvot*) with vitality and a deeper sense of your own essence. Without *teshuvah*, Torah study and *mitzvah* performance can become ordinary and mechanical. *Teshuvah* polishes and refines all your activities and makes them sparkle with the fire of the deepest recesses of your soul, reaching upward, returning to its source.

The Thirteen Attributes of Compassion

As we petition G-d to forgive us, we repeatedly recite the Thirteen Attributes of Compassion.

These Thirteen Attributes of Compassion were revealed to Moses when he pleaded for G-d's forgiveness after the sin of the Golden Calf. And they radiate during the month of *Elul*, when we relive Moses' experience.[1]

Moses was dealing with the aftermath of a very grave thing—idolatry, a betrayal of G-d Himself. And this act of idolatry was quite intentional—the Israelites knew the consequences. Nevertheless, Moses asked G-d to restore the special relationship between Himself and His treasured people.

To Moses' entreaty, G-d responded with an unprecedented gift. He revealed His Thirteen Attributes of Compassion—thirteen secrets of G-d's "personality" that only He could have revealed.[2]

We recite these Thirteen Attributes many times during the High Holidays: "*Hashem, Hashem*, Almighty, compassionate and gracious, slow to anger, and abundant in kindness and truth, keeper of kindness for thousands of generations, endurer of iniquity and transgression and sin, and cleanser [of those who repent]." (Exodus 34:6-7)[3]

Each one of these words is profoundly mystical and contains enormous Divine energy. The Thirteen Attributes of Compassion are described in the *Zohar*, the classical work of the Kabbalah, as the "thirteen-petalled rose" —the greatest secret of life, the key to repairing whatever is broken.

According to the Talmud (*Rosh Hashana* 17b), G-d told Moses: "Whenever Israel sins, let them recite this and I will forgive them."

The repetition of G-d's name—*Hashem, Hashem*—indicates that G-d is telling us, "I am the same G-d before you sin as I am after you sin and repent." This is a solemn assurance that the invocation of the Thirteen Attributes will never be without effect.

This assurance means that repentance is always possible. The implication is also plain: if we emulate G-d's compassionate ways, He will treat us compassionately in return.

Ask yourself: Do you consciously emulate G-d's compassionate ways? If so, how? If not, why not?

Exercise of the day:

Do one deed today which expresses compassion, especially to someone who may have wronged you. Describe how it felt to do it.

"What is the rose? It is the collective soul of Israel. For there is a rose (above) and a rose (below) ... Just as a rose has thirteen petals, so does the collective soul of Israel have thirteen measures of compassion encompassing it on all its sides." **(Opening of Zohar)**

Elul 24

Countdown
Six days left to Rosh Hashana. Today is the day of accounting for the month of *Nissan*—the month of Passover and liberation.

Events

Noah sends forth the dove from the ark for the second time; this time the dove returns carrying an olive branch.

1933—*Yahrzeit* of the Torah scholar and Jewish leader Rabbi Yisrael Meir Kagan (1838-1933) of Radin (Poland), author of *Chafetz Chaim* (a work on the evils of gossip and slander and on guidelines to proper speech) and *Mishna Berurah* (a codification of Torah law).

Facts ◉

In mystical texts,[4] this day—the day before creation on *Elul* 25—is referred to as the "Shabbat" which precedes and blesses all creation.

The Countdown to Rosh Hashana

אלול

Less than a week remains until Rosh Hashana, which is called "the birthday of the world." In fact, Rosh Hashana is the birthday of the first humans—Adam and Eve—who came into being on the sixth day of creation. This means that the first day of creation coincides with the 25th of Elul.[1]

Today is the day in the Hebrew calendar which carries with it nothing less than the energy of the creation of existence—time, space, matter, darkness, and light. Today we begin preparing the world for its rendezvous with G-d on Rosh Hashana.

If thus far you have not taken full advantage of the opportunities inherent in *Elul* to prepare for the High Holidays, the time to start is now. Preparation is essential for success in anything in life—be it material or spiritual, be it an audit of your taxes, or an audit of your soul.

Imagine yourself arriving in the reception room of a big corporation.

"Can I help you?" says the receptionist.

"Oh, I guess so," you answer yawning and surveying the ceiling.

The receptionist looks quizzically at you. "Well ... why are you here?"

"I'm not exactly sure."

"Are you here to apply for a job, perhaps?"

"Yes I think that's it."

"Okay, did you bring a resume?"

You look at her feeling a little stupid. "No, I didn't bring anything."

"Well, then perhaps you can come back when you've prepared for this."

If you arrived at a big corporation that ill prepared, you'd expect nothing to happen. Similarly, if you arrive at a synagogue on Rosh Hashana without preparation, without knowing what you are there for, or what this is all about, what can you truly expect?

Moses was on the mountain for 80 days. You don't have to physically go to the mountain, but you have to climb. Rosh Hashana and Yom Kippur will be only the sum total of what you do today.

Ask yourself: How well prepared are you for the High Holidays?

Exercise for the day:

Identify the strengths and weaknesses in your preparatory work thus far.

Recreate day one of creation, and bring a little light into your corner of the world.

Elul Month of Consolation

"In the beginning, G-d created the heavens and the earth. The earth was unformed and desolate and darkness covered the face of the abyss. The spirit of G-d hovered above the water's surface. G-d said, 'Let there be light.' And there was light. G-d saw that the light was good and G-d separated between the light and the darkness. G-d called the light day, and the darkness He named night. And it was evening and it was morning, day one." **(Genesis 1:1-5)**

Day One of Creation Countdown

Five days left to Rosh Hashana. Today is the day of accounting for the month of *Iyar*—the month when we fulfill the *mitzvah* of Counting the Omer and refining our personalities.

Events

3761 BCE—Creation of existence

3426 (335 BCE)— The rebuilding of the walls of Jerusalem—which had been in ruins since the destruction of the First Temple by the Babylonians 88 years earlier—was completed by Nechemia, as related in the Book of Nechemia (chapter 6).

3862 (102 CE)—*Yahrzeit* of the Talmudic sage Rabbi Eliezer, son of Rabbi Shimon bar Yochai, and of Rabbi Yechiel Michel of Zlotchev (1721?-1786), disciple of the Baal Shem Tov.

Laws and Customs

Selichot (all week)

After reciting the first *Selichot* after midnight Saturday night before Rosh Hashana, we continue to do so each morning at dawn (before the morning prayers) until the day before Rosh Hashana, in preparation for the "Days of Awe."

In these days when the universe was created some have the custom to read each day the chapter in Genesis that corresponds to that respective day of creation: on *Elul* 25 the verses that discuss day one of creation; on *Elul* 26 day two of creation; and so on.[2]

Cultivating Compassion

Part of the preparatory work of *Elul*—as we recite the Thirteen Attributes of Compassion—is to examine how compassionate we are in our own actions.

Elul is a month when G-d's compassion is flowing. But to tap into this flow of compassion, you must reach up from below to channel it down in your direction.

This is the secret of *Ani l'dodi*, "I am for my beloved"—I take initiative, I show that I am for my beloved, rather than waiting for my beloved to make a move.

It is true that G-d told Moses (Exodus 33:19): "I will be gracious to whom I will be gracious, and I will show compassion to whom I will show compassion." Therefore, sometimes you can experience G-d's compassion without having done anything yourself. But you can't expect it. You still have to do your part.

As compassionate as you may be now you can always be more compassionate. (As they say, if good is good, is better not better?) Compassion is a trait that can be cultivated—you become compassionate when you act compassionately.

Make no mistake, as people often do in the Western world—compassion doesn't mean that you look the other way and ignore crimes committed against you or others; compassion is not a contradiction of justice. It is true that forgiveness is part of compassion, but compassion is a great deal more than that.

First, compassion means being sensitive to another person's soul; it requires remembering that each one of us—however coarse and imperfect we may be on the outside—is endowed with a perfect Divine soul on the inside. And second, compassion means transcending our own comfort zone out of love for another.

Ask yourself: How sensitive are you to the souls of others? Do you see the Divine soul in others?

Exercise for the day:

Identify what it would mean for you to transcend your comfort zone for the sake of compassion.

Reach out in compassion to someone whose Divine soul you have a hard time seeing.

Recreate day two of creation, by reviewing whether you have healthy boundaries in your life.

"G-d said, 'Let there be a canopy in the midst of the waters and let it separate between waters and waters.' G-d made the canopy and separated between the waters which were beneath the canopy and the waters which were above the canopy. And it was so. G-d named the canopy heaven. And it was evening and it was morning, a second day."

(Genesis 1:6-8)

Day Two of Creation Countdown
Four days left to Rosh Hashana. Today is the day of accounting for the month of *Sivan*—the month when Moses began his 120-day journey, and the month in which the Torah was given on Mt. Sinai.

Facts ◉

We recite *Selichot* a minimum of four days (in Ashkenazic communities) because offerings brought to the Temple had to be examined for disqualifying flaws for four days prior to their offering.[1] Another reason is that just as the receiving of the Torah required three days of preparation, so too with Rosh Hashana, the Day of Judgment, the day in which we proclaim and reaffirm the sovereignty of G-d.[2]

The *Selichot* prayers for forgiveness are divided into three sections: a) the introduction, which is the same every day; b) the conclusion, which is also the same every day; c) the middle part which has selections of various prayers (*piyutim*) mixed in with supplications, including repeated appeals to G-d's Thirteen Attributes of Compassion.

Compassion as Love

Compassion means transcending your own comfort zone out of love for another. Compassion is love in the purest sense of the word.

The Book of Genesis (18:1-2) relates that shortly after his circumcision, G-d appeared to Abraham while he sat recuperating in the groves of Mamrei. While he was communing with G-d, Abraham noticed, off in the distance, three nomads approaching across the desert. Without so much as an "Excuse me" to G-d, he immediately stood up and ran to greet them and to prepare a meal for them.

From this strange incident, the Talmud derives the equally strange lesson that "welcoming guests is more powerful than welcoming G-d."

The Talmud does not ponder if this was the right thing to do, because clearly Abraham *knew*—without hesitation—that this was the right thing to do.

But how did Abraham know this? How did he know his actions would not offend G-d?

Abraham knew because Abraham was a holy man. Selfishly, he would have liked to spend more time with G-d. He could have asked him a lot of questions. But a holy person doesn't do just what's good for him, he does what's good

for reality. He is capable of transcending his personal comfort zone for the greater good—for the love of others.

The truth is that when Abraham turned to greet his guests, he didn't turn away from G-d-he turned away from one level of G-d to experience a higher level of G-d. This higher level is defined by selflessness, by doing for others.

To love G-d and to love other people is the same thing. Your love of G-d has to bring more love to others. And fundamentally, it goes even deeper than that. When you love G-d, you will love other people more. And that's the whole point of it.

Ask yourself: Do you feel that loving G-d and loving people is the same thing? Have you been able to apply this in your life? With what result?

Exercise for the day:

Demonstrate your love for your neighbor and your love for G-d in one specific act.

Recreate day three of creation by planting a "seed" today that will make things grow—do a good deed that will have perpetual effects.

Elul   Month of Consolation

℧ "G-d said, 'Let the waters beneath the heavens be gathered into one place, and let the dryness be visible.' It was so. G-d named the dryness 'earth,' and the gathering of the waters, He named 'seas.' And G-d saw that it was good. G-d said, 'Let the earth sprout grass, seed-yielding herbs, fruit trees bearing fruit of its own kind, with its seed within, upon the earth.' And it was so. The earth brought forth sprouts, herbs yielding seed of its kind, and trees making fruit which has in it seeds of its kind. And G-d saw that it was good. And it was evening and it was morning, a third day." **(Genesis 1:9-13)**

Day Three of Creation Countdown
Three days left to Rosh Hashana. Today is the day of accounting for the month of *Tammuz*—the month when Moses began his fateful climb to confront G-d, and the month in which we remember some very sad occasions.

Events

1855—*Yahrzeit* of Rabbi Shalom Rokeach, founder of the Belz Chassidic dynasty.

Facts ◎

Selichot prayers seeking forgiveness go back to the beginning of human history, when Adam, and then later Cain, prayed to G-d for forgiveness. The Torah is replete with supplications on behalf of individuals and the community. Similar prayers, composed in later times, are found in Talmudic texts. The first reference to, and text for, *Selichot* in connection with the "Days of Awe" is found in the early medieval era of the *Geonim*, in the writings of Rav Amram Gaon.

Three days before Rosh Hashana (and the same with Yom Kippur) the one who will lead the prayer service and the one who will sound the shofar should sanctify and prepare themselves and study the intentions of the prayers and shofar sounding.[1] As Rabbi Eliezer said: "My father, Rabbi Shimeon (Bar Yochai) would not listen to anyone leading the prayers on Rosh Hashana and Yom Kippur unless they prepared themselves three days before." Rabbi Shimeon explained that he did so because these prayers atone for the entire world, and the sounding of the shofar requires a special wisdom to know the mystery of the sound.[2]

Loving Unconditionally

To build a new structure takes talent and strength. To rebuild a ruin takes compassion —compassion which flows from unconditional love.

Moses rebuilt the ruin of a relationship between G-d and the Jewish people because he so profoundly touched G-d with his unconditional love—both his love for the Jews and his love for the Creator.

In the face of rebuff, Moses simply refused to accept that all was lost. With absolute conviction he believed that despite the break on the surface, both G-d and the people truly loved each other.

In a loving relationship, there will be times, perhaps, where one will want to give up. But the other will say: "We can't give up, we must try again." Love is tested in those times. In many cases it won't hold up to the challenge. But true love passes the test when one person says to the other, "My love for you is unconditional, no matter what you do. Even if you leave me, I will still be there for you."

Most of us don't want to be the ones who are abandoned. As a matter of fact, we try to be the ones who leave first—to be the ones who do the rejecting, not the rejected ones.

Even if we end up being abandoned by the other person, how many of us have had the strength and courage to say in the face of rejection, "I still love you."

But Moses said to G-d, "I don't accept that You say it's too late and the Jewish people can't be forgiven. I will stay here until You relent. I know that you truly love them and they love you." And so he prevailed.

In the final days before Rosh Hashana, to win pardon for our transgressions, we must demonstrate to G-d that we love Him and each other with that kind of relentless, unconditional love. That we forgive each other as we hope He will forgive us, that we are compassionate toward each other as we hope He will be compassionate with us. This is the best insurance for success.

Ask yourself: Can you demonstrate that you have loved others unconditionally—that you have loved G-d unconditionally?

Exercise for the day:

Express unconditional love to someone in your life.

Recreate day four of creation by being a "light" that illuminates and warms other people.

"G-d said, 'Let there be light in the canopy of heaven to separate between the day and between the night, and they will serve as signs for seasons, days and years. They will be lights in the canopy of heaven to illuminate the earth.' And it was so. G-d made the two great lights, the large light to rule the day, and the small light to rule the night, and the stars. G-d set them in the canopy of the heaven to illuminate the earth, to rule the day and the night, and to divide between the light and the darkness, and G-d saw that it was good. And it was evening and it was morning, a fourth day." **(Genesis 1:14-19)**

Day Four of Creation Countdown

Two days left to Rosh Hashana. Today is the day of accounting for the month of *Av*—the month which contains the saddest day in the Hebrew calendar, the 9th of Av.

In this, the seventh and final week of the Seven Weeks of Consolation, the people reply to G-d's words of comfort: "I will greatly rejoice in G-d, my soul will exult in my G-d, for He clothed me with the garments of salvation…

"For Zion's sake I will not keep silent, and for Jerusalem's sake I will not be still, until her righteousness shines forth like radiance… The nations will see your righteousness. And all the kings your glory…O Jerusalem, I have set watchmen on your walls. They will never be silent day or night… Behold G-d has proclaimed to the end of earth: Say to the daughter of Zion: Behold, your salvation comes… They will call them 'The Holy People,' G-d's redeemed; and you will be called "Sought Out," a city not forsaken.

"Who is this that comes from Edom…In all their affliction He was afflicted…In His love and pity He redeemed them; He lifted them up and carried them through all the years." (Isaiah, chapter 61)

Malchut ("sovereignty") radiates during this fourth and final week of Elul (the last of the Seven Weeks of Consolation), as we prepare to rebuild malchut on Rosh Hashana.

Facts ◎

On the final Shabbat of *Elul*—the Shabbat just before Rosh Hashana—we always read the Torah portion of *Netzavim*.[1] The practical reason is in order to separate between the curses of the previous portion and Rosh Hashana.[2] The Baal Shem Tov says[3] that on this Shabbat we don't bless the new month (as we do during the rest of the year) because G-d Himself blesses it, and this empowers us to bless the other eleven months.[4]

And G-d's blessing consists of the opening verse of this week's Torah portion: "You are all standing today…." "Today" refers to Rosh Hashana, the Day of Judgment…. You stand fast and upright on this day; i.e., you are judged favorably. This is G-d's blessing on the Shabbat when we bless the "seventh month," (a month) that is satiated and satiates all of us with abundant goodness all year round."

The Balanced Ledger

A Chassidic rebbe once sent his students to observe a local innkeeper as part of their preparation work for Rosh Hashana.

The students dutifully checked into the inn, but the first day observed nothing remarkable. They went to sleep, only to be awakened at midnight by someone praying loudly.

They tip-toed out of their rooms to find the innkeeper fervently reciting Psalms. When he finished, he opened up a cabinet and removed two big ledgers.

From one ledger he proceeded to read all his sins of the past year: he confessed that he was insensitive to his wife; that he didn't fulfill all his obligation to his community; that he didn't study enough Torah; he once came late to prayers, etc.

Then he opened the second ledger, saying to G-d, "These are my failings, now here's what You didn't do ... I asked for a better living wage this year and you didn't give it to me. My wife is still ill. My children need shoes..."

In the end he concluded, "Look, I didn't live up to my obligations and You didn't live up to Yours. So let's call it even. I'll close my book, You'll close Your book, and we'll start a new year again with a clean slate."

We learn from this story that the relationship between us and G-d is a partnership. When G-d created human beings in His image, He invested something Divine in us. There is a partnership between us and Him to perfect the world.

It is as if He founded a business, and said to us: "I am the investor, but you stand behind the counter."

Partners are accountable to each other. In the month of *Elul*, we take out our ledgers and make sure our accounts are in order. Rosh Hashana is audit day. G-d checks the books to see how we took care of His investment in us.

In so doing He doesn't look for perfection. He didn't create imperfect human beings to ask, "Why weren't you perfect?" He asks us only, "Why aren't you as much as you could have been?" But that's a tough question and tonight each individual must know how to answer it.

Elul Month of Consolation

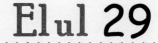

"G-d said, 'Let the waters teem with swarms of living creatures, and let birds fly above the earth, in the open canopy of the heaven.' And thus G-d created the great whales and every living creature that creeps with which the waters teem of its kind, and every winged bird of its kind. And G-d saw that it was good. G-d blessed them saying, 'Be fruitful and multiply, fill the waters of the seas, and let the birds multiply on the earth.' And it was evening and it was morning, a fifth day." **(Genesis 1:20-23)**

Day Five of Creation Countdown

One day left to Rosh Hashana. Look over the past month of *Elul*, which we are just finishing. Did you take full advantage of the energy of this remarkable month—its energy of love and compassion, its energy of accounting and preparation?

Events

5549 (1789)—The birthday of the third Chabad Rebbe, Rabbi Menachem Mendel Schneersohn, known as the "Tzemach Tzedek" (1789-1866).[1]

Laws and Customs

Selichot are recited before the morning prayers.

The **shofar** is not sounded today, to separate between the shofar soundings of the month of *Elul* (which are a "custom") and the Rosh Hashana soundings (which are a Biblically ordained commandment).[2]

Following the morning services, **Hatarat Nedarim**, the annulment of vows, is performed.[3]

It is customary to visit and pray at the **graves** of the righteous on this day.[4]

"My custom is to send **gifts** to the poor on Erev Rosh Hashana."[5]

Facts ◎

Before the onset of Rosh Hashana—when the feminine *malchut* ("kingship") is built—some great Rebbes would approach their Rebbetzins to bless them and receive a blessing from them.

as the SUN
does down

before Rosh Hashana

the universe

goes into a comatose
state

A slumber descends
on ALL existence,
everything comes to a standstill
in cosmic silence,
in apprehension of its contract
being renewed.

reaching

beginning

TISHREI

returning

uniting

Introduction
BEGINNING of the YEAR

The month of *Tishrei*—which marks the beginning of the Jewish New Year—is the most critical of all the months. Its awesome energy impacts our lives, not just during its 30 days but throughout the year that follows.

Tishrei is the month in which the first human beings—Adam and Eve—were created. It is the month in which the Patriarchs—Abraham, Isaac, and Jacob—were born. It is the month in which the barren women—Sarah, Rachel and Chana—were remembered by G-d and their wombs opened. It is the month when Joseph came out of prison.[1] In short, it is the month when many of the biggest events in biblical history took place.

The name of this unique month hints at its pivotal role in the Hebrew calendar. *Tishrei* is a permutation of the word *reishit*,[2] meaning "beginning," which in turn is taken from the root *rosh*, meaning "head." (Indeed, the very first day of *Tishrei* is Rosh Hashana, which literally means "head of the year.")

The head is the beginning/top of the body but its function is far greater than that. The head, which contains the brain, controls the central nervous system and, via its components, all the functions and movements of the body.

If time is like a body, then *Tishrei*, as head of that body, controls and energizes the entire cycle of time that follows it. Whatever we experience throughout this month in the High Holiday season—during the holidays of Rosh Hashana, Yom

Kippur, Sukkot, Shemini Atzeret and Simchat Torah—is meant to give us energy and strength for the next eleven months. The mood and environment we find ourselves in, the resolutions that we make at this time, have a cosmic and personal effect on all the days of the year.

COSMIC NERVOUS SYSTEM

The entire month of *Tishrei* and all its holidays are the main energy centers—the cosmic nervous system—controlling the entire year:[3]

Rosh Hashana infuses us with the ability all year round to accept and connect to our Divine calling. It gives us the power to renew our lives and reconnect to our life's mission each day of the year.

Yom Kippur is the source of holiness and *teshuvah* (returning to G-d in repentance after a transgression) for the entire upcoming year.

Sukkot is the source of joy for the entire year.

Accordingly, our behavior every day throughout this one month of *Tishrei* affects our lives for all the days of the twelve months that follow! Hence, the importance of truly using these days to their fullest and not squandering them.

Tishrei is packed with holidays[4] just like the head is packed with more functions than any other body part.[5]

In addition to controlling the function and movement of the body, the head controls the senses (sight, hearing, taste, smell, and touch), as well as our chief mode of expression (speech)—all of which are vested in the organs of the head (eyes, ears, mouth, nose). Relatively speaking, it seems disproportionate that the head should have gotten so much. And it seems disproportionate that *Tishrei* should have gotten such an abundance of holidays.

But if we consider that in Jewish thought, a human being is seen as a universe in microcosm, and that which exists within the human being is also paralleled in time and space, then we see that what is true of the human head must also be true of the head of the year.

Packed as it is with holidays, *Tishrei* generates the spiritual energy necessary for the work of perfecting the world which it initiates.

In the first five days of Creation (which we counted in the last days of *Elul*), G-d had created a stationary world, and on the sixth day—the first day of *Tishrei*—He created humanity to complete the work He had started by turning the world into a dynamic universe filled with meaning and higher purpose.

Thus *Tishrei* is a month that initiates and energizes the work of *tikun*—it presents the finest opportunity to repair, realign and rebuild our fundamental psycho-spiritual structure both on a personal and cosmic level.

And since a human being is a universe in microcosm, we include in ourselves (in microcosm) the entire world. When we repair ourselves, we repair the world.

The stakes are high:

How we behave in *Tishrei* determines our destiny for the year ahead. We are particularly aware of this in the Days of Awe, as—after an entire month of preparation with the "King in the field"—we now enter the "palace."

remembering

rebuilding

השנה

ראש

ROSH HASHANA '77

Introduction
The MEANING of ROSH HASHANA

The simple, literal meaning of Rosh Hashana is "head of the year," an appropriate name for the day that begins the Jewish New Year. However, this simple meaning belies the deeper, more profound content of this great two-day holiday:

~ It is a holiday when we celebrate the birthday of the world[1]—the day that humanity came into existence.[2] We set out lavish feasts, dipping apples in honey, for a sweet new year.

~ It is a holiday when the earth trembles as the shofar is blown, its heart-rending sounds vibrating through us. It reminds us that this is the day when G-d sits in judgment of us.

~ It is a holiday when, after a month "in the field," the King returns to His palace, and we come to Him to pay homage and to acknowledge Him as our King.

~ It is a holiday when we ask G-d to remember us for life and to inscribe us in the Book of Life.

~ Regardless of background or affiliation, it is a holiday when people feel compelled to attend a synagogue, any synagogue, in order to fulfill some obligation, even though they are not even sure what it might be.

And yet when they get there, many inevitably get lost in the hundreds of pages of prayers, which are moving at a brisk pace in Hebrew, a language that many don't understand well enough to truly connect to the meaning of the words.

If you feel like this on Rosh Hashana, the key is not to be intimidated. It's definitely good to follow along with the cantor and to pray with the group. But even when you are able to do that, you'll find that there are times when the cantor falls silent and you are on your own before G-d. Ultimately, this is what counts.

Rosh Hashana is the day when G-d judges you, and only you—not the cantor, not the rabbi, not anyone else—can know how to answer Him.

JUDGMENT DAY

Rosh Hashana is called the "Day of Judgment."[3] But what does this mean exactly? Many people believe that it means we should be trembling before G-d. If we sinned (and who hasn't?), G-d's wrath and punishment are imminent.

But that kind of thinking is a religious distortion. It is a perpetuation of the negative stereotype that G-d is "angry" and "vengeful," filled with rage and determined to "get even with us."

Yes, Rosh Hashana is a day of judgment, but not the kind of judgment we imagine. It is the ultimate insult—and nothing more than anthropomorphic projection imposed by human beings upon G-d—to think that G-d judges us the way we judge each other.

Instead of imposing our ideas of judgment upon G-d, we should be seeking to discover how G-d judges us. In fact, the better question might be: "*Does* G-d judge us?"

G-d created a universe of mortal, imperfect human beings. Does He now demand to know why we are not perfect? Clearly that can't be.

The truth is that the relationship between us and G-d is a partnership. Partners are accountable to each other. In the month of Elul, we do our accounting. Rosh Hashana is audit day. G-d checks the books to see how we took care of His investment in us.

This is the true meaning of Divine judgment.

Thus Rosh Hashana is actually a day of compassion—a holiday and cause for celebration. On this day G-d gives us the opportunity to face Him and report on our progress in fulfilling the Divine mission we were charged with. And we are given the power to renew our "contract" with G-d.[4]

Even if we feel uncomfortable with how little we have accomplished, there is nothing to fear. G-d's judgment is filled with wisdom and mercy. He doesn't look for perfection. He knows that He created imperfect human beings. He doesn't ask, "Why weren't you perfect?" He asks us only, "Why aren't you as much as you could have been?"

The judgment of Rosh Hashana is thus really a great gift: G-d's vote of confidence in us that we can live up to our greatest potential.

This is what we should keep in focus on Rosh Hashana as we open our hearts to G-d in prayer.

All key Rosh Hashana prayers are explained in detail at the back of this book. See PRAYER SECTION.

The Day of Remembering

When we usher in Rosh Hashana, just before sunset tonight, we light candles and we say a blessing:

"Blessed are You, O G-d, King of the Universe, who has sanctified us with Your commandments and commanded us to light the flame of the Day of Remembering."

Rosh Hashana is a "Day of Remembering" because it's a day when G-d reviews our ledgers for the past year and remembers why He sent us to earth. But since G-d doesn't need to be told to remember anything, this means more than that. In effect, this is a day when we ask G-d, "Please remember me, and through doing that, remind me of my mission on earth so that I may never forget it."

When we arrive at the synagogue, the usual afternoon prayers—*Mincha*—are recited just before Rosh Hashana formally begins. While these prayers are being said, a very special thing begins to happen. Jewish mystics explain that as the sun goes down before Rosh Hashana, the universe goes into a comatose state. A slumber descends on all existence, everything comes to a standstill in cosmic silence, in apprehension of its contract being renewed.

Then, as Rosh Hashana begins, the awakening starts. It begins slowly until the full awakening the next morning, when the ram's horn known as the shofar is blown.[1]

The shofar is like an "alarm clock" that wakes up the universe and us from this cosmic sleep. We needed this sleep to wake up refreshed; it holds the secret to our renewal. It is rather like exhaling in order to inhale. And this is, in fact, exactly what happens on Rosh Hashana. As the year ends, there is a cosmic exhaling and then a cosmic inhaling of fresh air.

As Rosh Hashana begins, take a deep breath! Now you are ready to recite the unique words of the key Rosh Hashana prayer, which asks G-d to remember why He sent us to this earth and that our mission here is not yet completed:

"Remember us for life, King Who desires life, inscribe us in the Book of Life, for Your sake, O Living G-d."

Erev Rosh Hashana

 "What nation is so great that they have G-d close to it? What nation is like this nation, that knows the 'personality' of G-d? The custom of the world is that when you stand in judgment, you don't know what the verdict will be. But the Jewish people are different. They dress in white and wrap themselves in white, and they eat and drink and celebrate on Rosh Hashana, because they know that G-d will rescue them, and find them innocent and destroy any negative decree."[2]

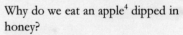

Laws and Customs

Light Festival Candles before sunset with two blessings: 1) "Blessed are You, O G-d, King of the Universe, who has sanctified us with Your commandments and commanded us to light the flame of the Day of Remembering." (When Rosh Hashana is on Shabbat, say: "to light the flame of Shabbat and the flame of the Day of Remembering.") 2) *Shehecheyanu*: "Blessed are You, O G-d, King of the Universe, Who has kept us alive and sustained us and brought us to this season."

Evening prayer—see Prayer Section.

Following evening prayers, it is customary to greet one another: *L'shana tovah tikoteiv v'teichoteim*, "May you be inscribed and sealed for a good year."

Upon returning home, a special Rosh Hashana *Kiddush* is made that ends with the words: "Blessed are You G-d, King over all the earth, who

sanctifies Israel and the Day of Remembering."

It is then followed by another recitation of *Shehecheyanu*. (On Shabbat, the usual *Kiddush* is said, with the addition of "this Day of Remembering, a day for sounding the Shofar" plus the special blessings above.)

Kiddush is followed by the washing of the hands and the blessing (*Hamotzi*) over *challah* dipped in honey. We then partake in the festive Rosh Hashana meal, which begins with eating an apple dipped in honey and other foods signifying a sweet year. Before eating the apple we recite the blessing over fruit and then say: "May it be Your will to renew us for a good and sweet year."

Grace After the Meal[3] is recited with the additional Rosh Hashana *yaaleh v'yavo*.

Facts

Why do we eat an apple[4] dipped in honey?

1. It alludes to the cosmic apple orchard ("field of holy apples"), the level of *malchut* ("kingship") which is rebuilt on Rosh Hashana.[5]

2. The apple manifests a very high spiritual level which is conceived on Rosh Hashana and revealed at the end of Sukkot.[6]

3. The apple represents a circle, symbol of eternity. By dipping the apple in honey, we create a kind of sweet eternity.

The Day the World Trembles,
The Day the World Is Born

The two meanings of the Rosh Hashana prayer, *Hayom harat olam*, communicate succinctly the essence of the day: "Today the world trembles; Today the world is born."

We feel this message most acutely when the shofar is blown. On the anniversary of the day on which the first human being possessing a Divine soul was created, we blow the shofar, which mirrors the cry of that soul—our soul.

On this day G-d breathed the soul of life into man. And now every Rosh Hashana man blows *his* breath—the breath that G-d breathed into him—through a ram's horn in order to hear the sound of his soul reverberate.

The ram, a male sheep (the animal that Abraham offered in sacrifice in place of his son Isaac), is the most gentle and innocent of creatures, untainted by the aggressive nature of other animals. The ram reminds us that our soul is that part of ourselves that is gentle and innocent, untainted by the aggressive, manipulative world we inhabit. And the ram's horn is the simplest of instruments—not carved, molded or strung like other instruments which testify to the ingenuity of man—and it produces the haunting, resonating, piercing cry that most closely approximates the pure sound of the soul.

The prayer that we recite before the blowing of the shofar further unlocks its secret: "From my narrow place, from my depths and constraints, I call to You, and You respond to me from Your expansive place."

The pressures and challenges of life that force us into a "narrow place"—a place of difficulty, pain, frustration, regret, or sorrow—are meant to be catalysts that compel us to cry out to G-d for something more than our earthbound materialistic reality.

This prayer assures us that when we cry from our "narrow place," the response flows from G-d's most expansive generosity. In fact, the shape of the shofar—narrow at one end and wide at the other—mirrors this experience.

The purest cry that is emitted from the constraints of our lives reaches the purest place in heaven and opens up the channel of all blessings.

Rosh Hashana

"Every year there descends and radiates a new and renewed light which has never yet shone. For the light of every year withdraws to its source in the Essence of the *Ein Sof* on the eve of Rosh Hashana, 'when the moon is covered.' Afterwards, by means of the sounding of the shofar and the prayers, a new and superior light is elicited... a new and more sublime light that has never yet shone since the beginning of time. Its manifestation, however, depends on the actions of those below, and on their merits and penitence during the Ten Days of *Teshuvah*."

(Tanya, Iggeret HaKodesh, ch. 14)

First Day of Rosh Hashana

First of the Ten Days of *Teshuvah*. In these ten days we rebuild *malchut* (kingship) in all its Ten *Sefirot*—the ten channels of Divine energy which permeate all forms of existence.[1]

According to the Ramak, this day corresponds to *malchut* (kingship).[2] According to the Ari, this day corresponds to *keter* (crown).

Events

3760 BCE—Creation of the first human beings, Adam and Eve.[3] On the same day, they sin by eating from the "Tree of Knowledge." They are then judged and banished from Eden. On that day they repent and are pardoned.

2084 (1677 BCE)— *Akeidat Yitzchak*: Abraham's supreme test of faith, his binding of Isaac. On the same day, when news of this event reaches Isaac's mother, Sarah, she passes away at age 127.

5683 (1923)—Launch of the *Daf Yomi* daily regimen of Talmud study (one studies a folio a day to complete the entire Talmud in 7 years), initiated by Rabbi Meir Shapiro of Lublin.

Laws and Customs

Rosh Hashana morning and special *Musaf* prayers, Torah readings and shofar blowing (except on Shabbat) — see Prayer Section.

Following the prayers, we go home for lunch and make a special *Kiddush*, prefacing with the verse *Tiku ba'chodesh shofar, b'keseh l'yom chageinu. Ki chok l'Yisrael hu, mishpat l'Elokei Yaakov* (*Psalms* 81:45). (On Shabbat, add references to Shabbat.)

Following *Mincha* service, the *Tashlich* ceremony is performed—see Prayer Section.

Tonight, the second eve of Rosh Hashana, before sunset, light candles, transferring the fire from a pre-existing flame. When Rosh Hashana falls on Shabbat, candle lighting must be done after nightfall.

Evening service and *Kiddush*: same as the first night.

A new garment is worn and/or a new fruit (i.e., one that has not yet been tasted this season) is placed on the table and eaten after *Kiddush*, in order to enable us to make the *Shehecheyanu* blessing.[4] (When the second eve of Rosh Hashana is on Saturday night, we add in *Kiddush* a special *havdalah* prayer.[5])

The Day of Coronation

Rosh Hashana

The idea of Rosh Hashana as the day when we "coronate" G-d as the King of the Universe, may be one of the strangest and hardest to accept for those of us raised in modern, democratic societies. To us, kings are corrupt despots at worst, and characters out of fairy tales at best.

Yet this idea is essential to the observance of Rosh Hashana, because in the language of Judaism, a king is a metaphor for absolute authority. On Rosh Hashana we accept upon ourselves G-d as the one and only absolute authority who rules over every aspect of our lives, and we submit to His judgment, which we believe will be merciful because our King is also our Father.

When we accept G-d's absolute authority over us, we do not annihilate our own individuality. On the contrary, we only empower it. When we acknowledge G-d as our King, we simultaneously recognize the nobility in ourselves—the dignity and majesty of having been created in the Divine image.

This idea fills us with unbridled joy and points out the paradox of Rosh Hashana, because Rosh Hashana is a day when we stand before the Supreme King and tremulously accept the "burden of His sovereignty," but it is also a festival, which we celebrate amidst much feasting and rejoicing.[1]

Such is the nature of a coronation: it is an event that combines trepidation and joy, awe and celebration. For true kingship, as opposed to mere rulership, derives from the *willful* submission of a people to their sovereign. So the coronation of a king includes a display of reverence and awe on the part of the people, conveying their submission to the king, as well as the joy which affirms that their submission is something they wholeheartedly desire.

The joy and celebration of Rosh Hashana is called *v'gilu b'roadah*, "celebration wrapped in trembling."

When we stand before the king, we feel such joy that we want to dance, but we cannot in respect of the king. So the joy must be packaged in a more appropriate expression. Only after we leave the palace (on Sukkot) can we begin celebrating with unbridled expression.

Rosh Hashana

"May everything that has been made know that You made it, everything that has been created understand that You created it" **(Rosh Hashana prayer)**
"On this day the destiny of nations is determined: which for war and which for peace…. Who is not recalled on this day? For the remembrance of every living created being comes before You—a person's deed and his task, his actions and movements, his thoughts and his schemes and motives." **(Rosh Hashana Zichronot prayer)**

Second Day of Rosh Hashana
Second of the Ten Days of *Teshuvah*

According to the Ramak, this day corresponds to *yesod* (bonding or foundation).

According to the Ari, this day corresponds to *chochmah* (wisdom).

Laws and Customs

Morning and Musaf prayers—similar to day one, with variations—see Prayer Section.

Shofar blowing—same as day one—see Prayer Section.

Lunch and Kiddush—same as day one.

Mincha, afternoon service—same as day one.

Following the **Maariv** evening service and *havdalah*, the holiday comes to an end.

Facts

On the very day they were created, the first man and woman committed the first sin of history. They were then judged and banished from the Garden of Eden, and humanity became subject to death, labor and moral confusion. But on that day they also repented their sin and were pardoned, introducing the concept and opportunities of *teshuvah* into the human experience. This day of judgment and repentance is replayed each year on Rosh Hashana.[2]

Both days of Rosh Hashana are considered "one long day."[3] Both days are kept even in Israel, and were kept even in the time of the Temple.[4]

The second day of Rosh Hashana corresponds to the first Shabbat of creation. This is the reason that Shabbat has the same letters as *tashev* ("return"), the root of the word *teshuvah*.

In a letter to his brother-in-law, Rabbi Gershon Kitover, the Baal Shem Tov relates: "On Rosh Hashana of the year 5507, I made an 'ascent of soul' in the manner known to you… I ascended level after level until I reached the chamber of Moshiach… And I asked Moshiach: 'When will the Master come?' And he replied: 'When your teachings will be disseminated and revealed in the world, and your wellsprings will spread to the outside.' "[5]

85

Rebuilding the Kingdom

Today begins the countdown to Yom Kippur. Today is the third day of the Ten Days of *Teshuvah*, which will culminate on this most awesome of days. This is possibly the most intense time in the Hebrew calendar when each individual is granted the power of a group of ten.

We are vested with this power because in these ten days, having crowned G-d as our King, we now undertake the task of rebuilding His kingdom—both in the spiritual realm "above" and in our world "below"—known in the language of Kabbalah as *Binyan HaMalchut*.

Malchut ("kingship") refers to the tenth of the Ten *Sefirot*, the ten spheres or channels of Divine energy with which G-d created the world and which flow through every aspect of reality including our own souls. This means that to rebuild *malchut* we must rebuild ourselves—our own nobility, our own dignity, that very aspect of ourselves which was created in the image of G-d. By building our own *malchut*, we rebuild G-d's *malchut* in the universe.

We know our *malchut* is in need of rebuilding when we feel afraid and insecure, because our personal sense of security and insecurity in life depends on it.

When children are raised in dysfunctional homes where their dignity is trampled upon, their *malchut* is eroded. They can grow up to be adults with great minds and great hearts, but they may be insecure adults who lack the courage for the suspension of self that is necessary to truly grow, because they feel they must fight for whatever scrap of dignity they can grab.

So the rebuilding of *malchut* in effect means the building of dignity, majesty, and security in a world that's very insecure. And we are given special power during these ten days to do it. It is not as hard as we might imagine, because to build it all we need do is access the place in ourselves that was never wounded in the first place—the place of our Divine soul.

Ask yourself: Do you generally feel secure or insecure in life? Are you someone whose *malchut* has been eroded by life experiences?

Exercise for the day:

Describe the part of yourself that was never wounded—your Divine soul.

Do something Divine today, something that makes you proud and builds your *malchut*, your dignity.

"Although *teshuvah* and pleading are always effective, during the ten days from Rosh Hashana till Yom Kippur they are especially potent and are immediately accepted, as it says, 'Search for Hashem when He is present.' "
(Rambam, Laws of Teshuvah 2:6)

Third of the Ten Days of *Teshuvah*. Seven days left until Yom Kippur.

According to the Ramak, this day corresponds to *hod* (humility or splendor).

According to the Ari, this day corresponds to *binah* (understanding).

Events

423 BCE—Today's fast day mourns the assassination of Gedaliah ben Achikam, the Jewish governor of the Land of Israel for a short period following the destruction of the First Temple. Gedaliah's killing spelled the end of the small remnant of a Jewish community that remained in the Holy Land after the destruction. After the assasination, the Jews fled to Egypt.

Laws and Customs

Fast day: Mourning the killing of Gedaliah, we abstain from food and drink from dawn to nightfall; *Selichot* prayers are included in the morning service.

During the Ten Days of *Teshuvah* (beginning with Rosh Hashana and ending Yom Kippur) special inserts and additions are included in our daily prayers (in addition to Psalm 27 which is said from Rosh Chodesh Elul through Hoshana Rabba):

1. Psalm 130 (after *Yishtabach* in the morning service).[1]

2. In the *Amidah* service, we add phrases in the first and last two blessings (see Prayer Section), "the Holy King" in the third blessing, and "the King of Judgment" in the eleventh blessing (said only on weekdays).

Returning to Pure Essence

In our earlier exploration of the meaning of *teshuvah* (see Elul 18), we defined *teshuvah* as having two levels—repentance and return:

Repentance means regretting a wrongful action, resolving not to repeat it, asking forgiveness, making amends.

Return means coming back to one's soul, one's Divine essence, to one's source in G-d.

The first level—which is what we should have been working on during the month of Elul—is only the means to achieve the second, which is our focus now, during the Ten Days of *Teshuvah*.

During these special days, we should be working to return to the quintessential self that we really are. *Teshuvah* (which literally means "return") implies that there is a part of us that is always healthy and good and pure, as we say in the morning prayer, "The soul that You gave me is pure ..." And no matter what damage had been done to us in life—to our sense of self, to our personal dignity—no matter what damage we ourselves have done, we can always return to the soul that remains undamaged, intact, pure.

The great 16th century Kabbalist Rabbi Moshe Cordevero of Safed, better known as the Ramak, suggests that the best way to return to our pure essence is to isolate ourselves for a period of time each day during the Ten Days of *Teshuvah* in order to meditate on the Ten *Sefirot*, which he calls the "Gates of *Teshuvah*." In this way it is possible to enter a different "gate" each day, thereby connecting the soul with its root in a given *sefirah*, each of which serves as a channel for Divine energy into creation and, of course, into the soul.

Ask yourself: How much do you want to connect with the purest, holiest part of yourself? Are you willing to invest the effort and the time to make this possible?

Exercise for the day:

Review the attributes listed on the calendar pages for each day of the Ten Days of *Teshuvah*.

Meditate today on the *sefirah* of *netzach* ("endurance"). In doing so, assess your level of endurance and your ambition. Is it being used for the proper things?

Tishrei

"A person must see himself and the world as equally balanced on two ends of the scale—by doing one good deed, he tips the scale and brings himself and the entire world redemption and salvation. Therefore in the days between Rosh Hashana and Yom Kippur, more than all year round, it is customary to increase charity and good deeds and the performance of the *mitzvot*."

(Rambam, Laws of Teshuvah 3:4)

Fourth of the Ten Days of *Teshuvah*. Six days left until Yom Kippur.

According to the Ramak, this day corresponds to *netzach* (endurance or victory).

According to the Ari, this day corresponds to *daat* (knowledge).

Facts

The word "depths" in the verse from Psalm 130 (which we recite in these days)—"Out of the depths, I call to You G-d"—has two meanings: 1) it can be read to refer to the depths of our heart and soul, or 2) to the depths above, the deepest levels of G-dliness.[1] When we call out from the depths of our heart we reach the depths of G-d's heart.[2] Indeed, the Ten Days of *Teshuvah* correspond to ten levels of depths, each day reaching deeper and deeper into the Divine, as we get closer to Yom Kippur.[3]

The Personal Holy of Holies

Before the destruction of the Temple in Jerusalem, the pinnacle of the Yom Kippur service was the moment when the High Priest (the *Kohen Gadol*) would enter the Holy of Holies.

This was the only time of the year that anyone could enter this holiest of inner sanctums and only the High Priest was permitted to do so and only for a short duration.

It was such an intense moment that if the High Priest was not completely pure—if he had committed even one transgression for which he had not previously atoned—he would die immediately.

This was because the Holy of Holies was a place so pure that even one blemish was intolerable. An eye cannot tolerate even one small eyelash, because it is so sensitive. And the Holy of Holies was the most sensitive, purest place in existence.

If he died, the other *kohanim* would have to pull his body out by a rope that had been previously attached to him. But if he succeeded in his mission to obtain G-d's forgiveness for the Jewish people, he emerged radiating a special glow that is vividly described in the Yom Kippur prayers.[1]

Today we have no High Priest and no Temple. But the Holy of Holies still exists—in the depths of our own soul. On Yom Kippur we attempt to reach that purest part of our selves and to connect with G-d there.

We might not be able to stay in that pure place for a long time. It might be only a few minutes. But, as we know, the most special experiences last only a moment. We prepare for these most special times for hours, years, and even decades, and the effort of the preparation is well worth that split second they last.

Ask yourself: Have you prepared sufficiently for Yom Kippur to be able to make the most of the experience?

Exercise for the day:

Begin reviewing the Yom Kippur prayers (see Prayer Section) in order to connect fully with the words when the time comes to enter your personal Holy of Holies.

Tishrei

"One who doesn't cry during the Ten Days of *Teshuvah*—
his soul is not complete. When one cries, it is a sign that he
is being judged above at that moment."
(The Ari)[2]

Tishrei 5

Fifth of the Ten Days of *Teshuvah*.
Five days left until Yom Kippur.

According to the Ramak, this day
corresponds to *tiferet*
(beauty, harmony and compassion).

According to the Ari, this day
corresponds to *chesed*
(loving-kindness).

Events

3894 (133 CE)—The great Talmudic
sage, Rabbi Akiva, is taken captive by
the Romans. His subsequent torture
and execution is recalled in the stirring
Eleh Ezkarah poem of the Yom
Kippur afternoon service.

Facts

There are two types of *teshuvah*: *teshuvah* out of fear and *teshuvah* out of love.
The former only affects the present and on. The latter however has
the power to transform the past; it actually transforms intentional sins into
merits! (Talmud, *Yoma* 86b). That is the power of *teshuvah* that comes from
love—not fear of punishment or guilt, but out of love to get closer to
our Source.

Tishrei begins the six months of winter, which correspond to six levels of
"reflected light," the light generated by human initiative ("arousal from
below"). This is alluded to in the name *Tishrei,* which begins with the three
letters *tav—shin—reish*, in the "reflected" order of the *aleph-beit* (from end to
beginning).[3]

In the Ten Days of *Teshuvah,* an individual has the power of a quorum
(*tzibbur*). Obviously, a quorum is that much more powerful.

Approaching the Source

We have now reached the midpoint of the Ten Days of *Teshuvah*. This is the period, say the sages of the Talmud,[1] of which the Prophet Isaiah (55:6) speaks when he proclaims: "Seek G-d when He is to be found; call on Him when He is near."

But isn't G-d omnipresent at all times and all places in the world. How could we say that now He is closer to us?

However, Isaiah is not speaking from G-d's perspective but from the soul's perspective. Chassidic teachings explain that this special time of the year is compared to the "source drawing near to the spark."[2] The "source" is G-d; the "spark" is each of our souls, which is called "the flame of G-d."

All year round the "source" is spiritually "distant," i.e., concealed, from the "spark." In the early days of *Av*, the "source" is at its "farthest" (most concealed) point; so far away that the spark can hardly sense its connection to the mother flame. In Elul—when Moses begins his final climb—the "source" begins to draw nearer, becomes more revealed. On each progressive day of Elul, the "source" draws closer and closer to the "spark." The closest point is on Yom Kippur, specifically during *Neilah* ("Locking of the Gates"), the final prayer at sundown.

Thus, the Ten Days of *Teshuvah* represent a type of "coming home" experience.

When the source gets closer to the spark, the spark begins to feel the warmth and it is drawn toward the larger, mother flame. It's like when you put your hand closer to a flame, you start feeling the warmth.

This is the reason that in these Ten Days of *Teshuvah* there is more consciousness of G-d among Jews, even those who are not familiar with the meaning of the High Holidays.

Ask yourself: Are you feeling the warmth of the mother flame—the warmth of G-d—as the time draws closer to Yom Kippur? If not, why not?

Exercise for the day:

Meditate on the verse from *Proverbs* (20:27): "The flame of G-d is the soul of the human being."

Identify some aspect(s) of your life that reflects the tug of your soul to its source.

"The world is mistaken when it thinks that *teshuvah* is only for sins. True *teshuvah* is from the expression 'and the spirit shall return to G-d.'[3] *Teshuvah* is a thirsty soul's longing to connect to its Source. With this in mind, *teshuvah* becomes an exciting and joyous experience, rather than one just of bitterness and remorse, because there is nothing more gratifying than returning to your true self."[4]

Today is the 6th day of the Ten Days of *Teshuvah*. There are now four days left until Yom Kippur.

According to the Ramak, this day corresponds to *gevurah* (discipline, might, or justice).

According to the Ari, this day also corresponds to *gevurah*.

Events

5725 (1964)—*Yahrzeit* of Rebbetzin Chana Schneerson (1879-1964), mother of Rabbi Menachem Mendel Schneerson, the seventh Chabad Rebbe.

Facts

"And Abraham drew near and said: 'Perhaps there are fifty righteous (individuals) in the city… perhaps there are ten' "(Genesis 18:24;32): 'Abraham drew near' means he was ready to plead. He began with the number fifty, the entrance to understanding (which has fifty gates), and ended with ten, the last of all the grades. R. Isaac said: "Abraham stopped at ten as the number symbolic of the Ten Days of *Teshuvah* between Rosh Hashana and Yom Kippur. Reaching that number, Abraham said, as it were, 'After this there is no more room for penitence,' and therefore he did not descend further.' "[5]

The Cycle of Forgiveness

Yom Kippur, which is only three days away, is called the "Day of Forgiveness" because this is the day when Moses, after pleading with G-d for 80 days to forgive the Israelites for the Sin of the Golden Calf, finally succeeded. On this day, G-d finally said to him: "I will forgive as you have asked."

On Yom Kippur we seek to connect to the energy of this awesome day and win forgiveness for ourselves as well. But we can hardly expect to be forgiven by G-d if we ourselves have not been willing to forgive others.

Forgiveness is not easy; it requires work. But, most importantly, it requires a connection to G-d, the Giver of Life (and now, as the mother flame draws close to the spark, is the ideal time to feel this connection).

The secret of being able to forgive others is to remember that G-d gave you life because you matter to Him—you have a vital and irreplaceable role to play in the perfection of His world. When you remember that, you can have the strength to rise above the pain others have caused you and forgive both them and yourself.

The word for "forgiveness" in Hebrew—mechilah—is related to the word machol meaning "circle." Life is meant to be a circle encompassing all our experiences and relationships in one harmonious, seamless whole. When someone hurts us, the circle is broken. Forgiveness is the way we mend the fracture.

Forgiveness means not merely forgiving the person who hurt us, but forgiving ourselves, forgiving G-d, forgiving even life itself with all its bizarre and often cruel twists and turns.

When you forgive, the circle is again complete and you find yourself encompassed by the wholeness of G-d's creation of which you are an integral part. And then you can have the confidence that this Yom Kippur you will hear G-d saying to you: "I will forgive as you have asked."

Ask yourself: Whom have you hurt? Who has hurt you?

Exercise for the day:

Make a list of those whom you must forgive.

Make a list of those whom you must ask for forgiveness.

Begin.

Tishrei

"When Elazar ben Durdaia (a notorious sinner) found that all his appeals for assistance had been turned down, he said: 'It all depends entirely on myself.' He placed his head between his knees and wept until his soul departed from him. A voice from heaven then announced: 'Rabbi Elazar ben Durdaya is destined for life in the world to come!' Hearing this, Rabbi (Judah HaNassi) wept: 'There are those who acquire their world in many years, and there are those who acquire their world in a single moment.'" **(The Talmud)**[1]

Tishrei 7

Seventh of the Ten Days of *Teshuvah*. Only three days left to Yom Kippur.

According to the Ramak, this day corresponds to *chesed* (loving-kindness).

According to the Ari, this day corresponds to *tiferet* (beauty, harmony or compassion).

Laws and Customs

"Yom Kippur does not atone for sins between one person and another, until one appeases his friend."[2]

Therefore, before Yom Kippur you should do everything possible to apologize and ask forgiveness from anyone you may have hurt, even with words. If the person is not appeased, you must try a second and a third time, each time employing new methods to gain the intended forgiveness.

The one who was hurt must not be cruel and refuse to forgive, unless he feels that not forgiving immediately will help humble the callousness of the person who has hurt him, or he believes that by forgiving, he himself will be hurt in the process.[3]

Facts

"He made the letter *lamed* king over intimacy, and He bound a crown to it, and he combined one with another, and with them he formed Libra in the universe, *Tishrei* in the year, and the gall bladder (or liver) in the Soul, male and female" (*Sefer Yetzirah* 5:9). The *mazal* (sign) for this month is *moznayim* (Libra/scale), which symbolizes the Divine judgment that takes place in this month, beginning with Rosh Hashana.

The Birth of Hope

It took Moses only 40 days to receive the entire Torah from G-d on Mt. Sinai, but it took him double that time—80 days—to win forgiveness for the Jewish people after the sin of the Golden Calf.

But when Moses finally returned from the mountain on Yom Kippur, the new set of tablets that he brought with him was greater than the first. The second set was carved from the depths of pain and demonstrated hope after loss—the second set was indestructible.

This teaches us that it takes much more effort to rebuild a relationship after it has been broken than to build it in the first place. But when we succeed, the new structure is much stronger and it can never be broken again.

Yom Kippur, which is only two days away, is the holiest day of the year because it is the birthday of the single most important ingredient in life—hope. The hope that there is healing after loss; that there is rebirth after destruction; that we can always rebuild what was broken and make it stronger than ever before.

And Yom Kippur teaches us *how* we can achieve all of this—by connecting to G-d, to immortality.

This is the ultimate message that we have to share with the world as we become more and more aware that we live in a period of time when the ultimate battle between good and evil is being waged. Into this battle we can carry the message of Yom Kippur:

"Everything is possible. With persistence you can overcome any challenge and adversary. Put your faith and hope in G-d because good can and will prevail."

The Shabbat of the Ten Days of *Teshuvah* each year repeats this message in the words of the Torah portion read at that time:

"Be strong and brave. Do not be afraid or feel insecure before them (your enemies), because G-d is the One Who is going with you, and He will not fail you or forsake you." (Deuteronomy 31:6)

Ask yourself: Do you feel hopeful for yourself and for the world? Do you allow yourself to become resigned?

Exercise for the day:

Inspire someone who feels broken. Give him/her hope.

Meditate on the words of the Torah portion quoted above.

Tishrei

"Let us proclaim the mighty holiness of this day, for it is awesome and formidable.... On Rosh Hashana it will be inscribed, and on Yom Kippur it will be sealed: How many shall pass on, and how many shall be born.... who will rest and who will wander, who will live in harmony and who will be harried... who will be impoverished and who will be enriched. But repentance (*teshuvah*), and prayer (*tefillah*), and charity (*tzedaka*) avert the severity of the decree."

(Rosh Hashana/Yom Kippur U'netaneh Tokef prayer)

Tishrei 8

Eighth of the Ten Days of *Teshuvah*. Only two days left to Yom Kippur.

According to the Ramak, this day corresponds to *binah* (understanding).

According to the Ari, this day corresponds to *netzach* (endurance or victory).

Events

2935 (826 BCE)—Commencement of the 14-day dedication festivities celebrating the completion of the Holy Temple in Jerusalem built by King Solomon. The First Temple served as the epicenter of Jewish national and spiritual life for 410 years, until its destruction by the Babylonians in 423 BCE.

1791—*Yahrzeit* of Rabbi Baruch, father of the founder of Chabad, Rabbi Schneur Zalman of Liadi.

Facts

The Shabbat of the Ten Days of *Teshuvah* is called Shabbat *Teshuvah* (or *Shuva*), "The Shabbat of Return." Its name is derived from its Haftorah, which opens with the words (*Hosea* 14:2), "Return O Israel to your G-d..." This Shabbat is considered the most auspicious time to rectify the failings and missed opportunities of the past and positively influence the coming year.

According to the Ari,[1] the seven days between Rosh Hashana and Yom Kippur (which will always include one Sunday, one Monday, etc.)—which correspond to the seven days of the week—repair and atone for all the days of the year. The Sunday between Rosh Hashana and Yom Kippur repairs all Sundays of the year; the Monday repairs all Mondays, and so on. Shabbat *Teshuvah* is thus the archetypal Shabbat—the juncture in time at which we are empowered to influence every Shabbat of our year.

When Rosh Hashana falls on Monday or Tuesday, we read the Torah portion *Vayeilech* on Shabbat *Teshuvah* (which is then *Tishrei* 6 or 5). When Rosh Hashana is on Thursday or Shabbat (Shabbat *Teshuvah* is then *Tishrei* 3 or 8) we read *Haazinu*.

The Haftorah of this Shabbat is one of the "two of return"—the final series in the Haftorahs that began with the Three Weeks of Affliction, followed by the Seven Weeks of Consolation.

To Be Like Angels

Tishrei 9

Tonight we will begin a 25-hour fast of Yom Kippur. We don't do this in order to afflict ourselves, which is the purpose of the fast of *Tisha B'Av* when we mourn the destruction of the Temple—indeed Yom Kippur is not a day of mourning but a day of joy. We fast on Yom Kippur because on this day we want to transcend our physical limitations and be like angels,[1] and food and other physical concerns distract us from our spiritual selves.

Some people may complain that the hunger distracts them from concentrating on the prayers and rituals of the day. But this is precisely the Yom Kippur challenge—not to be overly focused on the physical.

Use the opportunity of not eating and not drinking to allow yourself to experience the food and drink that comes from deep within. Fasting will then become a very freeing experience.

Yom Kippur is one day in the year when you can access the deepest part of your soul. But this is only possible if you create the space for it. Your soul—every soul—has a still, soft voice[2] that emits a unique hum. This sound can only be heard if you lower the noise in your life that usually drowns out your inner voice.

On Yom Kippur, when the "source" is nearest to the "spark" of your soul, you want to remove as many material distractions as you can, so that your soul can sing freely and your "spark" can dance.

When you experience Yom Kippur this way —which does take effort, and that's why you need to prepare for it—then it will not be a day when you feel hungry, but a day when you feel angelic.

The same holds true for the other prohibitions of Yom Kippur—against bathing, anointing, marital relations, wearing leather, etc.—all of which are meant to detach us as much as possible from the physical realm so that we can be free to experience the spiritual one.

Instead of indulging in physical pleasures, we spend the day in the cocoon of a synagogue where we are cut off from the outside world. We spend the day in prayer—our whole intention being to transcend the physical world, our material home, and to travel inward toward our purest spiritual selves— toward our true home in G-d.

"All who eat and drink on the ninth are considered to have fasted on the ninth and the tenth." **(Talmud, Yoma 81b)**

"On Yom Kippur we experience the mystery of the 'internal (spiritual) meal.' On Erev Yom Kippur we experience an 'external (physical) meal.' The meal we eat on Erev Yom Kippur allows us to then experience the 'internal' meal of Yom Kippur." **(The Ari)** [5]

"Erev Yom Kippur thus has the power to infuse our material life with the profound intimate spirituality of Yom Kippur." [4]

Ninth of the Ten Days of *Teshuvah*. This is the last day before Yom Kippur.

According to the Ramak, this day corresponds to *chochmah* (wisdom).

According to the Ari, this day corresponds to *hod* (humility or splendor).

Laws and Customs

Kapparot (Expiations)

We awake at dawn—when a "thread of Divine kindness prevails in the world." [5] Each member of the family takes a *kapparah*—a white rooster for each male, a hen for each female. (A pregnant woman takes three fowls, a hen for herself, and a rooster and hen for the unknown gender of the child]. The *B'nei Adam* prayer is recited three times. After each time, the fowl is waved over the head. A *shochet* then performs the *shechita* (the Torah ritual of elevating the animal)—in order to subdue and sweeten the supernal severities. [6] This is called *kapparah*, similar to the Yom Kippur "scapegoat" (Leviticus 16:5-22). If this cannot be done at dawn of *Erev* Yom Kippur, the custom is preformed in

the preceding days. Some perform the custom with money.

Eat more on this day, as if eating both for *Erev* Yom Kippur as well as for Yom Kippur.

Request from a parent or friend *lekach*—a sweet piece of honey cake, for a sweet year.

Immerse in a *mikveh* (ritual pool), symbol of rebirth and renewal achieved through *teshuvah*. Some have the custom to immerse three times during the day.

Increase in giving to charity, which helps repeal negative forces.

Ask each other for forgiveness: Sins committed against another person cannot be atoned for—even on Yom

Kippur—until one has first sought forgiveness from the person he/she has wronged. Thus it is customary to visit (or at least call) friends, family, associates and any person whom one may have somehow wronged or spoken ill of in the past year and ask forgiveness. (see *Tishrei* 7)

Malkot—symbolic lashes, while reciting the thirteen words (like the 13 Attributes of Divine Compassion) of *V'Hu Rachum* (*Psalms* 78:38) three times, for a total of thirty-nine words (13x3=39), corresponding to thirty-nine lashes.

Mincha service—in which we add, at the end of the *Amidah* prayer, the special *Vidui* (confession) prayer. See Prayer Section

The Holy of Holies is the place where HEAVEN meets EARTH where the DIVINE presence SHINES UNCONCEALED...

This is the place where we can meet

G-D

forgiving

uniting

YOM KIPPUR

Introduction
HOLIEST DAY of the YEAR

Yom Kippur is the holiest and most awesome of all the days of the Jewish year, the peak experience of the Days of Awe (*Yomim Nora'im*) as the High Holidays are called:

~ It is the day when the verdict that was written on Rosh Hashana (the Day of Judgment)—"who shall live and who shall die ... who by fire and who by water ..."— is finally sealed.

~ It is the day when we confess our sins to G-d and beg that they will be forgiven—banking on the energy of forgiveness which Moses brought down on this day more than 3,000 years ago when he won forgiveness from G-d for the Israelites' sin of the Golden Calf.

~ It is the day when the Ten Days of *Teshuvah* come to an end, and we are presented with the last and best opportunity to return to our own Divine essence, and by virtue of doing so, to return to G-d.

~ It is the "wedding day" between G-d and the Jewish people, as Moses comes down from Mt. Sinai with the second set of Tablets.[1]

On Yom Kippur we touch the holiest part of ourselves—our souls. In emulation of the High Priest of the days of old, we have the opportu-nity to enter our personal Holy of Holies. The Holy of Holies is the place where heaven meets the earth, where the Divine Presence shines unconcealed. This is the intimate place where we can meet G-d.

Yom Kippur is the convergence of the holiest in space, time and man—when the holiest part of man enters the holiest space on the holiest day.

We are able to do so when we take away all the materialism, all the physicality, all the external tools and expose what is left—the sacredness of our inner selves.

You don't feel sacred when you are working, and you don't feel sacred when you're consuming a meal, no matter how good it tastes. You may feel good or satisfied, but you don't feel sacred or unique or uplifted.

You feel sacred only when you experience your soul, the part of you that was created in the image of G-d. It is your true self, though you probably don't recognize it as such. But once you do, once you experience the fullness of Yom Kippur, you will never settle for less again.

DAY of LIMITLESS POSSIBILITIES

Yom Kippur is the only day in the year when each soul on earth comes closest to feeling its source. The innermost dimension of the soul is revealed and shines forth only on this day. This dimension of the soul—*yechidah* ("oneness")—represents the inner unity of our souls, transcending all fragmentation, compartmentalization, all our dualities and pluralities. It emerges only on Yom Kippur, "the Day of Oneness," [2] which falls on the 10th of *Tishrei*.

Ten is considered a complete number, encompassing all of existence and the entire cycle of time and space. It is signified in the Hebrew alphabet by the letter *yud*, the first letter of the essential four-letter name of G-d, the Tetragrammaton, which we are forbidden to pronounce. *Yud* is written as a dot—the unifying point that fuses everything into the sacred oneness of G-d. [3]

Sacredness/holiness, therefore, is the theme of this day, on which we try to be like angels. As the 16th-century scholar, the Maharal of Prague, put it, "All of the *mitzvot* that G-d commanded us on Yom Kippur are designed to remove, as much as possible, a person's relationship to physicality, until he is completely like an angel."

On this day, we immerse ourselves entirely into the world of the sublime, minimizing in every way our interaction with the material, pluralistic, fragmented world. We consume no food or drink, nor do we engage in marital relations. We do not bathe or anoint ourselves with creams or perfumes, and we do not wear leather shoes, which symbolize luxury. We wear white and spend almost the entire day in the cocoon of the synagogue immersed in prayer.

We invest all our energy in this day, because on Yom Kippur anything is possible. This we know from the very first Yom Kippur, the day which gave birth to hope. If ever there was a day to begin anew, it is on Yom Kippur. This is the day when we have the power to ask for anything we want—to achieve our deepest goals and dreams. Yom Kippur is the single most important day in our lives.

So make sure that you use this most special of days to the fullest. But if for some reason you cannot, at least participate in the opening prayer, *Kol Nidrei*, and in the closing prayer, *Neilah*. (And if you have lost a parent, be sure to also participate in *Yizkor*, the memorial prayer.)

All these and other Yom Kippur prayers are explained in detail in the PRAYER SECTION.

Breaking the Ties that Bind

Before darkness falls, marking the official beginning of the 10th day of *Tishrei* which is Yom Kippur, in every synagogue in the world a haunting melody is sung—*Kol Nidrei*.

Kol Nidrei means "All Vows" and its classic text, repeated three times, each time louder, is a renunciation of all oaths and vows.

It seems strange to begin the holiest day of the year—the day which we spend asking G-d to forgive us for all transgressions—by breaking former promises.

But *Kol Nidrei* is not that.[1] *Kol Nidrei* is the process through which we enter the holiest day of the year.

A *neder* is not just the vow or promise that you vocalize to another person, it is a word that denotes all commitments, attachments and ties that bind you.

By renouncing "all vows" you are declaring your commitment to break the bonds that keep you from traveling on the journey within, that keep you from opening yourself to the Yom Kippur experience.

Obviously, this does not mean forsaking healthy commitments and responsibilities—it means forsaking those attachments that limit you, that entangle and entrap you.

That is the essential focus of *Kol Nidrei*. It is a perfect prayer with which to begin Yom Kippur because unless you free yourself from such traps you cannot travel inward; with a ball and chain attached to you, you are not going to be able to get anywhere.

Kol Nidrei is repeated three times to relate to vows in speech, vows in deed, and vows in thought:

All vows and self-imposed prohibitions ... we regret having made them, may they all be permitted, forgiven, eradicated and nullified, and may they not be valid or exist any longer. Our vows shall no longer be vows, and our prohibitions shall no longer be prohibited, and our oaths are no longer oaths.

(This and all other Yom Kippur prayers are explained in detail in the Prayer Section.)

"Light is sown for the righteous and for the upright in heart—joy." **(Psalms 97:11)**

"Pardon us, forgive us, grant us atonement—for we are Your people and You are our G-d; we are Your children and You are our Father; ... we are Your congregation and You are our portion; we are Your inheritance and You are our lot; we are Your flock and You are our Shepherd; we are Your vineyard and You are our Watchman; we are Your handiwork and You are our Creator; we are Your beloved ones and You are our Beloved; we are Your treasure and You are our G-d" **(Yom Kippur prayer)**

Laws and Customs

Before going to the synagogue, eat a festive meal (*seudah hamfseket*).

Light a *yahrzeit* candle for the departed souls.

Light the candles for the holiday, and say: "Blessed are You, O G-d, King of the Universe, who has sanctified us with Your commandments and commanded us to light the flame of the Day of Atonement." (If Yom Kippur falls on Shabbat say, "to light the flame of Shabbat and the flame of the Day of Atonement.") Then say the *Shehecheyanu* blessing: "Blessed are You, O G-d, King of the Universe, Who has kept us alive and sustained us and brought us to this season."

Begin a 25-hour fast—no eating or drinking until sundown the next day. Some have a custom of fasting 26 hours, as 26 is the *gematria* (numerical value) of the essential four-letter name of G-d, the Tetragrammaton.

Bless your children before the evening *Kol Nidrei* service.[2]

Dress in white.[3] Married men wear a white robe called a *kittel* for the entire Yom Kippur as they do under the *chuppa*. In the first year of marriage, the *kittel* is not worn on Yom Kippur since it was worn at the *chuppa*.

The *tallit* (prayer shawl) is worn during the evening service (unlike all year round).

105

The Day of Oneness

Yom Kippur

The preparation work in advance of Yom Kippur is a journey inward which culminates in the fifth and final prayer of the Yom Kippur service—*Neilah* (the "Locking of the Gates").

Every day we have three prayers—*Maariv* (the evening prayer), *Shacharit* (the morning prayer), *Mincha* (the afternoon prayer). On Shabbat and every other Jewish holiday we have a fourth— *Musaf* (the additional prayer). But only on Yom Kippur is there a fifth— *Neilah*.

This is because *Neilah* corresponds to the fifth and highest dimension of the soul—the Holy of Holies of the soul—which we access only on this one day at this one time.

The five dimensions of the soul are:

Yechidah	"Oneness"	Essence
Chayah	"Life"	Transcendental life
Neshamah	"Soul"	Intellectual life
Ruach	"Breath"	Emotional life
Nefesh	"Spirit"	Biological life

All days of the year we're able to access the three dimensions of our soul; on Shabbat we access the fourth, *chayah*, but only on Yom Kippur can we access the fifth, *yechidah*— oneness with G-d.

This is because during *Neilah*, before the gates are locked, everything is open and we are able to reach even *yechidah* which is the most intimate, vulnerable, gentle part of the soul of the human being, unshielded by the defenses of the other levels. We reach it at the precise moment when *Neilah* is said, and when, at its conclusion, we declare: *Shema Israel* ..."Hear O Israel, G-d is our L-rd, G-d is One."

The Shaloh, the great medieval 16th-century sage writes that "there is no higher experience for the Jew—as when he acknowledges the oneness of G-d and his readiness to give his entire life to G-d." This is the moment when the spark and the flame come closest all year round. This is the most powerful moment of the year. This is the moment that you are the closest that you can come to the essence of everything, to G-d.

(This and all other Yom Kippur prayers are explained in detail in the Prayer Section.)

"Once a year...once a year he will make atonement for you, for all generations" **(Exodus 30:10).**

"This shall be an eternal law for you. Each year on the tenth day of the seventh month you must fast and do no work... For on this day, you shall have all your sins atoned, so that you will be cleansed. Before G-d you will be cleansed of all your sins. It is a Sabbath of Sabbaths to you, and a day upon which you must fast. This is a law for all time." **(Leviticus 16:29-31)**

"The needs of your people are numerous and their knowledge is scant; they are unable to express their needs and desires. We beseech you to consider our thoughts, even before we call out." **(Yom Kippur Neilah prayer)**

Yom Kippur
Holy of Holies

According to the Ramak, this day corresponds to *keter* (crown).

According to the Ari, this day corresponds to *yesod* (foundation) and to *malchut* (kingship or nobility)

Laws and Customs

Five prohibitions (*inuiim*): Eating and drinking. Washing. Anointing. Wearing leather shoes. Marital relations.

A complete day of prayer and atonement: **Five prayers (for detailed explanations, see Prayer Section).** Remember, if you are unable to follow all the prayers, don't feel guilty or forlorn. We are told that it is "better to say a few prayers for forgiveness slowly than to say many hurriedly." (*Shulchan Aruch HaRav, Laws of Yom HaKippurim* 600:2.)

**

After the evening prayer, make a blessing on the New Moon.

Wash hands after the fast—as we leave the sanctity of Yom Kippur and enter the mundane world, we wash our hands to protect from the effects of the mundane.[1]

Return home and break the fast in a festive meal. *Motzo'ei* Yom Kippur is celebrated as a holiday.

It is customary to begin building one's sukkah (or at least to discuss the laws of sukkah) on the night following Yom Kippur.

The evening following Yom Kippur corresponds to the tip above the letter *yud*, the first letter of G-d's Name, which is a brilliant light.[2]

From Awe to Joy

Today begin four days of transition between the "Days of Awe" (Rosh Hashana and Yom Kippur) and "Days of Joy" (Sukkot, Shemini Atzeret, Simchat Torah).

The first half of the month of *Tishrei*—which, as the first month of the Hebrew calendar, functions like a cosmic nervous system controlling the rest of the year—mandates that we allow ourselves to experience G-d as so much greater than we are: our King, our Judge, the one and only Absolute Authority over our lives.

Why is that not enough?

Because what is missing in that experience is the element of closeness, of love, and most importantly, of integration. [1]

To use an example from nature, when we stand in awe of an ocean in a thunderstorm, we may feel inspired and uplifted, but we are most likely relating to that awesome sight from a distance. To plunge in and immerse in the water, we cannot stand there awe-struck, afraid of the might of the ocean.

So too in our relationship with G-d. For this reason, *Tishrei* gives us these Days of Joy.

The Days of Awe represent the yearning for something greater. They peak on Yom Kippur, a day which is totally beyond us—a 25-hour period when we don't eat, when we barely sleep, and when we confine ourselves to the synagogue praying. In doing so, we try to free ourselves from the material life that keeps us from being uplifted.

But then comes the second half of the month—the time to integrate what we just experienced—the time to celebrate.

Why are we celebrating? Because we came into the palace of the King, and passed His judgment. Now we have left the palace, and we are ready to begin to dance in the streets.

Ask yourself: Are you ready to start celebrating? Do you feel joy emerging following your experiences of the High Holidays?

Exercise for the day:

If you can answer yes, make a list of what you need to get ready for the celebration. If you cannot answer yes, describe why.

Find a parallel in your personal life of love that has/needs these two elements: respect (awe) and closeness (joy).

Said Rabbi Yosef Yitzchak: "After Yom Kippur I went into my father and asked him: 'What now? (What is one to do now once Yom Kippur is over?).' He answered me: 'Now, one has to just begin doing *teshuvah*!' "[2]

G-d's Name

The first day following Yom Kippur corresponds to the letter *yud*, the first letter of G-d's name, reflecting on the initial spark (*chochmah*, "wisdom"), reborn after Yom Kippur.[3]

Events

2448 (1313 BCE)—Moses begins the process of building the Sanctuary in the wilderness. After Moses had secured G-d's complete forgiveness, he was commanded to build the Sanctuary (which demonstrated that the Jews were forgiven for their sin of the Golden Calf).[4] The following day the process begins. We recreate this today by building a sukkah following Yom Kippur.

Facts

According to an old tradition mentioned in the writings of the Baal Shem Tov, the day after Yom Kippur is referred to as "G-d's Name." (The Baal Shem Tov explains that each of the various Divine names describes G-d's involvement in a specific "world" or realm of reality, but the designation "G-d's Name," without reference to any particular name, connotes a Divine effluence that transcends all realms and particulars.) On Yom Kippur, we access and reveal the very essence of our soul, which is one with the very essence of G-d; thus the day after Yom Kippur carries the designation "G-d's Name."

Each of the four days between Yom Kippur and Sukkot correspond to one of the four letters in the essential Name of G-d known as the Tetragrammaton:[5]

day one: yud

day two: hei

day three: vav

day four: hei

Building a Sukkah

An essential component of preparation for the joy of Sukkot is the building of a sukkah—a hut with a roof of palm fronds, branches, reeds or bamboo—in which we are commanded to dwell during Sukkot week. Some people have the custom to begin building their sukkah on the night immediately following Yom Kippur; others build it between the 11th and 14th of *Tishrei*.

What is the significance of this *mitzvah*? While it might be nice to get together in this quaint setting with family and friends, have a party, camp out (if it isn't pouring), etc.—is there really any personal relevance to us today in this strange *mitzvah*?

The story of the 18th-century Chassidic Master, the Maggid of Mezritch, gives one answer to this question.

A wealthy man came to visit the great sage and was shocked to find him living in a sparsely furnished shack on the outskirts of town. Dismayed, he offered to personally provide the Maggid with quarters befitting his stature.

In reply, the Maggid asked the wealthy man to describe his home—which, of course, was a mansion—and then to describe his accommodations while traveling. When he finished, the Maggid said, "I see that your accommodations while traveling on business are much more modest than the place you call home. It's the same with me. Someday, you'll come to my true home and you will see how completely different it is."

The sukkah reminds us that we are just travelers in this material world. Our true home is not here. Our dwelling places, as beautiful as they may be, are not our true home, which is much more grand and beautiful than anything that money could buy or that we could even imagine.

Ask yourself: Do you relate to your house as your real home? How often are you reminded that this is not your true home?

Exercise for the day:

If you have not already done so, investigate the possibility of building a sukkah this year or at least arranging to eat in one during Sukkot.

"The four days between Yom Kippur and Sukkot is a time when the Jewish people are preoccupied with *mitzvot* ... this one is occupied with (building) his sukkah, this one is occupied with (acquiring) his *lulav*... (they thus continue to carry the purity of Yom Kippur). **(The Midrash)**[1]

Today corresponds to the *hei* of G-d's Name which is represented by *binah* ("understanding") i.e., developing and expanding the initial spark of *chochmah* into a full concept. On this day we begin to develop the power generated by Yom Kippur.

Events	Laws and Customs
5536 (1776)—*Yahrzeit* of Rabbi Abraham "The Angel" (1740-1776), the son of Rabbi DovBer of Mezeritch and study partner of Rabbi Schneur Zalman of Liadi. Known as "Rabbi Abraham the Angel" for his saintliness and asceticism.	Build a sukkah during these days preceding the holiday of Sukkot. A sukkah is a hut of temporary construction, with a roof-covering of branches, reeds, bamboo, etc., signifying the temporality and fragility of human habitation and man-made shelter, and our utter dependence upon G-d's protection and providence. The sukkah is symbolic of the "Clouds of Glory" that surrounded and protected the Jewish people after they left Egypt.

Acquiring the "Four Kinds"

The second most important component of preparation for the joy of Sukkot is the acquisition of the "four kinds"—three myrtle branches (*hadassim*), two willow twigs (*aravot*), one palm frond (*lulav*) and one citron (*etrog*)—which we bind together and then wave in six directions every day during the week of Sukkot (except on Shabbat).

The "four kinds," says the *Midrash*, correspond to four types of people:

~ The citron, which has both a delicious taste and a delightful aroma, represents the individual who both learns and achieves.

~ The palm frond produces fruit that has a taste but no aroma; this is the portrait of the scholar who shuns the world of action.

~ The myrtle, which is fragrant but tasteless, is the activist whose profusion of good deeds overshadows his scholarship.

~ The willow, which is tasteless and scentless, represents the person who neither learns nor achieves, actualizing neither his intellectual potential nor his capacity to improve the world.

On Sukkot, these "four kinds" are "all bound together in one bundle," each an integral part of the community of G-d. They are all indispensable, each contributing to the others.[1]

King Solomon, who was mystified by the meaning of the "four kinds," observed that the citron was a "tormented fruit." It remained on the tree all year round being subjected to all kinds of climatic conditions. But so too in life do we find that the greatest people are beset by travail and challenge, that the most balanced personalities are forged by the constant need to adapt to new climates and environments.

And the willow, which does not openly exhibit any positive qualities, nevertheless grows in clumps by the river. In the same way, some people might not display any positive traits, but their roots are imbedded in the banks of their ancestral river and nourished by the waters of their heritage. Observed alone they may not yet express their virtues, but when gathered in a community, their souls shine.[2]

Ask yourself: Which one of the "four kinds" are you? Do you recognize the virtue in others unlike yourself?

> *Exercise for the day:*
>
> Purchase the "four kinds" or make arrangements to borrow them in order to wave them during Sukkot.

"Three things are wondrous to me, and four I do not know."
(Proverbs 30:18)

"Despite all the wisdom granted to Solomon... he was mystified by the 'four kinds.' As it is written: 'Three things are wondrous to me'—these are the Passover offering, *matzah* and *maror* (eaten at the Passover *seder*]; 'and four I do not know'—these are the 'four kinds' (taken on Sukkot].
(The Midrash)[5]

Today corresponds to the *vav* of G-d's Name. The *vav*, shaped like a straight vertical line, transmits the Yom Kippur energy. This is the level of the emotions (*z'eir Anpin*), which transmits the concept conceived in the *yud* and developed in the *hei*.

Events	Facts
5596 (1837)—*Yahrzeit* of Rabbi Akiva Eiger (1761-1837), outstanding Talmudist and Halachic authority	The days between Yom Kippur and Sukkot are days of joy, because in the time of King Solomon, the First Temple was dedicated in these days.[4]
5643 (1882)—*Yahrzeit* of Rabbi Shmuel Schneersohn (1834-1882), the fourth Chabad Rebbe, known as "Maharash" .	

Climbing Higher

The Baal Shem Tov was fond of saying that for every question there is an answer, and for every answer there is another question.

As we traverse from awe to joy, we should remember that every time we internalize a higher form of energy, we realize that another, still higher form, eludes us.

So it is a ladder that we climb.

When the Tzemach Tzedek, the third Chabad Rebbe, was a child, he was playing on a ladder with other children. All the children climbed half way up, and he was the only child who climbed all the way to the top.

Afterwards, his grandfather, Rabbi Schneur Zalman of Liadi, who was standing by the window watching, asked him, "Why is it that you were not afraid to climb to the top when all your friends gave up?"

He answered, "Simple. I never looked down. I just kept looking up. When I saw how low I was, that motivated me to climb higher."

It's a question of setting your sights. The difference between a human being and an animal is that typically animals walk on all fours and never look up to heaven. Human beings walk upright, and that means their heads are up and they can look heavenward. As the Prophet Isaiah says, "Raise your eyes on high and behold Who has created these things." (Isaiah 40:26)

The fact that we can look up motivates us to continuously grow and climb higher in order to transcend our lowly state.

In this holiday season we acquire all the tools we need for the entire year. But it's up to us to utilize them. Our relationship with G-d is not out of reach. Our relationship with G-d is a partnership, a two-way street, and this is a great reason to celebrate.

May we all have a very enlightening and meaningful and uplifting celebration this Sukkot.

Ask yourself: Are you ready to reach higher? Are you ready to celebrate?

Exercise for the day:

Finalize your preparations for the celebration of Sukkot.

Today corresponds to the last *hei* of G-d' Name. This last *hei* signifies that the Yom Kippur experience is received by the recipient (*malchut*, "kingship") and is ready to blossom and be celebrated in full glory on Sukkot.

"The world says if one cannot enter from below you enter from above; I say *L'chatchila ariber*—begin by entering from above!" **(The Rebbe Maharash)**

Laws and Customs

Give additional charity.[1]

If you have not done so already, prepare the "four kinds" for use on Sukkot. Bind three *hadassim* (myrtle branches) and two *aravot* (willow twigs) to one *lulav* (palm frond) on the afternoon preceding the festival.

Facts

"Only one thing I ask of G-d, this I seek: May I dwell in G-d's home all the days of my life, to behold the pleasantness of G-d and to visit in His Sanctuary" (Psalm 27). All our prayers and supplications on Rosh Hashana and Yom Kippur are for "only one thing": To "dwell in G-d's home" during the days of Sukkot ("all the days of my life"), with pleasantness and joy (*Panim Yafot*).[2]

When a MAN

sits in the sukkah

of the SHADOW of FAITH

The Shechinah (G-d's Presence)

spreads its wings over him

from above...

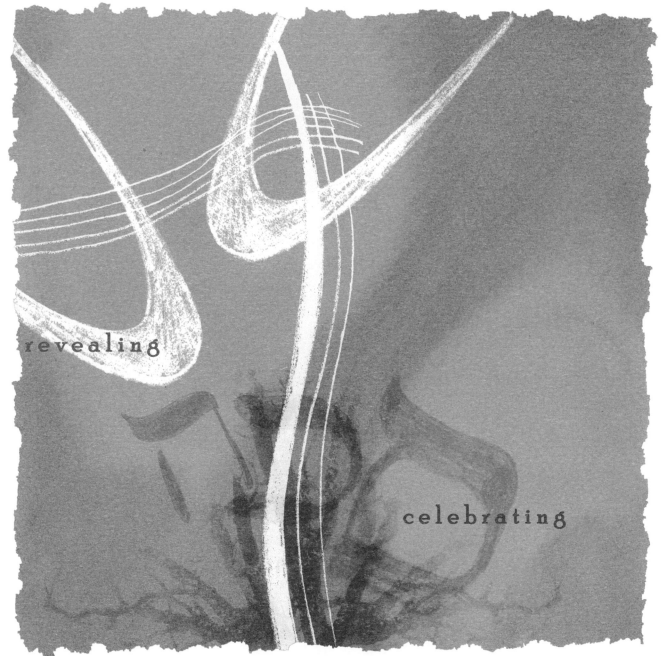

revealing

celebrating

SUKKOT

Introduction
The CELEBRATION of SUKKOT

Now, we are ready to celebrate. Now we are ready to unleash all the energy of *Tishrei* into a celebration of joy and unity on Sukkot.

Sukkot ("Festival of Booths") is a name for a period of time beginning on the night of the 14th of *Tishrei* and officially ending on the 21st of *Tishrei* (but really extending until the 23rd) which is best known for its joy.

During this time, we dwell in little huts (or booths) with a roof of palm fronds, branches, reeds or bamboo, in which we are eat all our meals and conduct all the activities of the day which we would regularly do at home.[1]

These huts remind us of our total dependency on G-d—that our seemingly sturdy man-made shelters are nothing in the absence of His care. These huts also remind us of the "Clouds of Glory" which hovered over and protected the Israelites as they wandered in the desert on the way to the Land of Israel.

During this time, we also have the custom to wave in six directions (after having pronounced the proper blessing) the "four kinds"—namely, three myrtle branches (*hadassim*), two willow twigs (*aravot*), a palm frond (*lulav*) and a citron (*etrog*).

These "four kinds" remind us of the four kinds of people who comprise and are essential to the Nation of Israel. (See the essay for the 13th of *Tishrei* for more on this subject.)

During this time, we also observe the festivities of:

- **Simchat Beit HaSho'eva** ("Happiness of the House of Water Drawing") when we commemorate with great joy and celebration the ceremony of water libations in the Temple.

- **Hoshana Rabba** (the day of "Great Salvation" when the verdict written on Rosh Hashana and sealed on Yom Kippur is made final). We recite the complete *Hoshana*—prayers in which the word *hosha-na* ("save us please") is repeated over and over.

- **Shemini Atzeret** (the "Eighth Day of Assembly"), an extra day added after the seven days of Sukkot when we celebrate alone with G-d because we and G-d cannot bear to "say goodbye" after the long holiday season. It is also the day when the messengers go out to deliver the judgment issued on the High Holidays.

- **Simchat Torah** ("Happiness of/with Torah") when we dance with the Torah in our arms, celebrating the second Tablets that we received on Yom Kippur, as we finish reading the last chapter of Deuteronomy and we begin anew with the first chapter of Genesis.

EVEN MORE THAN THAT

With all that happening, there is even more to Sukkot.

It is a holiday when we celebrate the unity of the Jewish people and the unity of the people all over the world. It is a holiday when we integrate the awe of Rosh Hashana and Yom Kippur into our lives—by bridging the Divine energies of *makif* (surrounding light) and *pnimi* (internal light).

The special joy of Sukkot derives from its coinciding with the appearance of the "full moon" in the middle of *Tishrei*. Rosh Hashana, which began *Tishrei*, coincided with the birth of the new moon. Sukkot, when the moon is fully visible, represents the revelation of what was hidden and concealed on Rosh Hashana.

Revelation makes us joyful. "There is no greater joy than the resolution of doubt," says the Talmud. Before the revelation we might have possessed all the ingredients of happiness, but without clear vision of how to direct our potential, we could not experience true joy. Sukkot is "the time of our rejoicing" because it brings with it the full revelation of what we have experienced and achieved during the first half of the month of *Tishrei*.

On Rosh Hashana and Yom Kippur, we touched base with the very quintessence of our souls and bonded with G-d. In those Days of Awe we crowned G-d the King of the Universe, actualized the power of *teshuvah* to transform the past and invigorate the future, and drew forth from heaven: life, sustenance and well-being for the year to come.

But the trepidation in standing before the Divine throne eclipsed the joy we felt. On Sukkot, the veil of trepidation recedes and the Days of Awe erupt into a week-long Festival of Joy—a joy that reaches its climax in the celebrations of Shemini Atzeret and Simchat Torah.

Oct. 10, 2022

Inviting Guests

Celebrating cannot be done alone. We celebrate with other people. That is why we are commanded by the Torah to welcome guests —the *mitzvah* of *hachnosat orchim*.[1] It is very basic that we must share our joy.

In addition to welcoming friends into our sukkah and eating a festive meal in cheerful company, we also welcome, in accordance with Kabbalistic tradition, seven mystical guests (*ushpizin*)—also known as the seven "faithful shepherds"—Abraham, Isaac, Jacob, Moses, Aaron, Joseph, and David. As the *Zohar* explains:

When a man sits in the sukkah of the shadow of faith, the *Shechinah* (G-d's Presence) spreads its wings over him from above ... and Abraham and five righteous ones and David with them, make their abode with him. A man should rejoice each day of the festival with these guests who abide with him (*Zohar, Emor* 103a).

These "exalted holy guests" come to feed us with spiritual nourishment, each imparting the quality unique to him. On our part, there is no greater hospitality that we can accord them than to emulate their lives.

On each of the seven days of the festival, another one of the seven *ushpizin* leads the group.[2]

Tonight's honored guest is Abraham. We welcome him along with the other *ushpizin* with these words:

May it please you, Abraham, my exalted guest, that all the other exalted guests dwell here with me and with you—Isaac, Jacob, Moses, Aaron, Joseph and David.

Abraham represents loving-kindness (*chesed*). Abraham's presence blesses the people gathered in the sukkah with the words from the Book of Isaiah (Isaiah 58:14): "I will take pleasure with G-d."

This then is the theme to focus on for the first day of Sukkot which begins tonight: love, kindness, and bringing pleasure to each other.

In keeping with the theme of loving-kindness, we should also invite to our sukkah some needy people (earthly guests "from below" to correspond to the mystical guests "from above"). If inviting poor strangers is not possible, we should at least provide food or money to help them celebrate elsewhere.

"On the fifteenth day of the seventh month, when you harvest the produce of the Land, celebrate the Holiday of G-d for seven days .... You shall dwell in booths for seven days .... In order that your generations shall know that I housed the Children of Israel in booths when I took them out of the Land of Egypt."
(Leviticus 39: 42-43)

Laws and Customs

Light candles for festival before sunset. When lighting the candles say "Blessed are You, O G-d, King of the Universe, who has sanctified us with Your commandments and commanded us to light the flame of the holiday." (On Shabbat say, "to light the flame of Shabbat and the flame of the holiday.") Then say the *Shehecheyanu* blessing: "Blessed are You, O G-d, King of the Universe, Who has kept us alive and sustained us and brought us to this season."

(For the special Sukkot prayers, see Prayer Section.)

Facts

The festival of Sukkot, commemorating G-d's enveloping protection of the Children of Israel during their 40-year journey through the desert (1313-1273 BCE), is celebrated for seven days, beginning from nightfall tonight. During this time, we are commanded to "dwell" in a sukkah. "How (does one fulfill) the *mitzvah* of dwelling in the sukkah? One should eat, drink and live in the sukkah, both day and night, as one lives in one's house on the other days of the year: for seven days a person should make his home his temporary dwelling, and his sukkah his permanent dwelling."[3]

Tonight's meal—and all the subsequent holiday meals—is eaten entirely in the sukkah. There the *Kiddush* is made holiday style with special mention of the holiday, and additional two blessings: *Leishev baSukkah* and *Shehecheyanu*.

See the *Code of Jewish Law* or consult a *halachic* authority for more details regarding the meals eaten in the sukkah. Some have the custom to refrain from eating or drinking anything outside of the sukkah, even a glass of water.

Oct. 16, 2022

March of Conquest

Earlier (on *Tishrei* 13) we examined the meaning of the "four kinds"—myrtle branches (*hadassim*), willow twigs (*aravot*), the palm frond (*lulav*) and the citron (*etrog*)—which we bind together and then wave in six directions every day during Sukkot week. Another way of understanding the "four kinds" is to compare them to the human body:

~the citron resembles, in its shape, the heart, the driving force behind all our actions.

~the palm frond resembles the spine, which holds the body together and creates balance, without which we would be unable to move.

~the myrtle leaves resemble, in their almond-shape, the eyes with which we behold G-d's world.

~the willow leaves resemble the lips, with which we give expression to our thoughts and feelings.

By holding these four together, we show that a person should devote all of his or her strengths and capacities to the service of G-d.

During the recitation of *Hallel*, the Psalms of Praise we recite on holidays, these "four kinds" are held together and waved in six different directions of space (south, north, east, up, down, west) for a total of eighteen movements—

three times to and fro in each of the six directions. These movements manifest the unity of the "four kinds"—and the Divine unity—in all the parameters of space in the entire universe, which it is our responsibility to elevate.[1]

After we raise the "four kinds" upwards we then lower the bundle somewhat earthwards before bringing it back to touch the chest, suggesting drawing Divine light downward into this world. When we lower the "four kinds" down, we first extend it somewhat upwards before bringing it back, suggesting elevating worldliness heavenward.

Following *Hallel*, on each day of Sukkot, we recite *Hoshanot*—prayers in which the word *hosha-na* ("save us please") is repeated over and over. As we do so, we circle the platform (*bimah*) where the Torah is read.

The circling is a march of conquest, compared to the circling of the city of Jericho in order to conquer the city. We march with the "four kinds," armed with our spiritual arsenal resolute to fight and win any battle.[2]

"And you shall take for you on the first day, the fruit of a beautiful tree and branches of date palms, and twigs of the plaited tree, and willows of the brook, and you shall rejoice before G-d, seven days." (Leviticus 23:40—41)

"First day" implies a new beginning: After we have completely wiped clean the slate of the past year, the first day of Sukkot begins a new year of accounting. (The Midrash)[5]

First Day of Sukkot
Full Moon

The honored guest for the first day of Sukkot is Abraham. Abraham represents loving-kindness (*chesed*). He blesses us (Isaiah 58:14): "I will take pleasure with G-d." This is the theme to focus on today: love, kindness and bringing pleasure to each other.

Laws and Customs

Sukkot Observances:

Continue to eat all your meals in the sukkah.

Bless and wave the "four kinds."

Celebrate with great joy.

THE "FOUR KINDS"

Each morning of Sukkot we take the "four kinds" and make a blessing on them, preferably in the sukkah in the morning before prayers. Two blessings are said the first day; on subsequent days the second blessing, *Shehecheyanu*, is omitted: "Blessed are You, O G-d, King of the Universe, Who has sanctified us with Your commandments and commanded us to raise the *lulav*."

"Blessed are You, O G-d, King of the Universe, Who has kept us alive and sustained us and brought us to this season."

After morning (*Shacharit*) prayers, *Hallel* (the special hymn of praise to G-d) is recited, during which we perform the *mitzvah* of *naanuim* ("movements")—waving of the "four kinds." This is done on each day of Sukkot (except Shabbat when the "four kinds" are not taken; Shabbat compensates for the energy of this mitzvah).

Please see the Prayer Section for an explanation of the special Sukkot prayers.

For the Torah reading of every day of Sukkot, two Torah scrolls are taken out. In the first we read the portion about holidays in Leviticus (11:26-23:44). In the second scroll we read for *Maftir*, the portion about Sukkot in Numbers (29:12-16).

The Haftorah is the last chapter of the Book of *Zechariah*. It discusses the transformation of the world and its nations in the End of Days. This Haftorah identifies Sukkot as the time when the ultimate redemption of the world will take place. An essential part of this redemption will be the gathering of all of the nations of the world in Jerusalem where all of the nations will announce their acknowledgment of G-d. (For more on this subject, see the essays for *Tishrei* 17 and 18, i.e., day 3 and 4 of Sukkot week.)

On the second night of Sukkot a special celebration began in the Temple, called *Simchat Beit Hasho'eva*, the great joyous celebration that took place nightly when they drew water to pour on the altar. It is therefore customary to celebrate every night of Sukkot with dance and song. (See tomorrow.)

The Taste of Water

Sukkot

When the Temple stood in Jerusalem, the "pouring of the water" was an important feature of the festival of Sukkot.

Throughout the year, the daily offerings in the Temple were accompanied by the pouring of wine on the altar, but on Sukkot, water was poured in addition to the wine.

The drawing of water for this purpose was preceded by all-night celebrations in the Temple courtyard. The singing and dancing went on until daybreak,[1] when the merry-makers would make their way to the nearby *Shiloach* Spring to draw the water, which was then brought to the Temple.

Declares the Talmud, "One who did not see the joy of the water-drawing celebrations has not seen joy in his life."[2]

Wine and water represent the two elements of our service of G-d. Water—which is tasteless, scentless and colorless, yet a basic necessity of life—symbolizes the intellectually and emotionally bland, yet fundamentally crucial, "acceptance of the burden of heaven." Wine—which is pleasing to the eye, nose and palate, intoxicating to the brain and exhilarating to the heart—is the sensually gratifying aspect of our Divine service: our understanding of the inner significance of the Torah's commandments and the fulfillment and joy we experience in our relationship with G-d.

But, if water represents the "flavorless," emotionally devoid aspect of our service of G-d, why did the pouring of water upon the altar on Sukkot yield such joy?

To a thirsty person, a cup of water is tastier than the most delectable wine. In the spiritual sense, this means that when a soul experiences a thirst for G-d—when it recognizes how vital its connection to G-d is—it undergoes an exhilarating experience that is like a feast for its senses. To such a soul, the "water" it draws from its deepest self to pour onto its altar of service to G-d is a greater source of joy than any intoxicating wine could ever be.

Sukkot is the time when we are most open to experiencing pleasure and joy in the simple act of "accepting the burden of the sovereignty of heaven."

"Draw water with joy, from the wellsprings of salvation."
(Isaiah 12:3)

"The great joy of Sukkot is the revelation of energy that was hidden in the Days of Awe. We see this alluded to in the *gematria* (numerical value) of the word *s'chach* (sukkah covering) which is made up of the letters *samech* (60), *chof* (20), *chof* (20) totalling 100. This number reveals the power of the 100 sounds of the shofar on Rosh Hashana.[3] The "Clouds of Glory" of the *s'chach* come from the clouds of incense offered on Yom Kippur. The seven days of Sukkot correspond to the seven days between Rosh Hashana and Yom Kippur."[4]

Second Day of Sukkot

Today's honored Sukkot guest is Isaac, who represents discipline (*gevurah*). He blesses us with the verse (Psalms 112:2-3): "Your children will be powerful in the land… with abundance and wealth in their homes." This is the theme for today: recognizing our abundant blessings, resulting from the power of discipline that channels the light so that we can contain it.

Laws and Customs

In Israel, today is the first day of *Chol HaMoed* ("intermediary" days between the beginning and end of a festival week). Outside of Israel, we add a second day to the holiday, in order to be able to absorb its entire energy. (The following are the laws and customs for everywhere outside Israel.)

The prayer service and Torah reading are the same as on day one (see yesterday).

The Haftorah on the second day of Sukkot (*Kings* I 8:2-21) is about the Temple dedication that took place in these days during the reign of King Solomon.

Following the service, we go home, make *Kiddush,* and partake in yet another festive meal as we did yesterday.

The Afternoon and Evening prayer services are the same as yesterday.

Tonight officially begins *Simchat Beit Hasho'eva,* commemorating the celebration connected with the pouring of the water on the Temple altar.

Night-long singing and dancing, reminiscent of the celebrations held in the Temple courtyard, are held throughout the festival in synagogues and streets of Jewish neighborhoods. In fact, there are aspects of these joyous celebrations that are possible only today, precisely because they cannot be held in the prescribed manner.

Due to the prohibition against the use of musical instruments on Yom Tov (the opening and closing days of the festival), the water pouring celebrations in the Temple did not begin until the second night of Sukkot. For the same reason, it was not held on Shabbat. Today, however, since our observance is only commemorative, we can celebrate without the music. So a negative situation results in an even greater, and deeper, jubilation. We hold celebrations on all nights of Sukkot, including Shabbat, calling forth from within ourselves a quintessential joy that does not require any mechanical aids to inspire it. And each night we intensify the great joy, in accordance with the teaching of our sages[5] that one should constantly elevate in holy and good deeds.

Transforming the World

During Sukkot week we read various excerpts from the writings of the prophets (*Haftorot*). These writings, particularly the prophecies of Zechariah and Ezekiel, speak of the transformation of the world and its nations which will take place in the End of Days.

The world will then have to undergo a day of reckoning before G-d:

And the fishes of the sea, and the birds of the sky, and the beasts of the field, and all creeping things that creep upon the earth, and all the men who are upon the face of the earth, shall tremble at My presence, and the mountains shall be thrown down, and the steep places shall fall, and every wall shall fall to the ground. (Ezekiel 38:20)

Finally, G-d will reveal Himself in all His majesty. When that happens all the nations of the world will recognize His supreme sovereignty, and they will make pilgrimages to Jerusalem to worship Him:

And it shall come to pass that every one that is left of the nations which came against Jerusalem, shall go up from year to year to worship the King, the G-d of Hosts, and observe the Festival of Booths. (Zechariah 14:17)

Thus, Sukkot, the symbol of G-d's protection over Israel, will be especially recognized by the nations of the world, and they will be rewarded for it.

The Sukkot celebration always had a profound effect on the world. The seventy offerings brought in the Temple on Sukkot corresponded to and protected the seventy nations who were descended from the sons of Noah (whose descendants are the nations of modern day). The people of Israel brought these sacrifices as atonement for the nations, praying for their well being, as well as for universal peace and harmony among all humankind.[1]

Today these offerings are recreated through our prayers. Our joy and service during Sukkot continue to have, as they did in ancient times, a cosmic impact on the destiny of the world.

Thus we see that the celebration of Sukkot is about transforming not just ourselves but the entire planet—to finally achieve peace for all of humankind.

"On that day G-d will be One and His Name will be One."
(Zechariah 14:9)

"If the nations of the world had known the value of the
Temple for them (the seventy Temple offerings on Sukkot
protected the seventy nations of the world), they would
have surrounded it with fortresses in order to protect it.
For it was of greater value for them than for Israel…"
(Rabbi Yehoshua Ben Levi)[2]

Third Day of Sukkot
Today's honored Sukkot guest is Jacob,
who represents compassion (*tiferet*).
He blesses us (Isaiah 58:8): "Then
Your light will pierce like the dawn."
In Hebrew, Jacob (*Yaakov*) contains
the same letters as the word "pierce"
(*yiboka*). This is the theme for today:
compassion and empathy have the
power to pierce through any darkness.

Laws and Customs

Chol HaMoed: Quasi-holiday. Work is allowed, yet it is still part of the holiday—we eat in the sukkah, bless and wave the "four kinds" and say special prayers. Some don't put on *tefillin*.

Chol HaMoed (literally meaning "weekday of the holiday") is a type of intermediary day that bridges the holiday proper with our mundane workday lives. (In Israel, where the first day of the holiday is one day, *Chol Hamoed* began yesterday).

The Torah is read on each of the days of *Chol HaMoed*. Four people are called up to each reading. (On Shabbat during Sukkot, seven people are called up, and an eighth for *Maftir*). Each day we read (from Numbers 29:17-34) about the daily Temple offerings for the corresponding day of Sukkot. These are the same verses we recite in the *Musaf* service of the holiday, which include the descending number of bullock offerings on each of the remaining six days of Sukkot, all totaling 70 bullocks.

On Shabbat of *Chol HaMoed* we read the well-known portion (Exodus 33:12-34:26) in which Moses asks G-d to reveal to him a deeper understanding of the Divine. G-d reveals to him the "Thirteen Attributes of Compassion" (see Elul 24). The special connection with Sukkot lies in the verses which refer to the Three Pilgrim Festivals: Passover, Shavuot and Sukkot.

The Haftorah for Shabbat of *Chol HaMoed* is Ezekiel 38, which contains a prophecy of the war of Gog and Magog. Following this war will come a new era of peace, when G-d will be recognized by all nations of the world. The prophecy is similar to that of Zechariah 14, read on the first day of Sukkot.

The Joy of Unity

Armies once had the custom of singing victory songs as they went to war. Why would they sing a victory song when they had not yet begun to fight? To express the conviction that they would win. This conviction lifted the soldiers' morale and inspired them to fight more valiantly, secure in certain victory.

Sukkot is this victory song. We march with the "four kinds," armed with our spiritual weapons resolute to fight any battle, confident we will prevail.

Sukkot gives us the power to transcend our uncertainty, our fears and vulnerabilities. It helps us access a greater strength that inspires us to be joyous. (Conversely, lack of this awareness is the root of insecurity, fear, uncertainty and the inevitable resulting despondency.)

Joy is a revealed expression of the soul's innate celebration of life—of our indispensable purpose in life, of our connection to our Divine mission. On Sukkot we celebrate this connection. We dance and sing with unadulterated joy in expression of genuine happiness from the essence of our being.

Sukkot is "the time of *our* rejoicing" because we do not celebrate alone—G-d also joins the celebration and rejoices with us, His creatures.

Joy unites us with G-d and with other people. Indeed, because joy cannot be celebrated alone, we are obligated to invite guests to our sukkahs.

"It is fitting that all of Israel should dwell in a single sukkah," says the Talmud.[1] Though physically we might sit in separate sukkot, spiritually we all sit together in one unifying sukkah. We bind together the "four kinds" which symbolize different personalities, acknowledging that our diversity is our strength, that it feeds our unity, and that each of us has a unique contribution to make to the greater good.

Let us gather together during the remaining days of Sukkot and celebrate—celebrate our lives and the gifts that G-d gives us every day. This message of hope, joy and unity is needed now more than ever. It is the ultimate fuel to be help us forge ahead, rebuild, and come out even greater.

"Sukkot is called the 'time of our rejoicing'—the rejoicing of G-d with Israel and the rejoicing of Israel with G-d. They both fuse into one harmonious celebration of heaven and earth."
(Rabbi Schneur Zalman)[2]

Fourth Day of Sukkot
Today's honored Sukkot guest is Moses, who represents endurance (*netzach*). He blesses us (Isaiah 58:11): "G-d shall always guide you, and satisfy your soul with refinements."
Today's theme: Moses brought down the Torah, G-d's guide for life that empowers us to endure any difficulty. It also allows us to reach the most sublime states in the cosmic order.

Facts

Eating festive meals and spending time outdoors in the sukkah is a powerful and unique spiritual experience. Some have the custom of decorating their sukkah with elaborate ornaments; others preserve its unadorned simplicity. But whatever one's style, the sukkah is the only *mitzvah* in which we are completely surrounded, from head to toe, by the *mitzvah* itself—enveloped, as it were, in the Divine presence.

In Psalm 27 (recited during these days) we read: "He will hide me in His tabernacle on a day of adversity; He will conceal me in the hidden place of His tent; He will lift me upon a rock." This refers to Sukkot, when we are surrounded and protected by the sukkah. This also refers to the "four kinds," which are alluded to in the word *ohalo* ("tent"), an acronym for *etrog, haddas, lulav, v'arovah*, and in the word *b'tzur* ("rock"), acronym for *beinonim, tzadikim, v'rashoim*, the different types of people symbolized by the "four kinds" (see *Tishrei* 13).[3]

Oct. 15, 2022

A Time to Laugh — A Time to Dance

The Rebbes tell us that what we accomplish on Rosh Hashana and Yom Kippur through tears, we can accomplish on Sukkot and Simchat Torah through joy.

The obvious question is, if you can accomplish the same thing with joy as with tears, who needs tears? Why not just skip Rosh Hashana and Yom Kippur and go straight to Sukkot?

But here's the secret—you can't reach the necessary state of joy unless you can cry first. True joy is not about denial or escape; it is a celebration of the gift of life and the mission with which we were charged. Such joy comes hand in hand with accountability and responsibility, and the need, when necessary, to be sensitive and shed some tears over our lost opportunities and mistakes.

In other words, there is a time to cry and a time to rejoice, as we learn from the famous book authored by King Solomon, the Book of Ecclesiastes (*Kohelet*) which some read during Sukkot:

To every thing there is a season, and a time to every purpose under the heaven: a time to be born, and a time to die ... a time to break down, and a time to build up; a time to weep, and a time to laugh; a time to mourn, and a time to dance... . (Ecclesiastes 3:1–8)

The secret we need to master is how to ride the rhythms of life. This holiday season teach us exactly that—because it is all about cycles. What particularly stands out is the cycle of seven: *Tishrei* is the seventh month. On Rosh Hashana and Yom Kippur important prayers are recited seven times. Seven days connect Rosh Hashana and Yom Kippur. And Sukkot lasts seven days.

On Hoshana Rabba we circle the *bimah* seven times, reciting seven *Hoshanot*. Then finally, on Shemini Atzeret, we celebrate Simchat Torah, circling the *bimah* seven times again, while reciting seven verses and dancing seven *hakafot* ("circlings").

Seven is the cycle of time, the cycle of existence, the cosmic cycle.[1]

The secret to a balanced life is aligning ourselves with the inner cycles/rhythms of existence. To know when to cry and when to dance. Because there is a time for everything.

"Joy has the power to transcend barriers ('*simcha poretz geder*'). When you dance with joy you break down walls and all forms of limits and constraints."
(The Rebbe Sholom Ber)[2]

Fifth Day of Sukkot

Today's honored Sukkot guest is Aaron, who represents humility (*hod*). Aaron and Moses come together as one. His blessing is therefore the same as Moses'.[3] Strength and endurance together with humility make us receptive to G-d's guidance and the deepest spiritual revelations: "G-d shall always guide you, and satisfy your soul with refinements."

Laws and Customs

Some have the custom to read the book of Ecclesiastes (*Kohelet*) on Sukkot.[4] Among the reasons for this custom:

1) Spending time in the sukkah teaches us about the temporal nature and futility of the material world, which is the theme of Ecclesiastes.

2) Ecclesiastes discusses the theme of joy.

3) It mentions seven and eight days, which allude to the seven days of Sukkot followed by the eighth, Shemini Atzeret.

Every seventh year (the year following the Sabbatical) during Sukkot we have the *mitzvah* of *Hakhel* ("gathering"). The entire nation—men, women and children—would gather at the Temple in Jerusalem, where the king would read to them from the Torah, words that would inspire and motivate them to get closer to G-d. *Hakhel* and Sukkot both share the mutual theme of unity.

Though the actual *mitzvah* cannot be performed today, it is appropriate to commemorate it by initiating special gatherings during the *Hakhel* year, and together study Torah, pray and give additional charity. *Hakhel* introduces the synergy of a group, which is more than the sum of the parts.

Being a microcosm of the universe, each person too should "gather" his/her faculties and activities into one united front, focused and directed toward fulfilling his/her particular mission in life.

Oct 18, 2022

The Power of Bonding

There are only two or three days left to sit in the sukkah. So now is the time to seize what remains of the opportunity to spend as much time in the sukkah as possible and make the most of the special energy that Sukkot brings.

When you are sitting in the sukkah, you're bound to become aware that something is surrounding you and everyone else is sitting there with you. As the _Song of Songs_ (2:6) says of this time: "His right hand embraces me."

This is the encompassing light of G-d. You sense that something beyond you is nevertheless with you.

This is the time to open yourself to something greater.

But remember that a cup that's filled has no room for anything in it. You have to empty your cup a little to allow something new in. If you want change, you cannot be filled only with yourself and only with your solutions, especially if they haven't worked.

But being inspired to change is not enough. The power of inspiration is limited; if the inspiration is not integrated it drifts away.

Integrating inspiration requires hard work, and this is where other people can help. When two people commit to do something together they form a bond and they become accountable to each other. The "four kinds," which we wave every day of Sukkot, represent the power of unity of different people all of whom we need to make the world go round. (See Introduction to Sukkot and Sukkot 1).

There are still a few precious days of Sukkot left. Use them wisely. Spend as much time as you can in a sukkah. Take up the "four kinds" and think about what they represent. Concentrate on one thing—an area in yourself that you want to change. The Divine presence will be with you and it will give you the energy to follow through with your plans for the rest of the year.

Tishrei

Tishrei 20

"G-d shall always guide you and satisfy your soul with refinements (*tzachzachot*, i.e. the highest levels of Divine energy), and make strong your bones; and you shall be like a watered garden, and like a spring of water, whose waters fail not."

(Isaiah 58:11)

Sixth Day of Sukkot

Today's honored Sukkot guest is Joseph, who represents bonding (*yesod*). His blessing is the same as Moses and Aaron, because Joseph channels endurance and humility down into the universe.

The theme for today is bonding with those you love.[1]

Laws and Customs

Tonight, the eve of Hoshana Rabba (see tomorrow), it is customary to stay awake and recite the *tikkun* service: portions of Torah and the *Book of Psalms*.

In some synagogues the custom is to distribute apples as a sign for a sweet year, being that Hoshana Rabba concludes the judgment entered on Rosh Hashana, when we also ate an apple dipped in honey.

Existence is essentially about building a LOVING relationship between MAN and MAN and man and G-d

integrating

penetrating

SHEMINI ATZERET   HOSHANA RABBA

SIMCHAT TORAH

Introduction
INTERNALIZING LOVE

The Hebrew calendar is a cycle of progressive growth. We see this especially clearly throughout the month of *Tishrei*.

In the early days of the month—in the Days of Awe—we stood with trepidation before G-d. Then we entered the embrace of the sukkah and we began to integrate the awesome intensity of the first half of the month.

The Kabbalah explains the psycho-spiritual nature of all developmental growth processes as two primary stages. First comes the *makif* stage, in which we surround ourselves with the experience. Next comes the *pnimi* stage, when we allow the experience to penetrate us, and be integrated and internalized.

All growth is about love. Indeed, all of life is about love. All of Torah, the blueprint for life, is about love. Everything else is commentary. Existence is essentially about building a loving relationship between man and man and man and G-d.

Every relationship consists of *makif* (the loving embrace, when we engulf each other in an all encompassing union) and *pnimi* (the personal experience, when we internalize the love within).[1]

Our relationship with G-d that has been renewed on Rosh Hashana, sanctified on Yom Kippur, and celebrated on Sukkot is consummated on Shemini Atzeret and Simchat Torah. (In Israel these two holidays are observed together on the same day, the "extra" day of the Sukkot festival; outside Israel they are observed on two separate days.)

SONG of SONGS

This progression is dramatically illustrated by the romantic words of the Song of Songs:[2]

~Elul, the preparation for *Tishrei*, corresponds to the words from the Song of Songs: "I am to my beloved and my beloved is to me." (6:3)

~The first ten days of *Tishrei*—the Ten Days of *Teshuvah* which begin with Rosh Hashana and end on Yom Kippur—correspond to "His left hand is under my head." (2:6)

~Sukkot corresponds to "His right hand embraces me." (2:6)

~Hoshana Rabba corresponds to "He shall kiss me with the kisses of His mouth." (1:2)

~And finally Shemini Atzeret and Simchat Torah correspond to the actual union itself, which begins the Divine state of "pregnancy" until the Divine birth of new souls of Israel on the seventh day of Passover, the day of the splitting of the Red Sea.

THREE LEVELS of LOVE

The observance of Hoshana Rabba, Shemini Atzeret and Simchat Torah stands out among the holidays because they are filled with customs that are not mandated by any commandments but which naturally evolved among the Jewish people.

These customs are indicative of the intense love that the children of Israel feel for their Creator.

Three levels of love are possible:

1) If you love someone dearly, anything that your beloved asks, you will do, even when it is uncomfortable or inconvenient.

2) If you love someone even more than that, you don't wait to be asked, you respond to the slightest hint in order to satisfy your beloved.

3) If you love someone with all your heart, you don't wait even for hints, you anticipate what might bring your beloved pleasure and you just do it.

The commandments mandated in the Torah are what G-d asks of us, and we fulfill them out of love (the first level)—in this category are the observances of Passover, Shavuot, Rosh Hashana, Yom Kippur and Sukkot.

Then there are commandments which are not explicitly stated in the Torah but are hinted at or implied, and we fulfill them out of an even greater love (the second level)—in this category are the observances of Chanukah, Purim and other derivative *mitzvot*.

Then there are the customs—*minhagei Yisrael*—which are not found anywhere in the Torah (directly or indirectly). These are observances that Jews simply initiated. These *minhagim* are the deepest expression of love of G-d (the highest level), because without being asked Jews anticipate what would give G-d pleasure and they do it.

This is especially true at Shemini Atzeret/Simchat Torah—when we dance wildly through the night and the following day, hugging the Torah in our arms and singing joyously.

Nowhere in the Torah does it command us to do this. But we do—and we put our hearts and souls and all our energy into it. Why? Out of our purest and deepest love for G-d.

One Twig and One Leaf

The word "simple," when applied to human beings or physical objects, usually implies an absence of something. A simple man, for example, is one who has not been blessed with much intelligence or depth of feeling.

There is, however, another application of the word "simple"—in the sense of something that is pure and singular, as opposed to something that consists of various parts and elements. Thus G-d is described as "simple oneness."

In our world, we have no model for such a simple oneness, for even the most homogeneous entity is a composite of various parts, qualities and aspects. G-d, however, is utterly and absolutely one.

And yet, the Baal Shem Tov draws a parallel between human "simplicity," defined by a lack of learning and spiritual sophistication, and the Divine "simplicity." He singles out for distinction the simple Jew who has a simple faith in G-d not observed in his more sophisticated fellows. This is not because scholars do not possess faith or commitment to G-d (which is intrinsic to every Jewish soul), but because, in them, its innocence is blurred by the sophistication of their understanding.

On Hoshana Rabba we celebrate the simple Jew by selecting the simple willow twig for a special *mitzvah*. Indeed, the day is called "Day of the Willow." Among the "four kinds," the willow twig stands for a Jew who neither excels in his wisdom nor his accomplishments, and it is the willow twig that makes Hoshana Rabba.

Generally, when the "four kinds" are waved, there must be at least two willow twigs, each with at least three leaves, but the special *mitzvah* of Hoshana Rabba is fulfilled with just one willow twig, which need only have one leaf.

This *mitzvah* is considered so important that the rabbis of the Talmud arranged the Jewish calendar in such a way that Hoshana Rabba never falls on Shabbat when the handling of tree branches or twigs would be forbidden.

Hoshana Rabba must be kept aloof of the changes and vacillations of this world. If the cycles of time threaten its consistency, we must divert these cycles, manipulating the calendar if necessary, to ensure that the simplicity of the willow twig—the simplicity of the Jew who puts all his trust in G-d—always assert itself on the seventh day of Sukkot.

Hoshana Rabba

"On Hoshana Rabba—the seventh day of the willow—the priests would circle the Temple altar with willows in hand."
(The Talmud) [1]

"This is the final day of judgment for water, source of all blessings (*Levush*). On the seventh day of Sukkot the judgment of the world is finalized and the edicts are sent forth from the King."
(The Zohar) [2]

Tishrei 21

Hoshana Rabba
Seventh Day of Sukkot
Today we welcome our final Sukkot guest, King David, who represents nobility (*malchut*). His blessing (Isaiah 44:17): "No weapon that is formed against you shall succeed." Today's focus is on cultivating our true dignity, built on the firm belief that "no weapon" can succeed in undermining our inherent connection with G-d.[3]

Laws and Customs

Special Prayers—see Prayer Section for details.

Some have the custom of wishing each other *pitka tova* or *gemar tov* being that Hoshana Rabba is the final day of sealing the decrees.

Festival clothes are worn. Some wear white clothes like Yom Kippur, and light the candles which remain from Yom Kippur.

We eat an especially festive meal. Ashkenazic Jews eat *kreplach* (small squares of rolled pasta dough filled with ground beef or chicken and folded into triangles). They are traditionally served at the pre-Yom Kippur meal, on Hoshana Rabba and on Purim.

Today is the last day on which we fulfill the *mitzvot* of the "four kinds" and dwelling in the sukkah (though many have the custom of dwelling in a sukkah on Shemini Atzeret as well[4]).

We conclude today reciting Psalm 27, which we began 51 days ago, on Rosh Chodesh Elul.[5]

***

Tonight begins Shemini Atzeret. We light festival candles before sunset.[6]

The Shemini Atzeret evening prayer is the same as on the other holidays, with special mention of this particular day.

Kiddush is made holiday style with special mention of the holiday, and *Shehecheyanu*.

Many communities begin the *hakafot* celebration with the Torah tonight, on the eve of Shemini Atzeret (see tomorrow).

Facts

Hoshana Rabba[7]—the day of "Great Salvation"—sets the final seal of judgment;[8] the verdict written on Rosh Hashana and sealed on Yom Kippur, is made final on this day.[9] The reason for this is because Hoshana Rabba is the seventh and final day of Sukkot, when the world is judged for water, upon which life is dependent. And since "all depends on the final decision," Hoshana Rabba, the final day of Sukkot, is the day when the final decision is made regarding the judgment for all of life. Hence it is a powerful day, compared in some ways to Yom Kippur, with additional prayers and customs.[10]

Although the Torah does not give this day special status, Jews traditionally observe many customs on this day and have invested it with a solemn character.

A Day Rich with Essence

The name of this holiday, Shemini Atzeret, has many meanings.

The Hebrew word *shemini* means "eighth" but it comes from the same root as *shuman* meaning "fat" or "rich." The Hebrew word *atzeret* can mean "retention/absorption" or "restraint/ retreat" or "in-gathering/assembly." And it can also mean "essence." Thus Shemini Atzeret represents the richness of the essence of the entire year, because this day consummates all the energy of the holidays of *Tishrei* and channels it into all the days of the year.

Rashi, in his commentary on Torah, explains the significance of Shemini Atzeret with the following parable:

There was once a king who invited his children for a banquet of several days. When it came time for them to go, he said to them: "My children, please, stay with me one more day—your parting is difficult for me...."[1]

In the parable, the king does not say, "*our* parting is difficult for me," but "*your* parting is difficult for me." Indeed, G-d is everywhere and so He never parts from us. It is we who part from G-d, moving on to a state of diminished awareness of our relationship with Him.

"Your parting" has yet another meaning— the parting we take from each other, which, in G-d's eyes, is synonymous with us parting from Him. When we are one with G-d, we are also one with each other, united as children of our royal father. The same applies in reverse: when we are one with each other, united in our common identity as G-d's children, we are one with G-d.

This parting is distressful to G-d. So He retains us one day longer, for an eighth day of "retention" or "absorption" or "ingathering"—a day on which dwelling in the sukkah is no longer a commandment but on which the unity of Sukkot suffuses us nonetheless.

On this day it is not we who are in the sukkah, but the sukkah is within us. On this day we are empowered to internalize the unity of Sukkot, to distill it into an essence, and store it in the pith of our souls so that we may draw on it in the months to come.

Shemini Atzeret

 "The fifteenth day of this seventh month shall be the festival of Sukkot for seven days ... The eighth day shall be a sacred calling to you ... it is an *atzeret* (a time of retention)." (Leviticus 23:33—36)

"On Shemini Atzeret the joy is reserved for Israel alone; they are the private guest of the king who can obtain any request which he makes."
(Zohar III 32a)

Shemini Atzeret
Shemini Atzeret, "Eighth Day of Assembly" or "Eighth Day of Retention," retains and absorbs the attainments of the seven days of Sukkot and the entire month of *Tishrei*.

Laws and Customs

Prayers are the same as on Sukkot, with Shemini Atzeret references.

Special rain prayer is said in *Musaf*.

Close to the end of the day it is customary to enter the sukkah for the final time and "say goodbye," by eating something.

Simchat Torah begins this evening (outside of Israel). Following the recitation of the 17 verses of *Atah Horeisa*, we take out the Torah scrolls from the ark and make a *hakafah* ("circling") around the *bimah* in the synagogue, singing and dancing with the Torah scrolls with great joy, in grand celebration of the special gift that G-d gave us—the Torah. We repeat this for seven *hakafot*. (For more on this subject see tomorrow's entry.)

For details regarding the prayers of Shemini Atzeret, see Prayer Section.

Facts

Shemini Atzeret is the conclusion and consummation of the entire holiday season; it retains the "conception" that results on this day from our union with G-d; it guarantees that birth will follow. Shemini Atzeret channels all the energy of the holiday into our lives so that it can bear fruit all year long.[2] This one day is therefore filled with enormous power:

1. The final day of all judgments,[3] when the decree and verdict is sent on its way.[4]

2. The day when we say the primary prayer for rain—source of all blessings.[5]

3. We dance with unbridled joy for the Torah, for the Second Tablets and the forgiveness we received on Yom Kippur.

Shemini Atzeret is unique in the fact that on this day single offerings were brought in the Temple ("one bullock, one ram"), unlike all other holidays, and especially Sukkot when each day these offerings were brought in multiple numbers. The Talmud explains the reason, with a parable of a king:

After asking his servants to join him for a large banquet (the seventy Sukkot offerings), on the last day the king asks his beloved: "Please join me for a small meal, so that I can take pleasure in you."[6] After elevating the entire world during Sukkot through the seventy offerings, Shemini Atzeret is the single day when everything else is put aside and we, "the single nation"—are alone and intimate with the King,[7] without any strangers present,[8] for one last time before entering the dark, cold days of winter.[9]

Celebration of the Indestructible

On Simchat Torah we complete the cycle of reading the Torah (the last verses of the Book of Deuteronomy) and we begin anew (with the Book of Genesis).

The very last words of the Torah read: "... and all the great deeds which Moses performed before the eyes of all Israel." (Deuteronomy 34:12)

Rashi states that this refers to Moses' breaking of the tablets.[1] But, surely, his breaking the tablets was a failing rather than an accomplishment. How could it be a great deed?

It was a great deed because his breaking of the tablets made possible the inscribing of the second tablets which were indestructible.

The first tablets can be compared to a *tzaddik*—a person who is born innocent and leads a holy life; the second to a *baal teshuvah* ("master of return")—a person who falls, but then gets up, repents and starts anew, and is infinitely stronger for the experience.

The second tablets—which came into being because the first ones were broken—reflect the challenge of life itself: the fall of man and his ability to rise to new, unprecedented heights.

The second tablets also reflect the power of human initiative: They were carved by Moses and were given by G-d on Yom Kippur after 80 days of Moses' tireless efforts. The second tablets therefore revealed a new dimension in our relationship with G-d. That even after we have fallen, through our efforts (of *teshuvah*), we can demonstrate the invincibility of our inherent connection with G-d and Torah, that transcends all our weaknesses. It was the breaking of the first tablets that uncovered this power and invincibility.

The second tablets, in short, revealed a new and unprecedented dimension within us, the Torah,[2] and our relationship with G-d.

Simchat Torah is the celebration of that new dimension. We therefore dance with absolute passion and no limits. Our legs carry us as our arms are wrapped around a Torah scroll. It is a dance that touches the very essence of the Jew, the very essence of the Torah, and the very essence of G-d. It is a dance that transcends our limited intellects and emotions, that encompasses all people, regardless of education, background and spiritual station. It is an infinite dance that touches immortality itself.

Simchat Torah

"The 48 hours of Shemini Atzeret and Simchat Torah should be greatly cherished. In every moment (of these two days) we can draw treasures in pitchers and barrels, materially and spiritually. And we do this through our dancing." **(The Rebbe Sholom Ber)**[3]

"Simchat Torah means two things: We celebrate (simcha) with the Torah, and the Torah celebrates with us." **(The Rebbe Yosef Yitzchak)**[4]

Facts

Simchat Torah[5]—though not specifically mentioned in the written or oral Torah[6]—marks the climax of the festival-rich month of *Tishrei*. As the final day of the holiday season, it epitomizes the power of the entire month of *Tishrei*. The awe of Rosh Hashana, the sacredness of Yom Kippur, the unity and joy of Sukkot, all reach their highest expression on Simchat Torah[7] as we rejoice in the Torah and the Torah rejoices in us. Thus, Simchat Torah represents, in many ways, the highest point of the year, certainly the most joyous one.

The *Hakafot* ("circlings") around the Torah platform are containers for the highest Divine revelations, which come in a form of "circles" (*iggulim* in Kabbalistic terms). They are too great to be restricted in limited containers;

they therefore can only be expressed in an explosive circling dance.[8]

Without experiencing it personally, it is impossible to describe the joyful exuberance of the Simchat Torah celebration in Jewish communities worldwide. What can be plainly stated is that the joy, the dancing and the singing is at the greatest possible level that mortals can achieve.

We dance with our legs, and they lift our entire beings—even our minds and hearts—to places that we could not have reached on our own. This dance is the "Dance of the Essence" —the essence that transcends all levels, layers and definitions. As we say in the verses recited before dancing: "You—in Your absolute Essence—have revealed Yourself so that we know You."

This essence—the "You"—cannot be accessed with the mind, the heart and any of our limited and defined tools. It can only be accessed by reaching into our own essence, and breaking into a dance with profound innocence, with no limits and constraints, with no considerations and no deliberations.

We dance with each other and with G-d. We dance and celebrate the very essence of life and the gift of our mission.

After all the outpouring of prayers during this month, all the *mitzvot,* all the different expressions of awe and love—it all comes down to an unadulterated celebration of dance and song that expresses most our absolute passion and fundamental connection with G-d.

For details regarding the Hakafot celebration and the prayers of Simchat Torah, see Prayer Section.

Eternal Moments

A story is told about the 19th-century Chassidic Master, the Rebbe Rashab, who was visited by a friend he had not seen for 37 years.

The re-union was strange—the two once-close friends had seemingly nothing to say to each other after all that time—and then the Rebbe began to sing. It was a song from another time, and he closed his eyes as he sang, transported to another place. In a trance-like state, he sang for a long while, and when he finished, he turned to his friend and asked, "Do you remember?" And the friend answered, "Yes, I remember." That's all they said to each other, and a week later the friend died.

Later the Rebbe explained to his students who had witnessed that moment: "Thirty-seven years ago, when we parted ways, this was the song that we sang. The song was, in a way, a time capsule that held for us all the years that passed. When my friend said that he remembered, I knew that we didn't need to reunite because we had never parted ways—that song lifted us to an eternal time and place as if these years had never passed."

Eternal moments have the power to transcend time and space because they capture inside them the fleeting connection between the finite and the infinite. Such moments are gifts from G-d and are extremely rare. We'd all love to experience such eternal moments, because immortality is what we all yearn for. But unfortunately, life is, for most of us, an accumulation not of eternal moments but of finite, "dying" moments.

As we process the experiences of this High Holiday season, we want to capture the eternal moments that we experienced, be able to recall them, and use them to return to the closeness we felt with our own soul and with G-d.

Ask yourself: What eternal moments did you experience in this High Holiday season? What will it take to recall them later at will and be transported above time and space once again?

Exercise for the day:

Describe in detail as many eternal moments as you can recall.

"It takes a seed three days to be completely retained, and ensure that it will bear fruit. Today, Isru Chag, is the third day from Shemini Atzeret, and is thus the conclusion of the retention of all the revelatory energies of *Tishrei*."

(The Ari)[1]

Isru Chag

No *Tachnun* until the end of the month

A Simchat Torah Story

The first time the Baal Shem Tov spoke to his disciples about Simchat Torah he related to them an episode that occurred in heaven on the morning of the holiday.

Simchat Torah morning, Jews sleep in a little because of their tremendous dancing during *hakafot* of the previous night. The heavenly angels, however, don't dance all night, so, that morning the angels awake at the usual time, all ready to sing their morning prayers.

Yet on this day the angels found themselves with nothing to do. The Talmud states that "the angels cannot sing G-d's praises in the heavens, until Israel sings G-d's praises on earth." Since the Jewish people were still asleep, the angels could not yet begin their daily service.

What did the angels do in the meantime? They proceeded to do some cleaning up in heaven's paradise known as the Garden of Eden. When they entered the Garden of Eden, they found it littered with strange objects: torn shoes and broken heels.

Now, in paradise, angels are accustomed to finding holy objects, like prayer books, prayer shawls, *tzitzit* ("fringes"), *tefillin* ("phylacteries"), Torah scrolls and similar sacred items. Never in their "career" had they come across… torn soles. "What are these bizarre objects doing here in paradise?" the angels wondered.

They turned to their senior colleague, the angel Michael, described as the supernal advocate of the Jewish people. "Yes," Michael admitted, "this is, in fact, my merchandise. These are the remains of last night's *hakafot* celebrations, during which Jews danced for hours and hours with their Torah scrolls."

The angel Michael proceeded to count and pile the tattered shoes according to the communities from which he "acquired" them. "These are the soles from the city of Kaminkeh, these are from the city of Mezeritch," and so on.

"The angel Matat," said Michael, referring to the most prestigious angel in the heavenly court, "ties crowns for G-d out of Israel's prayers. But today, I will do better," he boasted. "I shall fashion an even more glorious crown for the Almighty out of these torn shoes from the late-night Simchat Torah dancing."

This is the power, the Baal Shem Tov concluded, of the dance of a Jew on Simchat Torah. Even his torn soles pierce heaven…

Turning Inspiration into Action

If you want the inspiration of the High Holiday season not to dissipate but to be turned into eternal moments that you can draw on for the rest of the year and for the rest of your life, you have to *do* something about it.

While meditation can be very beneficial, action is more powerful than any meditation can be. Indeed, meditation only lays the groundwork for action. Action changes human beings, moves mountains, and ultimately changes the world.

How can action change the world? It melts the tension between matter and spirit, fusing them into one.

Matter (our material, earthly realm) is temporary but tangible. Spirit (our soul) is eternal but intangible. Hence the tension between them. The Jewish solution is to fuse the two—to spiritualize the material.

To do so, you must take your material life, which is the antithesis of anything eternal, and you must connect it to something eternal. That's the key.

Many people interpret this to mean that they should free up more moments in their life for eternal and spiritual activity—that, for example, instead of working fourteen hours a day, they should come home earlier and spend more time with the family.

That is very good but there is another way.

When you go to work you should transform your workplace into eternity. One suggestion, especially if your work is about making money, is to put a charity box on your desk. While it might seem like a token gesture, it becomes a constant reminder in the midst of financial deal-making that other things are more important.

Another suggestion—since so much attention is paid to food consumption—is to take the time to always make a blessing before and after eating. While it might seem like another token gesture, a blessing is a powerful reminder that the material world is not here for us to indulge in, but to be refined and transformed.

Ask yourself: How do you plan to capture the inspiration of the High Holidays? How can you turn it into action?

Exercise for the day:

Commit to one action that will fuse the material with the spiritual in your life.

Do it.

"(The verse in the Haftorah of Shemini Atzeret) 'On the eighth day he (King Solomon) sent the people away, and they … went to their tents joyful and glad of heart for all the goodness that God had done' is referring to the people returning home after the holiday season. Why "tents" and not "homes"? Because the spiritually rich *Tishrei* season has imbued us with the feeling that the material world is not our permanent abode; it is only like a "tent," temporal and impermanent in nature, and our true home is in our soul." **(The Rebbe Yosef Yitzchak)** [1]

Events

Yahrzeits—Rabbi Levi Yitzchak of Berditchev (1740-1810). Rabbi Aaron Strasheler (?-1833). Rabbi Moshe Sofer of Pressburg (1762-1839), the "Chatam Sofer."

Chassidic leader and advocate for the Jewish people, Rabbi Levi Yitzchak was a close disciple of the second leader of the Chassidic movement, Rabbi DovBer, the Maggid of Mezritch. He is best known for his unconditional love for every Jew and his impassioned words on their behalf before the Almighty.

Rabbi Moshe was an outstanding Halachic authority and community leader, and was at the forefront of the battle to preserve the integrity of traditional Judaism in face of the challenges of his time.

Rabbi Aaron was one of the greatest disciples of Rabbi Schneur Zalman of Liadi. He is the author of many profound Chassidic works.

Meeting the Challenge

Every challenge we are presented with in life packs a certain amount of energy. And to meet that challenge requires of us an amount of energy equal to that of the challenge. If the resistance is, say, 10 pounds, we need to counter it with 10 pounds. And we need 11 pounds, or more, to overcome it.

When it comes to the tension between matter and spirit (see essay for the 25th day of *Tishrei*), the spirit must apply that much energy, and then some, to overcome matter.

Physically speaking, two of us cannot sit in the same seat at the same time, because physicality by definition takes up time and space. So, in order to share with another, we have to give up something. If we have food, and we share with another, we have less. If we have money, and we share with another, we have less. That's how things are measured quantitatively in the world of matter.

But, spiritually speaking, two people can sit in two different seats a million miles apart, and their love is so deep that they're like one. For them to share food or money means not giving but gaining something far more precious.

So matter and spirit work in two different directions entirely. Matter (being selfish) always holds onto its own space, but spirit (being selfless) doesn't have a problem with giving up its space. The spirit understands that money runs out, food spoils, everything material eventually rots and erodes. But anything with spiritual value, by definition, is eternal, unchanging.

This means that every moment in life which becomes spiritualized is immortalized. So, if you dedicated extra time to the High Holidays, you have gained something eternal.

Ask yourself: How much energy did you put into this High Holiday season? How much did you get out of it?

Exercise for the day:

Calculate the time and effort you put into the preparation and celebration of the various High Holidays?

Know that in the coming year, this time and effort will be returned to you in manifold ways.

Watch for it.

"We stand now at the culmination of a month filled with uplifting experiences. We have stood in awe before the King of the universe; we have been forgiven and cleansed by His mercy; we have experienced the joy of uniting with G-dliness through His beautiful commandments; and we have all together rejoiced with His Torah. Now we take all these invaluable treasures that we have gathered together and 'unpack' them in the following months of the new year." **(The Rebbe Yosef Yitzchak)**

Facts

The power of *Tishrei*—a month filled with holidays—extends till the last day of this rich month. We therefore don't say *Tachnun* ("Supplication" for God's mercy) until *Tishrei* is over. This tells us that we still benefit from all the holiday experiences—especially as they were consummated and celebrated on Shemini Atzeret and Simchat Torah.

Leading a Holy Life

All this week the Torah portion being read is *Bereishit*—the opening of the Book of Genesis—which begins with the famous words: "In the beginning, G-d created the heavens and the earth."

In other words, this sentence states that G-d created both spirit and matter, which clearly means that G-d is neither spirit nor matter. This also means that the assumption most people make that they have a choice of leading *either* a materialistic life or a spiritual life is false. There is a third choice: a G-dly life—a holy life—which is another thing altogether.

G-dliness—or holiness—is not the same as spirituality. Spirituality can lead to holiness, but in itself it is not holiness.

Unless spirituality is a path to holiness, it can be as ego-centric as materialism. There are spiritual people who are quite arrogant—they see themselves as superior to everyone who is not as spiritual as they. Holiness, on the other hand, demands humility.

Another distinction between spirituality and holiness is action. Spirituality can take the shape of being a completely meditative experience, apart from the material world. Holiness means that you take upon yourself the task of living in the material world in order to transform it.

A story that aptly illustrates this point is told about two Chassidim: a father and son who were absorbed in studying Torah. Suddenly, a baby (the son's child who was sleeping in the next room) fell out of its crib and started crying. The son was concentrating so hard, he did not hear it. The father heard and went to tend to the baby. When he returned, he said, "If you don't hear the desperate crying of a child, what value is there to your Torah study? Torah study is meant to refine you, to teach you how to help another person, to hear the cry of one in need!"

Ask yourself: What kind of life are you leading: a materialistic life, a spiritual life, or a G-dly life?

Exercise for the day:

Describe how you need to change your life to make it G-dly.

Identify one G-dly act you can do today and do it.

Tishrei

Tishrei 27

"As one establishes oneself on Shabbat *Bereishit*, so goes the rest of the year." **(Chassidic Masters)**

"The edicts that are written on Rosh Hashana, sealed on Yom Kippur, finalized on Hoshana Rabba and sent out on Shemini Atzeret, don't leave the King's palace until after Shabbat *Bereishit*." **(The Rebbe Yosef Yitzchak)** [1]

Laws and Customs

The Shabbat following Simchat Torah is called Shabbat *Bereishit*, named after the Torah reading of this day: Bereishit (Genesis 1:1-6:8) This is the first Shabbat of the annual Torah reading cycle.

The Haftorah for Shabbat *Bereishit* is from Isaiah (42:5-22; some continue till 43:10), which discusses the creation of heaven and earth—the theme of the Torah portion read earlier.

When Shabbat *Bereishit* falls on *Tishrei* 29, the day directly preceding Rosh Chodesh, we read a special Haftorah (reading from the Prophets), which begins with the words *Machar Chodesh* meaning "Tomorrow is the new month" (Samuel 1 chapter 20)

Facts

The story of our life's struggles and achievements reflects the manner in which G-d chose to create the world: "In the beginning...the earth was without form and empty, with darkness on the face of the depths... G-d said, 'Let there be light,' and light came into existence."

We all enter life "in the dark:" confronting a "closed" world, overcoming the ignorance of infancy to uncover the hidden and illuminate the obscure.

The weekly Torah reading is what defines the Jewish week, serving as the guide and point of reference for the week's events, deeds and decisions. Rabbi Schneur Zalman of Liadi called this "living with the times." Hence the theme and tone of this week is one of beginning and renewal, as we launch into yet another cycle of Torah life.

The Hebrew calendar is arranged so that the last Shabbat of the month of *Tishrei* is always Shabbat *Bereishit*. Thus, at the end of all the festivals of *Tishrei* we come back to *Bereishit*, to the beginning. Here is an indication that the beginning of all wisdom is to know that G-d is the Creator and Master of the world. Coming back to the beginning further indicates that we never "finish," nor "graduate," as far as the Torah is concerned. Truly endless is the Torah, "longer than the earth, wider than the ocean," for it is the wisdom of G-d.

It is on this note that Jews leave the month of *Tishrei* and begin their daily life in the new year. Inspired and enriched by the spiritual experiences of every variety, they can face every challenge in their daily life with courage and fortitude, in the knowledge that they are a link in the eternal chain which unites Israel with G-d, through the Torah.

Doing What G-d Wants

During the time when the Temple stood in Jerusalem, the duties of the High Priest were minutely detailed in Torah law. This law mandated the High Priest to do something very strange. On Yom Kippur, when he entered the Holy of Holies—the most important service that he would perform all year—he was obliged to come out immediately if he heard a noise outside. Why? To see if anyone was hurt (even though there were many other priests around who could tend to such things). This was because he could never be so immersed in the Divine experience as to forget about the sanctity of life. He had to constantly remember that he was not there to enjoy the spiritual ecstasy but to do what G-d wants.

This is something we must be forever mindful of as we go about our task in life to spiritualize the material world.

For example, when we give to charity, why do we do it? Some people do it for the tax deduction. Others do it for the plaque and the honors. Still others do it because it makes them feel good. But there is only one good reason to do it: Because G-d said we should, and therefore it is the right thing to do—it makes the world work right. As the engineer of the world, G-d gave us instructions how to make the "machine" of life work at its best.

When we do it because G-d said so, we're essentially connecting to something that is beyond the money and beyond the charity. When we do it because G-d said so, we align our corner of this material world with the cosmic engineer's plan, thereby transforming it into a G-dly place.

If you live a life dedicated to doing what G-d wants, you are guaranteed to bring immortality into your life. Even more than that, you are guaranteed to change everything about you. Because every fiber of your body and every moment of your day is then infused with a new vitality. You are connecting to something that is so much higher than yourself and at the same time uncovering who you *really* are, and that is a very exciting thing.

Ask yourself: How much of your life is dictated by what G-d wants?

Exercise for the day:

Name one thing that G-d wants you to do that you don't do.

Do it.

"After the *Tishrei* holiday season begins the period of *Ve'Yaakov holoch le'darko*, meaning 'And Jacob went on his way.' Every Jew goes on his way, back to his work in fulfilling his unique mission in life. But now, he comes 'armed' with the deep inspiration and energy that he has received from celebrating all the holidays in this month."

(The Rebbe Sholom Dovber)

Emulating Abraham

Some people say that they don't have to keep the Torah and its commandments because it's good enough to be a Jew at heart. They say they love G-d, they meditate on the oneness of the universe a lot, and they are basically good people. The rituals and mandates of Judaism they don't need.

It is true that in most spiritual disciplines other than Judaism, the action is not as important as what is going on beneath the surface. But Judaism says that what is beneath the surface does not truly change unless there is an action above the surface. It's like a contract that is never signed and executed.

Imagine, for example, that you give a brilliant business presentation and your customer heartily responds: "What a wonderful project! I'm in! I'm with you 100% percent." But if he doesn't sign the contract, if he doesn't invest in your project, what do his words ultimately matter? It's nice that he gave you his emotional support but what you want and need is his active support.

The material world is about bottom lines; it is driven by action and it can only be transformed by action—not just any action, but action which spiritualizes the material. This is why it is not enough to be a Jew at heart.

The amazing thing is that through action, it is possible to spiritualize everything in life including your own body—it is possible to actually retard the aging process. The Book of Genesis tells us about Abraham, who lived to 175, that "Abraham aged, and he came into his days." And the *Zohar* explains that this means that Abraham aged very slowly because he spiritualized every moment. By doing so, his life became eternal.

Today, 4,000 years after he lived, millions of his descendants the world over remember not only his name but also everything he did which is recorded forever in the Torah. That's immortality.

Ask yourself: How much of your life will be remembered by others?

Exercise for the day:

List three things you did, or plan to do, for which you want to be remembered forever.

"He made the letter *nun* king over smell, and He bound a crown to it, and he combined one with another, and with them he formed Scorpio in the universe, *Cheshvan* in the year, and the intestine (or spleen) in the soul, male and female."

(Sefer Yetzirah 5:9)

Events

Yahrzeit of:

Shimeon HaTzaddik, one of the last of the Men of the Great Assembly (Avot 1:2). Shimeon HaTzaddik served as High Priest in the Temple for 40 years. His passing brought some fundamental changes in the service of Yom Kippur (*Yoma* 39b. *Menochot* 109b).

Don Isaac Abravanel (1437-1508), one of the leaders of Spanish Jewry at the time of the 1492 expulsion. A minister in the king's court , he chose to join his brethren in their exile. He began writing his extensive and highly regarded commentary on the Torah in 1503 in Venice (where it was published in 1579).

Laws and Customs

Blessing the New Month

The Shabbat before Rosh Chodesh is called Shabbat *Mevarchim* ("the Shabbat that blesses" the new month): a special prayer is recited blessing Rosh Chodesh ("Head of the Month") of the upcoming month of *Cheshvan*. Prior to the blessing, we announce the precise time of the new moon's "birth." Some have the custom to recite the entire Book of Psalms before morning prayers.

Some Sephardim have the custom to begin reciting *Borchi Nafshi* and the fifteen psalms beginning with *Shir HaMaalot* ("Song of Ascent") after *Mincha* on Shabbat *Bereishit*.[1]

Every *Erev* Rosh Chodesh (the day preceding the new month) is called Yom Kippur *Katan* ("the small Yom Kippur"). It is an appropriate time for additional study and prayer.

Facts

As the moon of *Tishrei* wanes, we are challenged to carry its energy into the new moon of the next month. Every diminishment is always meant to lead to greater growth. Every waning moon gives birth to a new one. Our efforts today have to go toward being unperturbed by the waning of *Tishrei*; rather we must use this new month as a catalyst that ignites our work of "unpacking" the treasures we have accumulated during *Tishrei* and integrating them into our daily lives during this month and the months ahead.

Everything You Do Matters

Once upon a time, the Baal Shem Tov sent a group of his students on an important mission to help a needy couple in another town. When they returned, he was not so interested in hearing about their mission as about the minutiae of their trip—what they ate, where the slept, how they traveled, etc.

They didn't understand the relevance of these details, but he insisted on hearing everything. When they related that one morning they sat down near a brook and drank some water there, his face lit up and he said, "That water was waiting from the beginning of time for someone to come and make a blessing over it and drink it."

In Jewish mystical thought, space, time and matter are understood to be forces of Divine energy—sparks which fell down to earth at the time of creation and which became embedded in all aspects of existence; these sparks must be elevated in holiness for the world to achieve perfection as per the Divine plan. This is why the little things you do in life are sometimes more important than the big things—the journey is sometimes as or more important than the final destination.

When you go to work tomorrow, take a moment to appreciate how you got there. Every second of your trip matters—the people you meet on the way, the cup of coffee you drink while waiting for the bus, the piece of paper you throw in the trashcan—all are changed by your actions.

Quite often the things that are seemingly beyond your control are really opportunities to elevate sparks of Divine energy trapped in the mundane, and by doing so, to spiritualize the material—to bring infinite to the finite.

It's a deeper way of looking at the world. And when you begin looking at life this way, a whole new world will be revealed to you—a G-dly world, an immortal world, the real world.

Ask yourself: Have you ever stopped to think that everything you do matters?

Exercise for the day:

Write down one final request you have of G-d for the new year.

Re-read the journal for the past two months. Enjoy all that you have accomplished. That matters too.

Today is a bridge—being the last day of *Tishrei* and the first day of Rosh Chodesh *Cheshvan*, it bridges the head of the year with its body (which begins in *Cheshvan*). Our behavior today can help fuse the two throughout the year.

Facts

Cheshvan always has a two-day Rosh Chodesh, the second of which, the first of the new month, always falls on a Monday, Wednesday, Thursday or Shabbat.

The transition from the month of *Tishrei*, which is filled with holidays, into the month of *Cheshvan*, which has no holidays, is a particularly difficult one. This is because it is a descent from a spiritual "high" to coping with mundane realities. Nevertheless, we have to know that G-d's plan and intention is precisely this: to bring the sublime experiences of *Tishrei* into our ordinary daily lives.

Cheshvan is called *Yerach Bul* (*Kings* I 6:38). Bul refers to the idea that during this month the grass withers (*baleh*) and feed is mixed (*bolelin*) in the house for the animals.[1] Others say that it may come from the word, *yevul*

("produce") for during this month plowing and planting begin in Israel. Still others see a reference to *mabul* ("flood") since Cheshvan is the "month of the flood," marking the beginning of the great flood during the time of Noah.[2] The flood began on the 17th of Cheshvan, and ended the following year on the 27th of *Cheshvan*. The following day, the 28th of *Cheshvan*, Noah brought his offering to G-d and G-d swore never again to bring a flood upon the earth to destroy all mankind. G-d then revealed the sign of His covenant with the world: the rainbow.

The popular name for this month is *Mar Cheshvan* (originating at the time that Jews returned to Israel after the Babylonian Exile). The prefix *Mar* (which means "bitter") is a reference to this month having no festivals or

rejoicing, but much suffering for Jews throughout the ages. *Mar* also means drop and refers to the first rains (the yoreh) which fall in *Cheshvan*.

On the 7th day of *Cheshvan* those living in Israel begin requesting rain by adding *Veten Tal U'Matar* to their *Amidah* prayers. If no rain has fallen by the 17th, a drought is feared and ritual fasting and special prayer begins.

Yet again, we see references to water —the water which we prayed for on Hoshana Rabba and Shemini Atzeret (see *Tishrei* 21, 22). Water is the symbol of love and of blessings. In the month of *Tishrei* we gather all the resources and build up all the reserves for an entire year of love and blessings. In *Cheshvan* our work is to "unpack" these rich resources, and internalize them into our lives.[3]

You have now concluded 60 days of hard, but exhilarating work. Feel proud.

As this rich season comes to a close, know that you have participated in an extraordinary journey — on a road that has been traveled for thousands of years.

Yet your journey this year covered a part of the road that has never before been tread upon:

Your unique journey.

And you have been blessed to reach here, empowered with all the wealth of the holidays: Rosh Hashana (renewal); Yom Kippur (sanctity); Sukkot (joy); and Simchat Torah (ecstasy).

The next step is yours.

May YOU be
BLESSED
with a HEALTHY, SWEET
and
MEANINGFUL
year. One filled with
JOY and HAPPINESS
for YOU and your
FAMILY
60 DAYS OF WORK —
A LIFETIME of blessings

159

PRAYER is
a Dialogue

between

YOU and

your

SOUL

between

your SOUL
and
G~d

developing courage

accessing your heart

expressing your feelings

PRAYERS

BEYOND LIP SERVICE

Let's be honest. Prayer is a difficult thing—not just for beginners but for everyone. Just because some people are fluent in Hebrew and have attended a synagogue all their lives doesn't mean that they know how to speak with G-d. We all are equally challenged to get beyond "lip service" and experience the "service of the heart"—to truly speak to G-d from the heart, heart to heart.

Jewish law dictates that before beginning to pray we prepare ourselves for an hour in order to focus our hearts properly.

If this is necessary with every daily prayer, how much more so when it comes to the holiday prayers, especially those of Rosh Hashana and Yom Kippur—which consist of hundreds of pages of prayers!

If you want to pray properly and derive maximum benefit from the beautiful and powerful High Holiday services, you need to prepare yourself accordingly.

This section will help you do so.

WHAT IS PRAYER?

Before getting into the complex prayer schedule of the High Holidays, it seems most appropriate to begin from the beginning—with the basic questions that every one of us asks:

What exactly is prayer? Why do we find it so hard to pray?

Prayer is a conversation, a dialogue between your heart and your soul, between your heart and G-d. It is hard because it takes practice and work to develop the skills necessary to converse from the heart. This is why prayer is called "service of the heart." As such, it is *not* an intellectual experience—it is an emotional experience.

Education and society today have programmed us to take control of things with our minds. We learn systems and rules that help us understand the universe in which we live so that we can manipulate it for our benefit. But we are not taught how to express our emotions —how to feel.

Of course, we all *have* emotions and feelings, but they are our natural ones, not something we have developed, cultivated or refined. That's why we can have a brilliant and evolved mind while having the emotional immaturity of a child.

If study is exercise for the mind, prayer is exercise for the heart.

162

This is precisely why prayer is so difficult. It is extremely hard to express emotions and especially to express emotions to someone invisible.

This, then, is the challenge of prayer: to learn how to access your heart, to develop courage to be vulnerable and to express your feelings, and to do so before G-d with no shame or fear.

How To

Here is an exercise that can help you begin:

~ **Free up real time. Find a quiet space away from any distracting sights or sounds. Get everything else out of your mind and release yourself, by focusing inward. Listen to yourself breathe. Close your eyes. Sing a song to yourself. Create the mood—an oasis.**

~ **The next step is to concentrate on your inner soul—the invisible force within that makes you tick. Allow yourself to feel and speak to your deepest essence. Then realize that your soul is part of a much larger essence. That larger essence is called G-d. If you were able to speak to your essence, what would you say?**

~ **Choose any prayer that speaks to you. As you recite the words, speak to G-d with the awareness that He is the essence which sustains and energizes your soul.**

~ **Allow the words of the prayer, formulated by prophets and ancient sages, to open up your deepest emotions before G-d.**

~ **Then, in your own words, ask Him for everything you need in life. Be completely open and vulnerable. Express your feelings about the most important matters in your life.**

Prayer—speaking from your heart to G-d—is not about saying big things. It is about saying small things in big ways. It is not about saying many words; it's about saying them with heartfelt sincerity. Don't feel that you have to begin big. Better to begin small, in digestible pieces. Slowly acclimate yourself to the experience.

Small, slow steps will lead you through the largest doors. This is especially true for the High Holiday prayers, when the doors in heaven are open, just waiting for our sincere call.

And this is why it is very important to choose the right synagogue for your High Holiday prayers.

Typically, when we enter a synagogue in America—more often than not—we enter a Jewish bureaucracy and we feel alienated, unable to fit in. Yet the very reason we go to a synagogue on Rosh Hashana and Yom Kippur is that we want to feel connected—connected to the Nation of Israel, connected to our Divine soul, connected to G-d. If we arrive in a strange place, and at the last moment, this is not likely to happen.

This means that you should not wait until the last moment to choose a synagogue. The time to find the place where you feel you belong, where you feel inspired, is as far in advance of the High Holidays as possible.

The second task is to become familiar with the High Holiday prayers. Buy or borrow the *Machzorim* (the special prayer books for the High Holidays) and become acquainted with the order of prayers.

This Prayer Section is meant to be of assistance in this regard.

The explanations contained here are not exhaustive and are not meant to replace the *Machzorim*. Their purpose is to serve as a companion guide to the prayers, helping you focus on the highlights of the services and to decipher some of their intricate structure.

At all times please keep in mind that the most important aspect of any prayer is your intention and spirit—your heart. Therefore, feel free to read the prayers in English or any language that comes easy to you. It is important

to know what you are saying. Yet, be aware that there is a special power when praying in the original Hebrew. Hebrew is a holy and mystical tongue that carries special power. Even if you do not know Hebrew, you can choose one or two prayers that are easy to follow, like the *Shema*. Don't worry if you can't keep up with the rest of the congregation; you are there to speak with G-d, and G-d hears you at your own pace.

G-d understands your heart and your sincerity. Above all, that is what you need to bring to the High Holidays.

"Better to say a few prayers patiently than to say many hastily" (*Shulchan Aruch HaRav*, Laws of Yom HaKippurim 600:2).

PRAYER BASICS

Jewish prayer follows a basic order every day, which is augmented somewhat on Shabbat and considerably expanded on the High Holidays. That is, the basic structure remains the same, but additional poems/hymns (*piyutim*) are included, as are special supplications that emphasize the theme of a given holiday.

Jews pray three times a day (and as a Jewish day begins at sunset, the first prayer of any given day is the evening prayer). These three prayer times are:

the evening service (Maariv)

the morning service (Shacharit)

the afternoon service (Mincha)

On Shabbat, the morning prayer is followed by an additional section called *Musaf*. In this regard the holiday prayers mirror Shabbat prayers, though Yom Kippur includes still another addition at the close of the holiday, called *Neilah* ("Locking of the Gates.")

These prayers correspond to the five levels of our soul, as follows:

1. Nefesh ("Spirit") Biological life
Evening, *Maariv*

2. Ruach ("Breath") Emotional life
Morning, *Shacharit*

3. Neshamah ("Soul") Intellectual life
Afternoon, *Mincha*

4. Chayah ("Life") Transcendental life
Shabbat/Holiday addition, *Musaf*

5. Yechidah ("Oneness") Essence
Close of Yom Kippur, *Neilah*

THE BASIC COMPONENTS OF JEWISH PRAYER INCLUDE:

~ **Preliminaries** (consisting of a selection of Psalms)
~ **Barchu** ("Bless G-d")—an invocation to prayer
~ **The Shema** ("Hear O'Israel")

The Shema—"Hear O'Israel, the Lord is our, G-d the Lord is One"—is the quintessential statement of Judaism and monotheism, expressing the unity of G-d. The sentence following the Shema—known as *Baruch Shem* ("Blessed is the Name")—is always read quietly (except on Yom Kippur as will be explained).

Three paragraphs from the Books of Deuteronomy and Numbers follow: the first (Deuteronomy 6:4-9) speaks of love of G-d, about teaching one's children Torah, and about the commandments of putting on phylacteries called *tefillin* and affixing words from the Torah to ones doorpost—the *mezuzah* scroll; the second (Deuteronomy 11:15-21) speaks of Divine righteousness, reward and punishment; the third (Numbers 15:30-41) speaks of the commandment of wearing fringes known as *tzitzit*, the 613 commandments of the Torah, and the liberation from Egypt.

~ **The Amidah (the "Standing" Prayer)**

The most important part of the prayer service, the *Amidah*, is recited in silence, with only the lips moving, standing in complete sublimation before G-d. Before we begin this prayer, we take three steps back and forth to remind ourselves that we are now entering the presence of G-d. We then ask permission to direct prayers to G-d: "O G-d, open my lips and my mouth shall declare Your praise." (At the end of the *Amidah* three steps are taken back signifying taking leave of G-d's presence.)

The *Amidah* consists of three sections: Praises, Petitions and Thanksgivings, thus fulfilling the dictum, "Let the praise of G-d precede any petition that we may address to Him." There are three opening praises and three closing thanksgivings, in between which we generally recite twelve intermediary petitions, making a total of eighteen blessings. However, on Shabbat and holidays only one intermediary prayer is said, regarding the sanctity of the day, making for a total of seven blessings—corresponding to the seven days of existence (six days of creation and Shabbat).

The repetition of the Amidah

Following the silent recitation of the *Amidah* by everyone, the cantor repeats this prayer aloud. On holidays various special hymns (*piyutim*) are added to the repetition.

The Torah Reading

As the Ark is being opened we recite: "Whenever the Ark set out, Moses would say: Arise G-d and Your enemies will be dispersed..." One or more Torah scrolls are taken out with great ceremony. As the cantor embraces the Torah scroll, declarations of

Divine unity are sung alternately by the cantor and the congregation, including the *Shema*.

The Torah portion (*parsha*) of the week is read aloud in several sections, each of which is marked by calling up (*aliyah*) an adult male to the Torah platform (*bimah*) where he recites a blessing before and after the reading of each section. Following the reading of the Torah portion, a short section of the second Torah scroll, called a *Maftir,* is read.

Following the Torah reading, a selection from the books of the prophets, called a Haftorah, is read which corresponds in theme to the Torah portion.

Musaf

This additional service, which follows the morning service on Shabbat and holidays, stands in place of the additional offerings made in the Temple on those days. The entire service consists of the *Amidah*—first the silent *Amidah* recited by each individual, followed by the cantor's repetition.

Conclusion

The conclusion consists of various hymns and psalms. Its main feature is the *Aleinu*—"It is our duty to praise the Master of all." At the close of this prayer, we repeat the promise of the prophet Zechariah: "G-d will be King over all the world; on that day, G-d will be

One and His Name will be One." (*Zechariah* 14:9)

Kaddish

A sanctification of G-d's Name, this special short prayer begins with *Yitgadal v'yitkadash Shmei Raba*—"Exalted and sanctified may His Great Name be." The *Kaddish* is recited by all (at times only by mourners) several times during every service.

In the following special Prayer Section we will examine how this basic structure is embellished and expanded on the High Holidays. We will choose selected prayers and special highlights of the service. Consult a complete prayer book or *Machzor* for the entire service.

If study
is EXERCISE
FOR THE
MIND,
Prayer
is exercise
FOR THE HEART

Prayers for Rosh Hashana

FOCUS OF PRAYERS

On Rosh Hashana we emphasize our acceptance of G-d's sovereignty over our personal lives, over the entire universe and a united world. In this context, each prayer helps us come more in touch with our Divine mission on this earth—which is our purpose and calling—and the ability to make it a viable reality in our lives.

> Like every Shabbat and holiday (except Yom Kippur) Rosh Hashana has four prayer services:
>
> ~ the evening service (Maariv)
>
> ~ the morning service (Shacharit)
>
> ~ an "additional" (Musaf) service, following the morning service
>
> ~ the afternoon service (Mincha), which is followed (on the first day of Rosh Hashana) by Tashlich for which we walk out of the synagogue to pray by a moving body of water

Each prayer helps us get in touch with another dimension of our soul's connection with G-d and its Divine mission. The special prayers of Rosh Hashana, including special *piyutim* ("hymns"), are recited both days of the holiday, with many variations as marked with special symbols. (When the holiday is on a Shabbat, additional Shabbat prayers are said.)

The focus below is only on certain key prayers and highlights of the service.

EVENING SERVICE (MAARIV)

Following the preliminary prayers, *Barchu* and *Shema*, we say the silent *Amidah*, which includes several additions which emphasize the themes of life's renewal,

G-d's sovereignty, remembrance and inscription for a good year.[1]

In the weekday *Amidah* we say twelve intermediary petitions, making a total of eighteen blessings. On Rosh Hashana (and every other holiday), only one intermediary prayer is said, regarding the sanctity of the day, making for a total of seven—corresponding to the seven days of existence (six days of creation and Shabbat), and the seven emotional attributes (from *chesed* through *malchut*) which are rebuilt on Rosh Hashana.

Additionally, the intermediary *Amidah* section contains four special prayers (corresponding to the four cosmic worlds which are renewed on Rosh Hashana), that divide into ten paragraphs (corresponding to the Ten *Sefirot* which each world is comprised of): four paragraphs—the four *U'vechein's*—regarding establishing G-d's sovereignty on earth;[2] two regarding sanctity of G-d and His people; two regarding the restoration of Jerusalem and the coming of *Moshiach;* two regarding the sanctity of the holiday.

MORNING SERVICE (SHACHARIT)

Following the recitation of the usual Psalms, the formal Rosh Hashana (and Yom Kippur) *Shacharit* prayer begins with the following declaration:

HaMelech yoshev —**"The King is seated upon a lofty and sublime throne."**

On Shabbat and holidays we say the passive *HaMelech hayoshev*, "the King who sits," but on Rosh Hashana and Yom Kippur G-d actually sits in judgment, so we say the active *HaMelech yoshev* with prolonged emphasis to stress the main theme of this holiday.[3]

The continuation of the prayers until the *Amidah* is

the same as on every Shabbat and holiday, with the obvious focus on the Rosh Hashana theme throughout.

Following *Barchu, Shema* and the silent *Amidah*, the cantor begins the repetition of the *Amidah*.

This is the most prominent feature of the service and includes numerous hymns (*piyutim*), interwoven in the blessings that emphasize the central theme of Rosh Hashana (and Yom Kippur): G-d as King of the universe sitting in judgment of the entire world. Most of these hymns are poems arranged with verses in alphabetical sequence, which demonstrates that the prayer is all-encompassing, including everything that begins with every letter of the alphabet. Often the author's identity is spelled out in the first letter of each verse. Besides elaborating on the theme of the holiday, the repetition also serves as an opportunity to include those that did not (or are unable to) adequately say their personal *Amidah*. It allows us all the ability to concentrate on the content of the prayers. The Ark is opened at various intervals throughout the service.

The cantor's repetition begins with the traditional opening, *Hashem sifsei tiftach* ("May G-d open my lips") and the blessing of the *Avot* (the Patriarchs Abraham, Isaac, and Jacob). The cantor then adds a special prayer. Since it is not permitted to interrupt any section of the *Amidah*, the cantor invokes a special formula requesting permission to enrich the service with hymns. The cantor, as representative of the congregation, pleads for Divine guidance and success in his mission:

Mi'Sod chachomim —"[With words] based on the teachings of the wise and the understanding and knowledge acquired from the discerning, I open my mouth in prayer and supplication, to beseech and implore the countenance of the supreme King of Kings and Master of Masters."

Yoreisee —"Trembling in awe I pour forth my impassioned plea as I open my lips to utter words of prayer, as I rise to plead before the most awesome One…"

On the second day of Rosh Hashana he says instead:

Osisi —"I have come to implore You with a torn and seething heart…"

Next come assorted hymns authored by various medieval sages, interspersed in the first three blessings. (On the second day different hymns are recited.) Customs vary as to the content and number of these hymns in different communities and congregations. Each hymn addresses different aspects and dimensions of the Day of Judgment and G-d's sovereignty over existence.

Kedusha —"Holy, holy, holy," a key feature of every *Amidah*, this special sanctification of G-d's Name with the songs of the celestial angels—as described by the prophets Isaiah (6:3) and Ezekiel (3:12)—is lengthened and embellished on Rosh Hashana.

The intermediary *Amidah* section is similar to that of the evening service.

Avinu Malkeinu

Following the *Amidah*, the special *Avinu Malkeinu*— "Our Father our King" is recited (but not on Shabbat), consisting of supplications for life and forgiveness, summarizing the trials and tribulations of the Jewish people. (*Taanit* 25b).

1-3	Introductory
4-7	Happy year free from evil decrees and enemies
8	Against false accusations

The Torah Reading

The Torah is a Divine blueprint for life. All Jewish experiences are grounded in the Torah given at Sinai. The Torah reading serves as a way of channeling the Divine wisdom of the Torah into our lives. The specific Torah readings teach us the theme of the holiday and open up inside of us deeper spiritual faculties that allow us to align ourselves with the energy and power of Rosh Hashana. We must listen closely

to the Torah reading, taking in its Divine music — absorbing its cosmic force, allowing its message to resonate and transform us—a message which has now been read exactly on this day for thousands of years.

On Rosh Hashana (and Yom Kippur) the Torah reading is read with a special heartrending tune, soul stirring and deliberate in its tone.

The Ark is opened with great ceremony. The standard opening—"Whenever the Ark set out, Moses would say: "Arise G-d and Your enemies will be dispersed…"—takes on deeper meaning on Rosh Hashana, referring to the dispersion of all enemies whether inner or outer, physical or psychological. Then the Thirteen Attributes of Compassion are recited three times (especially significant to Rosh Hashana).

Two Torah scrolls are taken out on Rosh Hashana, one for reading the holiday's theme, the other for reading the portion dealing with the holiday offering.

Day One

The Torah reading for the first day of Rosh Hashana is about the birth of Isaac.[4] It begins *V'Hashem pokad et Sarah.*[5] "G-d remembered Sarah…and He did for Sarah as He had spoken. Sarah conceived and bore Abraham a son."

The Torah reading divides into five sections (*aliyot*) on Rosh Hashana (like every holiday), except when it is a Shabbat we divide it into seven parts. Following the Torah reading in the first scroll, the second scroll is opened in which we read (both days of Rosh Hashana) the commandment to observe Rosh Hashana (from Numbers 29:1-6).

This is followed by the reading of the Haftorah. On day one we read[6] about Chana's prayer for a child, and the birth of Samuel her son (*Samuel I* 1-2:10).

The obvious connection between Rosh Hashana and the Torah and Haftorah readings is that both Sarah and Chana were childless until their prayers were answered on Rosh Hashana when they gave birth to a special son.[7] But the question is: Why did this happen specifically on Rosh Hashana? Answer: This is the precise theme of Rosh Hashana, the birth of the universe—i.e., opening new channels that allow the world to be born anew. In Kabbalistic terms this is called the building of *malchut* ("kingship/sovereignty"). Sarah and Chana both represent the feminine *malchut*, which, like the woman, is the source of all life. The channels of birth are often closed or blocked, as they are every year right before Rosh Hashana. On Rosh Hashana, through our prayers and blowing shofar, we eliminate these impediments and allow the new birthing to take place.[8]

* * *

Chana was a barren woman who came to pray for a child in the Sanctuary, which preceded the Temple. As she was praying, Eli, the High Priest, observed that her lips were moving but that no sound was coming out, and he rebuked her for being drunk.

She replied in a heart—wrenching way, "I am not drunk ... I am pouring out my soul before G-d."

When we examine this story, we find it's peculiar that Eli would assume that Chana was drunk just because she was unable to vocalize her prayer.

One explanation: Eli did not think that she was literally drunk, but that she was drunk with her own needs. It was Rosh Hashana when she came to pray, and Eli was indignant that she came there to indulge in her own selfish concerns.

But Chana told him in effect, "I'm not praying for my selfish needs ... My soul is yearning only to fulfill the will of G-d."

Chana wanted nothing more than to fulfill her Divine mission in this world—she wanted to give birth to a child that would be an emissary of G-d on earth. And this is indeed what happened. Chana's prayer was answered by G-d, and she gave birth to a baby who became the Prophet Samuel, a key figure in Jewish history.

This story teaches us what Rosh Hashana prayers are about.

Seemingly, we are praying for selfish things—for life, for health, for good livelihood, for peace.[9] But we are praying for these things so that we will be able to fulfill our Divine mission here on earth—that unique mission which G-d assigned to each one of us—because our fulfillment of it is necessary to the fulfillment of His plan of redemption.

Therefore, if you come to the synagogue and do your best to follow the group, but you get lost—don't worry. A group is only meant to enhance the individual prayer. But this isn't about the group. Ultimately, it's about you and G-d. "G-d desires the heart."[10] Pray from the heart and your prayer will be heard.

* * *

Day Two

The Torah reading of day two is *Akeidat Yitzchak*— the binding and offering of Isaac (from Genesis 22), and the Haftorah is Jeremiah's prophecy of hope and G-d's love for Israel (*Jeremiah* 31:1-20).[11] The Talmud explains the connection to Rosh Hashana: "G-d said, 'Sound before Me a shofar made of a ram's horn that I may remember for your sake the offering of Isaac, the son of Abraham, and I will consider it as if you bound yourselves before Me.' ”[12] Indeed, according to the *Midrash,* the *Akeidah* actually took place on Rosh Hashana.[13] And "Because you listened to Me," G-d promises Abraham, "I will bless you, and through your children all the nations of the world will be blessed."[14]

We are also told that in the merit of Abraham withholding his love and compassion for Isaac in order to fulfill G-d's command to offer Isaac, G-d too will withhold his 'wrath' and forgive us.[15]

The *Akeidah* (literally "binding")—the single greatest statement of faith in history—expresses the deepest connection we can have with G-d. A bond in which we completely dedicate ourselves to the Divine will and become transparent channels for G-d's plan on this earth. Abraham and Isaac epitomized this profound relationship.

When reading this portion in the Torah on Rosh Hashana, and then following it up with blowing the ram's horn, we both invoke the great merit of our ancestors as well as declare that we too are dedicating our very lives to our Divine calling, transcending all immediate material comforts and distractions.

The Torah reading for the second day of Rosh Hashana is followed by the Haftorah from the Book of *Jeremiah* (Ch.31). We read this on Rosh Hashana because it expresses G-d's abounding love for Israel: "Is Efraim not My beloved son, is he not a precious child that whenever I speak of him I recall him even more? Therefore My inner parts stir for him; I will surely have compassion on him…"[16] This is one of the themes of Rosh Hashana—G-d remembering us and showing us compassion.[17]

Shofar Blowing

The mitzvah of the day of Rosh Hashana is the blowing of the shofar. This mitzvah expresses the essence of the holiday.

In the course of the *Shacharit* and *Musaf* service, the shofar is sounded one hundred times, in various combinations of *tekiah* (a long blast), *shevarim* (a trio of broken sobs) and *teruah* (a staccato of short notes). At this point, the shofar is blown thirty times. It will be blown another thirty times during the silent *Musaf Amidah,* another thirty in the cantor's repetition, and the final ten before the end of *Musaf.* In addition, another thirty blasts are sounded at the end of the service to confuse the *Satan.*

When (the first day of) Rosh Hashana falls on Shabbat, the shofar is not sounded. Shabbat accomplishes the same effect that the shofar does.

The awesome moment of blowing shofar—which is sounded by the most pious man in the community—begins with both Torah scrolls being clutched by two people who stand at each side of the one who will blow the shofar.

Before the sounding of the shofar, several prayers are said with intense concentration, to prepare for the awesome moment of the shofar sounding:

Psalm 47—consisting of ten verses (corresponding to the Ten *Sefirot*)—is recited seven times, piercing the seven heavens and the seven emotions. Each time corresponds to one of the seven: *chesed* (love), *gevurah* (discipline), *tiferet* (compassion), *netzach* (endurance), *hod* (yielding), *yesod* (bonding), and finally *malchut* (sovereignty). Also, the Name of G-d, *Elokim* (which refers to *gevurah*) is mentioned seven times in this psalm. By saying this psalm we help eliminate and sweeten the seven severities (*gevurot*) of each of the seven emotions and each of the seven days of the week. And by repeating the psalm seven times, we sweeten the (7x7=) 49 dimensions of impurity.[18]

The one who blows the shofar then recites eight verses, verse by verse, and the congregation repeats them after him. The six middle verses form the acrostic *kera Satan*, which means "cut off the accuser," erase the sins of which we are accused.

This is followed by the *Yehi ratzon* said with special Kabbalistic intention, "May it be Your will, G-d...that the merit of certain Names...should tear asunder the screens and the accusers which separate between You and Your people Israel. I exalt You, my G-d, the King of judgment who hears the sound of the shofar of Your people Israel with mercy."

Then come the two blessings on the shofar: the blessing on the commandment to blow shofar; and the seasonal blessing, *Shehecheyanu*.

The sounding of the shofar, in three groups, for a total of thirty sounds:

Tekiah, Shevarim, Teruah, Tekiah
Tekiah, Shevarim, Teruah, Tekiah
Tekiah, Shevarim, Teruah, Tekiah

(the one who blows shofar confesses silently)

Tekiah, Shevorim, Tekiah
Tekiah, Shevorim, Tekiah
Tekiah, Shevorim, Tekiah

(the one who blows confesses silently)

Tekiah, Teruah, Tekiah
Tekiah, Teruah, Tekiah
Tekiah, Teruah, Tekiah Gedolah

Following the shofar sounding, we say: "And so may it be Your will, our G-d and G-d of our fathers, that the angels that are formed from the [blowing of the]

shofar; and from the *tekiah*, the *shevarim*, the *teruah* and the *tekiah*; and from the *tekiah-shevarim-teruah-tekiah*; and from the *tekiah-shevarim-tekiah*; and from the *tekiah-teruah-tekiah*, ascend before the Throne of Your Glory and intercede favorably in our behalf to atone for all our sins."

The one who blows the shofar recites three more verses, and the congregation repeats them after him verse by verse.

Ashrei—"Happy are those who dwell in Your house"—is recited, as the one who blew the shofar returns to his place. It is a custom that he then turns and looks at all the people in the congregation who just heard him blow shofar.

SHOFAR

TEN REASONS are given for sounding the SHOFAR on Rosh Hashana:[19]

1) Trumpets are sounded upon appointment of a new king. So too on Rosh Hashana, when G-d renews the creation of the universe and His kingship over it, and we coronate Him as our King.

2) As a call to repentance.

3) To remind us of Mt. Sinai where they heard "the sound of a shofar increasing in volume" (Exodus 19:19), and to "accept and then understand" as our ancestors did then.

4) To remind us of the words of our prophets that are compared to the sound of a shofar (Ezekiel 33:4).

5) To remind us of the destruction of the Temple

that took place amidst the sound of our enemy's trumpets. This is meant to arouse in us the yearning for the rebuilding of the Temple.

6) To remind us of *Akeidat Yitzchak* who gave his life for heaven, and we too are ready to do the same.

7) The sound of the shofar has the power to drive awe into our hearts before G-d.

8) To remind us of the upcoming great Day of Judgment, which is called a day of shofar and *teruah* (Z e p h a n i a h **1:16**).

9) To remind us of the ingathering of the exiles so that we yearn for it, as it says that "On that day they will sound the great shofar and those lost will return." (I s a i a h **27:13**).

10) To remind us and strengthen our faith in the Resurrection of the Dead, which will be heard like the sound of the shofar (I s a i a h **18:3**).

Shofar also contains in itself all three central Rosh Hashana themes (see below): *Malchiyot* — as coronation of the King. *Zichronot* — as symbol of the ram's horn that replaced Isaac to invoke G-d to remember us in the merit of *Akeidat Yitzchak. Shofarot* — the actual shofar is a call to t e s h u v a h.

SHOFAR AS A WAKE-UP CALL

Maimonides writes: Although blowing the shofar on Rosh Hashana is a divine decree, it contains a hidden message, namely: Slumberers, arise from your sleep, wake up from your deep sleep, you who are fast asleep; inspect your actions, repent, and remember your Creator. Those of you who forget the truth because of daily trivialities, indulging throughout the year in the useless things that cannot profit you nor save you, look into your souls, amend your ways and deeds. Let everyone give up his evil way and his bad purpose.[20]

All aspects of the shofar - its shape, makeup and sound - carry messages to us.

Shape

The shofar must be bent: To bend our hearts and spirits.

Narrow at mouthpiece, wide at other end: the call from the depths of our hearts pierces heaven and causes an expansive response.

Hollow: Hollow out our insides, to be receptive to a greater light.

Ram's horn: Docile and humble like the ram — *kabbalat ol.*

Not flesh, but bone: *Bittul* (selflessness) must not feel that it is part of something that still retains the life of the animal.

No cracks: For the sound to be heard, there can be no 'back door' escape hatches, no fissures or splits, only one seamless shofar.

Sounds

The Talmud explains,[21] that the three sounds, *tekiah, shevarim, teruah,* are three different cries: *Tekiah* is an unbroken, pure sound of hope. *Shevarim* are drawn out gasps, like someone who is ill. *Teruah* is the short outburst of cries.

There are several psycho-spiritual meanings behind the secret of the shofar sounds. Here is a selection of a few of the many applications. The spiritual significance of the shofar sounding is explained at length in Jewish mysticism, with a variety of different explanations. Generally its significance focuses on two elements:

1. Sweetening severe judgments (*hamtokot ha'gevurot*), and transforming them to forces of love and compassion. As the *Midrash* states, "When G-d is ready to judge He sits on the chair of judgment. But when the shofar is sounded, He rises from the chair of judgment and sits down in the chair of compassion, and He transforms the judgment to compassion."[22]

2. G-d is moved to do so because the sound of the shofar parallels and reflects the purest cry of the human soul in search of its Source.

The effect of the cry of the shofar is compounded by the distress of the soul which feels limited by the "narrow straits" and inhibited depths of life and its hardships. But precisely because it comes from "narrowness," the cry is so profound and reaches the widest expanses of heaven. In the words of one of the verses we recite before the sounding of the shofar: "From my narrow place, from my depths and constraints, I call to You, and You respond to me from Your expansive place."[23] This is actually mirrored in the shape of the shofar: one side is narrow, the other wide. Blowing into the narrow part is precisely what allows the powerful blast to be sounded.

Also, the three actual sounds of the shofar echo three different psycho-spiritual experiences. The long unbroken note of the *tekiah* (preceding the other sounds) reflects the simple cry of the soul from its depths (unlike the sound of words which are shaped by the mouth). The three broken notes, drawn out sobs of the *shevarim* is the sigh of the broken heart, gasping for hope. The staccato of short crying outbursts of the *teruah* is the crying soul eliciting compassion. It is not broken like the *shevorim*. The final, long drawn out blast of the *tekiah* (following all the other sounds) expresses the confidence that we have triumphed and G-d responds from the wide expanses above.[24]

According to the *Zohar*, the first three sounds correspond to the Patriarchs: The *tekiah* is Abraham (*chesed*, "love"). *Shevarim* is Isaac (*gevurah*, "discipline/severity"). *Teruah* is Jacob (*tiferet*, "compassion"). The first and last blasts—of love and compassion—refine, sublimate and sweeten the *gevurah* of *shevarim*.

In another place it states that the *teruah* corresponds to David (*malchut*, "sovereignty," which is built from *gevurah*, hence the staccato cries), and the final *tekiah* is Jacob.[26] Thus, all four sounds correspond to the building of *malchut* (a key theme of Rosh Hashana), which is constructed from *chesed*, *gevurah* and *tiferet*—representing the four legs of the celestial chariot, which in turn correspond to the four worlds.[27]

Chassidic teachings explain that the sequence of the sounds reflects the journey into deeper recesses of the heart and soul: the first *tekiah* is the cry of the soul that can still be expressed in a long drawn out sound. The *teruah* begins to lose its sound, because the cry from a deeper part of the soul cannot be expressed in sound. The *shevarim* is yet another deeper level, where the sound is breaking into very short cries. Finally the last *tekiah* is symbolic of the "voice that has no sound," from the deepest depths of the soul that cannot be expressed even in the slightest sound.[28]

There is also an opposite explanation: In order for the unbroken sound of the *tekiah* to be contained by us, we need the *shevarim* which breaks the sound into "digestible" parts. This also allows us to refine and sweeten the severity of Isaac, which cannot be contained unless it is diluted into containable parts.[29]

ADDITIONAL SERVICE (MUSAF)

What distinguishes the Rosh Hashana *Musaf Amidah* is that it consists of nine blessings[30] instead of the usual seven. This is because in the central petitions we say these groups of special blessings: the *malchiyot* (verses referring to G-d's kingship), the *zichronot* (verses referring to remembrance), and the *shofarot* (verses referring to the shofar), each of which consists of ten Biblical texts, followed by ten blasts of the shofar (except on Shabbat). For this reason this is the longest silent *Amidah* of the year.

The Talmud tells us that G-d said: "Recite before Me (on Rosh Hashana) *malchiyot, zichronot, shofarot. Malchiyot*, so that you proclaim Me King. *Zichronot*, so that your remembrance for good may come before Me. And how (shall this be done)? By the shofar.[31] Accordingly, we recite in *Musaf* three sets of prayers corresponding to these three central Rosh Hashana themes.

Each of the three groups is compiled in the same way:

Introduction

Ten Biblical texts comprising:

three texts from the Torah
three texts from the Writings
three texts from the Prophets
one text from the Torah

A supplication

Concluding blessing

Among the many explanations given for the *malchiyot, zichronot, shofarot*:

1) They represent the three basic principles of Jewish faith: the existence of G-d and G-d's sovereignty over the universe (*malchiyot*); Divine Providence and reward and punishment (*zichronot*); Divine Revelation (*shofarot*).[32]

2) Kabbalah and Chassidic thought teach that these three principles encompass the entire story of existence and its purpose to make this material world a home for G-d: *Malchiyot* is our work to reveal G-d's presence in every aspect of existence (*memaleh kol almin*). *Zichronot* is our work of revealing the transcendental dimension of G-d (*sovev kol almin*). *Shofarot* refers to the G-d's Essence, which is beyond any definition, and allows us to integrate *malchiyot* and *zichronot* so that the universe can be a true container and home for the highest dimensions of G-dliness, without compromising either of the two.[33]

3) The ten verses in each of the *malchiyot, zichronot* and *shofarot* rebuild the ten Divine utterances with which the world was created,[34] which evolve from the Ten *Sefirot*.[35]

Following each of the three groups, the ten blasts of the shofar are sounded (except on Shabbat).

The conclusion of the Amidah is the same as in the morning.

The repetition of the Amidah

As in the morning service, the cantor, following the first blessing, invokes the special formula requesting permission to enrich the service with hymns. Several hymns are recited, in which we invoke events that happened on Rosh Hashana, the merits of our ancestors, the fallible nature even of *tzadikim* and the blowing of the shofar—all as cause for G-d to accept our prayers and remember us only for good.

Upad mei'oz —"From of old this day was established for judgment." On this day Adam was created, he sinned and G-d interceded on his behalf and pardoned him. And thus G-d ordained this day as judgment day for all generations. The Patriarchs were born on this day, which is why the months is called *etanim* ("might ones"), in order to serve as righteous advocates for us.

Teifen b'mochon—"Accept the shofar blast to change the Throne of Judgment for that of the Throne of Mercy." In the merit of the binding of Isaac, may his descendants be graciously spared from judgment.

Melech elyon—"G-d as King." We describe and elicit different aspects of G-d's sovereignty.

[On day two, none of the above hymns are said. Following the opening blessings we say *L'kayl orech din* ("G-d as judge") instead of *Melech Elyon* ("G-d as King").]

U'nesaneh Tokef — (Composed by Rabbi Amnon of Mainz in Germany, about 1000 years ago) this heart-rending prayer, which is one of the most powerful in our liturgy, describes how the fate of all creatures is determined on Rosh Hashana. It is recorded on this day and sealed on Yom Kippur, concluding that repentance, prayer and charity avert the severity of the decree:

"On this day... You will remember all that was forgotten. You will open the Book of Memory, it will read itself, and everyone's signature is in it... and all mankind will pass before You like a flock of sheep.[36] *Like a shepherd inspecting his flock,*

making his sheep pass under his staff, so shall You run by, count, calculate, and consider the soul of all the living; You will apportion the fixed needs of all Your creatures, and inscribe their verdict. On Rosh Hashana it will be inscribed, and on Yom Kippur it will be sealed: How many shall pass on, and how many shall be born; who will live and who will die; who will die at his predestined time and who before his time; who by water and who by fire, who by sword, who by beast, who by famine, who by thirst, who by storm, who by plague, who by strangulation, and who by stoning; who will rest and who will wander, who will live in harmony and who will be harried; who will enjoy tranquility and who will suffer; who will be impoverished and who will be enriched; who will be degraded and who will be exalted. But repentance (teshuvah), and prayer (tefilah), and charity (tzedaka) avert the severity/evil of the decree."[37]

Following *Kedusha*-which is the same as in the morning-another special prayer is recited:

Ve'chol maaminim—"And all believe" listing different attributes of G-d as King, Rememberer and Judge.

A special Aleinu (in front of an opened Ark) is recited inside the *Amidah*. At the words "that He does not assign us" the Ark is closed. When we say "But when we bend the knee" it is reopened and the cantor and congregation kneel and prostrate themselves (even on Shabbat).

All year round we only bend our knees signifying behavioral humility; on Rosh Hashana and Yom Kippur we kneel and prostrate our entire bodies, signifying the sublimation of our mind and heart as well.

Then come the three sets of **malchiyot, zichronot, shofarot**—as in the silent *Amidah*, and the sounding of the shofar.

The Priestly Blessing is next (as in the *Musaf* of every holiday). Like in the times of the Temple, the *kohanim* (priests) assemble at the Ark and bless the entire congregation with the Priestly Blessing found in Numbers 6:24-26. The actual blessing consists of fifteen words, which are recited word by word, with two breaks in which the entire congregation answers *Amen*.

Hayom Ti'amtzaeinu—"On this day strengthen us…" Seven requests for blessing "on this day" corresponding to the seven emotions that build *malchut*: Strengthen us (*gevurah*); bless us (*chesed*); exalt us (*tiferet*); seek us out for good (*netzach*); hear our cry (*hod*); accept our prayers with mercy and goodwill (*yesod*); sustain us with the right hand of Your righteousness (*malchut*).

Ki'hayom hazeh—"As of this day bring us joyous and happy…"

Before the end, ten more blasts of the shofar are sounded, making for a total of one hundred blasts.

Conclusion

It is customary to sound thirty more shofar blasts, in order to "confuse the Satan."

TASHLICH

Following the *Mincha* service, the *Tashlich* prayer service, in which we ask G-d to "cast away our sins in the depths of the sea," is recited at a body of water, a well or spring, containing fish, "for water symbolizes kindness (*chesed*), and fish, an ever-open eye." The water is also a reminder that people cannot live without G-d, as a fish cannot live without water. In addition the fish's always-open eyes are a reminder that G-d always sees each person's actions, good or bad.

We recite the Thirteen Attributes of Compassion mentioned in the Book of *Micha* (7:18-20), which correspond to the Thirteen Attributes that G-d revealed to Moses (Exodus 34:6-7). Indeed, they reflect a higher level of the Divine attributes.[38]

The *Tashlich* ceremony is concluded with *Yehi ratzon*—"May it be Your will"—beseeching G-d to allow His Thirteen Attributes of Compassion to shine so that they sweeten all the severe judgments. Then we shake the corners of the *tallit katan* (the four-cornered, fringed garment worn by males).

When Rosh Hashana falls on Shabbat, *Tashlich* is postponed to the second day. If one is unable to perform this ceremony on Rosh Hashana, one may do it until the last day of Sukkot.

"Please REMEMBER me, and through and through doing that, REMIND me of my MISSION on earth so that I may **never** **for**g**et** IT."

Prayers for Yom Kippur

FOCUS OF PRAYERS

On Rosh Hashana we wish each other *Ketiva v'chatima tovah,* "to be written and sealed for the good." On Yom Kippur we amend that to *Gemar chatima tovah,* "the end of the sealing for the good."

Yom Kippur is the conclusion of Rosh Hashana and is sometimes called "the inner Rosh Hashana,"[1] because it concludes the judgment of the universe begun on Rosh Hashana. This is also why many of the prayers of the two holidays are similar, though their focus is different.

On Rosh Hashana, the birthday of the human race, the focus is on our acceptance of G-d's sovereignty over our personal lives, over the entire universe and a united world. In this context, each prayer helps us come more in touch with our Divine mission on this earth—which is our purpose and calling—and the ability to make it a viable reality in our lives.

On Yom Kippur, the holiest day of the year, the focus is on holiness (*kedusha*). In Temple times, this was the one and only day of the year when the High Priest entered the Holy of Holies. Now that the Temple is destroyed, we endeavor to enter instead into our personal "Holy of Holies" and by coming in touch with the most intimate part of our own Divine soul to connect with G-d.

Thus Yom Kippur is the day of the soul—when the soul is closest to its source in G-d. On Yom Kippur, more than on any other day, we have the ability to look at everything with the eyes of our soul, not with the eyes of our body.

This also explains why Yom Kippur is the day of forgiveness. (On this day some 3,000 years ago, G-d finally answered Moses prayers and agreed to forgive the Jews for the sin of the Golden Calf.) Because the soul is closest to its source, it feels its source and the source feels it; their essential connection is revealed and all barriers melt away.

Yom Kippur follows the structure of prayers of Shabbat and other holidays except that a fifth prayer service is added just before sundown:

the evening service (Maariv)

the morning service (Shacharit)

an "additional" (Musaf) service, following the morning service

the afternoon service (Mincha)

sundown service (Neilah)

As explained in the introduction to this Prayer Section, the soul has five levels. During the weekday, we access the three lower levels in our prayers. On Shabbat and holidays we access the fourth level. But it is only on Yom Kippur that it is possible for us to access the fifth, highest level—*yechidah*—oneness with G-d, and only during *Neilah* ("Locking of the Gates"), the final prayer service of the holiday.[2]

In addition to the prayers explained below, Chassidic Masters passed on a tradition to us, originating from the Baal Shem Tov, to recite nine special Psalms on Yom Kippur: before *Kol Nidrei* (Psalms 115-123), before retiring at night (124-132), after *Musaf* (133-141), and before *Neilah* (142-150).

EVENING SERVICE (MAARIV)

The evening service (Maariv) corresponds to the lowest level of soul—nefesh ("spirit")—which relates to our biological life.

Preliminaries—unique to Yom Kippur; the prayers begin before sunset with the hallmark hymn of this holiday, *Kol Nidrei* ("All Vows").

~ Kol Nidrei

All Torah scrolls are taken out of the ark. Two people clutching Torah scrolls stand one on each side of the cantor, as Aaron and Hur stood on either side of Moses and held up his hands to support him when he prayed to G-d for victory over the war with the Amalakites. (Exodus 17:2)

The *Kol Nidrei* is a prayer absolving all vows; it is recited because the first step to entering the world of the soul is to be free of the bounds of the material world. The lowest level of the soul—the *nefesh* level—is the survival level; to get beyond this requires that we free ourselves of all biological life demands and traps since the survival mode creates all types of "vows," habits and patterns that bind us; we must be free from them to truly grow.

Kol Nidrei is repeated three times, each time louder and stronger; the repetitions correspond to the three soul garments: thought, speech and action.

~ Barchu ("Bless G-d")—an invocation to prayer.

~ The Shema

This is the same as the evening service of Rosh Hashana with one key difference. The statement following "Hear O Israel, the Lord is our G-d, the Lord is One"-*Baruch shem* ("Blessed is the Name")-is gener-ally read quietly. Only on Yom Kippur is it read aloud. We are taught that Moses originally heard this prayer from the angels when he was on Mt. Sinai and brought it back down with him. He told the Israelites to say it quietly, because it was "stolen" from heaven. Thus we say it quietly all year round. But on Yom Kippur we are spiritually raised to the level of angels and we say the verse out loud and in public.[3]

~ The Amidah

This is the same as the evening service of Rosh Hashana except for the addition of the *Vidui* ("Confession"), which is recited twice in the evening service-once within the silent *Amidah* (which is not repeated) and once after the *Amidah*.

Vidui —"Confession"

This is meant to be an intimate moment when we acknowledge our iniquities before G-d who knows "the mysteries of the universe and the hidden secrets of every human being." The first essential step in *teshuvah* is acknowledgement of the wrongdoing—the exact antithesis of denial. Repentance cannot be just a fleeting thought like other thoughts that come and go in a person's mind. By acknowledging our sins in words, our repentance becomes much more real and helps us reach the complete understanding that our sins are wrong and cannot be rationalized away.

On Yom Kippur we say two types of *Vidui*—short and long—while gently beating the chest. The short is called *Ashamnu*—"We are guilty"—and is recited ten times during Yom Kippur, two times in each of the five services: M*aariv, Shacharit, Musaf, Mincha,and Neilah*. The long is called *Al Cheit*—"For the sin"—and is recited eight times, two times in each of the four services, but not in *Neilah* as at the fifth level of soul—*yechidah*, "oneness" with G-d—no sin

181

is possible.

Both the short and long *Vidui* alphabetically list all types of sins. *Ashamnu*, the short one, goes through the entire alphabet, listing 24 types or categories of sin. *Al Cheit*, the long one, includes a double alphabetical listing (each of the 22 letters of the Hebrew alphabet is listed twice, making for 44 kinds of sin). Al Cheit is broken down into four sections; in between each section we say: "For all these, G-d of Pardon, pardon us, wipe away our sins, atone for us." Pardon (*selach*) is the weakest of the three—it is for the sins that we committed without even personal benefit, therefore only pardon is possible. Wipe away (*mechal*) is stronger—for intentional sins done for personal benefit. Atone (*kapper*) is the strongest—for unintentional sins, which can be entirely atoned for. (See also the essay for Elul 23.)

Sins in general have to be understood not as mere transgressions but as disconnections. The Hebrew word for "commandment"—*mitzvah*—comes from the root meaning "connection." The Hebrew word for "sin"—*aveirah*—comes from the root meaning "disconnection" or "displacement." When we sin we actually displace and disconnect ourselves from our own true self. A sin is therefore not committed just against G-d, it is committed against the self. *Teshuvah*—which requires *Vidui*—confession or acknowledgement—is the process of realigning and returning to our real self, our Divine soul.

In the Yom Kippur service, sins are expressed in the plural not only to save individuals from embarrassment but so that the congregation as a whole might attain true atonement. We cannot confess only for ourselves, rather we have to beg forgiveness for all Jews who sin. As the great 16-th century Kabbalist, the Ari, said, "Confession is written in the plural, 'We have sinned' because all Israel is considered like one body and every person is a limb of that body. So we confess to all the sins of all the parts of our body."

The *Al Cheit* is a list of categories of sins that are the most common. Many relate to our misuse of speech and having the wrong type of thoughts or attitude. Some have to do with more concrete *mitzvot* like keeping Shabbat or keeping kosher. All relate to different aspects of our lives. Of course, we should not feel limited to confess only the list of sins printed in the prayer book, we should mention in the *Vidui* any specific sins which we may have committed.

Penitential Prayers

Exclusive to Yom Kippur is an entire selection of penitential prayers which are recited in each of the five prayers (after the silent *Amidah* in the evening service, and in the cantor's repetition in the other services). In the evening service the Ark is opened anew for each hymn, indicating opening a new dimension of the soul. Each hymn is followed by reciting the Thirteen Attributes of Compassion (which were revealed to Moses atop Mt. Sinai before he descended on Yom Kippur). In total the Ark is opened five times corresponding to the five levels of soul.

The penitential prayer (in each of the five prayers) consists of these special hymns :

Zachor Rachamecho—Remember Your mercies [In *Musaf* this is replaced with *Aleh Ezkerah*, the Ten Martyrs.]

Zachor Lanu —"Remember for us the covenant of the Patriarchs"-Biblical quotations promising forgiveness.

Shema Kolenu —"Hear our voice"-heart-rending petitions to G-d imploring that He not reject us.

Ki Anu Amecha -"For we are Your people."

Ashamnu - The short *Vidui*.

Al Chayt - The long *Vidui* (not said in *Neilah*).

V'David Avedecha - "And David Your servant".

Avinu Malkeinu - ("Our Father, Our King") (see Rosh Hashana prayers) [Not said in *Musaf*.]

Additionally, each of the five prayers contains its own special hymns. *Neilah* has its own unique penitential prayer.

~ Conclusion

It is a custom to say the entire Book of Psalms following the Yom Kippur evening service. Some stay awake praying all night. Those who retire, should first say the prayer before retiring, followed by Psalms 124-132.

MORNING SERVICE (SHACHARIT)

The morning service (Shacharit) corresponds to the second level of soul—ruach ("breath")—which relates to our emotional life, and the prayers of the morning service are seen through the lens of ruach. Although all prayer is about emoting with G-d, the root of it all begins in the morning service of Yom Kippur, which reveals the ruach dimension of your soul.

The morning service of Yom Kippur is essentially the same as for Rosh Hashana. The major differences occur in the cantor's repetition of the *Amidah*.

Following the preliminary prayers, *Borchu*, *Shema*, the silent *Amidah* (which includes *Vidui*), comes the cantor's repetition of the *Amidah*. As in the Rosh Hashana service, with the Ark open, the cantor invokes a special formula requesting permission to enrich the service with hymns. This is followed by the alphabetical poem (composed by Rabbi Kalonymus, in the 10th century) *Eimecha nasati*—"I am awestricken as I offer supplication."

Then the Ark is closed and the hymn *Imatzto Osoir*—"You have established the tenth [of *Tishrei*] to atone" is recited. (More *piyutim* are said here by different congregations.) When the Ark is next opened, the special prayers of Yom Kippur begin, followed by *Kedusha*.

From this point the Amidah continues the same as on Rosh Hashana.

Similar to the evening service, the final part of the *Amidah* consists of the special Penitential Prayers, which conclude with the *Vidui* ("Confession"), followed by several additional prayers. At the conclusion of the service we say *Avinu Malkeinu* ("Our Father, Our King").

~ Torah Reading

On the morning of Yom Kippur, two Torah Scrolls are removed from the Ark. In the first scroll we read (with the same special song of Rosh Hashana) the chapter in Leviticus (16:1-34) that discusses the instructions to Moses and Aaron concerning the procedure for the priestly service on Yom Kippur, which would enable them to achieve atonement for Israel. The Torah portion then details the laws of Yom Kippur.

The *Maftir* is read from a second Torah scroll and is from Numbers (29:7-11), which relates the sacrificial service for Yom Kippur.

Following *Maftir*, the Haftorah is read. The Haftorah is from Isaiah (57:14-58:14), which begins *Solu, Solu* "Make a path, make a path, clear the way remove any obstacle from the path of My people." Isaiah continues saying in the name of G-d: "I am with the broken hearted and humble of spirit, to revive the spirit of the humble, to revive the heart of the crushed." After giving them hope, the prophet then urges the Jewish people to return to G-d through good deeds, kindness and sincere *teshuvah*. Fasting alone, Isaiah says, is not enough without the spirit of devotion and return. It requires an emotional and spiritual vitality.

In this Haftorah we clearly see the focus on the *ruach* dimension of the soul—its emotional spirit, not just its biological one. As G-d says through Isaiah: "I will not contend forever, nor will I always be wrathful, for the spirit (*ruach*) in which I wrapped [the body] is from Me, and I have created the souls."

Yizkor

This is a special prayer for the souls of the departed which is said only on Yom Kippur and the festivals. (Those blessed with living parents are asked to walk out of the synagogue during this service.)

Yizkor (meaning literally "remember") celebrates our most powerful resource—the power of eternity, the power to remember those that came before us.

On the holiest day of the year, we perform one of the holiest things we can do as children: remembering our deceased parents. On Yom Kippur also departed souls have atonement. (The name of the day in Hebrew is *Yom Kippurim* in the plural, atonement both for those alive and those deceased.) And this atone-

ment is achieved through their children on earth, who commit to charity for the sake of their parents. Giving money (the epitome of materialism) has the power to atone and redeem the soul above.[4] Furthermore, it has the power to create a physical channel and "home" (a living memorial) for the departed soul.[5]

The *Yizkor* prayer is one of the most intimate and moving prayers in Jewish liturgy. A child, no matter how old or young, speaks to his or her father and/or mother in personal terms, calling them by name and invoking their memory before G-d.

This short but potent prayer is said with the Torah scrolls raised (held by two people) on the *bimah*.

Even if you cannot make it to the other services, *Yizkor* is a prayer that you should not miss. It is an enormous blessing and opportunity to connect to eternity—and it provides many blessings in return.

ADDITIONAL SERVICE (MUSAF)

The additional service (Musaf) corresponds to the fourth level of soul—Chaya ("life")—which relates to our transcendental life. All the prayers of this service (and even those that were said last night and this morning) are now seen through the lens of Chaya.

The *Musaf* service (as on Shabbat and all other holidays) consists only of the *Amidah* prayer. First we say the silent *Amidah* which is the same as *Musaf* of Rosh Hashana—with the variation that we now refer to the Yom Kippur day and its offerings—concluding with

Vidui, this time focusing on the inadequacies on the *Chaya* level of the soul. This is followed by the cantor's repetition of the *Amidah*, again with special focus on the *Chaya* level.

Before saying *Aleinu* the Ark is opened. At the words "that He does not assign us" the Ark is closed. When we say "but when we bend the knee" it is reopened and the cantor and congregation kneel and prostrate themselves (even on Shabbat).

The special part of Yom Kippur *Musaf*—during the cantor's repetition—is the recreation of the service of the High Priest in the Holy temple. This was a transcendental (*Chaya*) experience, which we recreate today by relating the story and meditating upon the service of the High Priest.

The Avodah — "Service of the High Priest in the Temple"

The story actually begins at the dawn of history as the opening hymn testifies. This hymn recounts (in alphabetical order): the creation of the universe and the human being; the fall of man and his return; the story of Noah and the covenant not to destroy the world again; the birth of Abraham and the introduction of a new light into the universe; the birth of Abraham's descendants, the Twelve Tribes; the selection of Levi for the priesthood; and finally the birth of Aaron, who would be consecrated to serve G-d, and would become the instrument of atonement for the entire human race.

The recitation continues with the events of Yom Kippur, detailing the special service to achieve atonement. This prayer is thus the story of history, the story of our lives, the story of our fall and rise, of loss and hope, of death and rebirth.

It is quite moving to read the account of the entire service. The awesome way that the High Priest prepared himself (and was escorted by his assistants) to the sacred Yom Kippur service. How he immersed himself in the sacred waters. How he prepared himself for seven days before Yom Kippur. The lessons for us, how we must sanctify our lives, are endless. The High Priest's service was both physically and mentally exhausting as it required both physical dexterity (while fasting and having no sleep) and total mental concentration.

The main highlight of the service is, of course, the entry of the High Priest all dressed in white into the Holy of Holies, preceded by his pronouncing aloud the four-letter Holy Name of G-d, the Tetragrammaton.[6] This only happened once a year, on the holiest day of the year, Yom Kippur. No one was ever allowed to enter the Holy of Holies nor pronounce the Holy Name.

The High Priest pronounced the Holy Name ten times on Yom Kippur-three times at each of his three confessions and one time when he drew lots as to which goat would become the sin-offering. Each time he pronounced the Holy Name, everyone who heard it would respond with *Baruch Shem* ("Blessed is the Name") as we relate the prayer:

"And the priests and the people standing in the Courtyard, when they would hear the glorious, awesome Name, the Ineffable one, emanating from the High Priest's mouth, in holiness and purity, they would kneel and prostrate themselves, give thanks and say, 'Blessed is the Name of His glorious kingdom for all eternity.'"

We recite the above paragraph four times, for each of the times that the High Priest pronounced the name, and we prostate ourselves three times (not when he threw the lots), as they did in the time of the Temple.

On the holiest day of the year, in the holiest place on earth, the holiest man on the planet, uttered the holiest word in the universe. We recreate this most sacred experience every Yom Kippur at this point in the prayer service. And this is the ultimate *Chaya* experience, not just the biological dimension of life, not just the emotional spectrum, not just the intellect, but the entire psyche of the spirit is involved—all the faculties are immersed in the all encompassing experience of entering the Holy of Holies.

When the High Priest emerged from the Holy of Holies unharmed, having successfully achieved atonement for the people, he offered a moving prayer for them. First he wished them a year filled with all the blessings of G-d and later he would prepare a celebration to thank the Almighty for allowing him to complete his monumental task.

After telling the story of the High Priest's service, we conclude: "And so, as You have listened to the prayer of the High Priests in the Sanctuary, so may you hear the prayer of our lips and deliver us."

We continue with a prayer that invokes G-d to bless us in the year to come with all the blessings included in all the letters of the alphabet.

We then go on to describe the majesty radiating from the High Priest as he came out of the Holy of Holies: "Like the resplendent canopy spread over the vaults of heaven… Like the lightning that flashes from the effulgence of the angels… was the appearance of the High Priest."

Following this, we describe, by contrast, the great tragedy of the destruction of the Temple. Yet we ask: "May the remembrance of these things bring us pardon?" Though, without a Temple we cannot now recreate the actual Yom Kippur service, we thank G-d for helping us atone and we implore G-d to recognize the deep void we experience.

Aleh Ezkiro ("These I will remember")

The service goes on now describing the troubles that have befallen us ever since the destruction of the Temple, ending with the heart-rending story of "Ten Rabbinic Martyrs" which begins: *Aleh Ezkiro*—"These I will remember."

In one of the most moving accounts, we recount the story of the cruel Roman emperor who decreed that the ten greatest Jewish leaders of the time should be brutally put to death. Rabbi Yishmael, the high priest, purifies himself and with reverence pronounces G-d's ineffable Name and ascends to the heavenly heights to inquire if this decree comes from G-d.

He ascends and inquires of the angel clothed in white, who answers him: "Take it upon yourselves, righteous, beloved Sages, for I have heard form behind the Curtain that this decree has been imposed upon you."

The prayer continues with a graphic description of the savage executions of the Ten great Martyrs: Rabbi Yishmael, Rabban Shimeon ben Gamliel, Rabbi Akiva, Rabbi Chananya ben Tradyon, Rabbi Chutzpis, Rabbi Elazar ben Shamua, Rabbi Chanina ben Chachinai, Rabbi Yeshevav the Scribe, Rabbi Yehudah ben Dama, and Rabbi Yehudah ben Bava.

The angels cry out in bitter grief: Is this the Torah and such its reward?! A voice from heaven responds: This is my decree; submit to it.

The angels resonating cry echoes through history—through all the deaths and persecutions we have endured. Their cry reverberates in our Yom Kippur prayers—prayers that continue to be said with tears that soak the very fibers of existence itself. Cries that have pierced the heavens, waiting for a response.

Yes, we have submitted to your decree. But we demand more. We appeal to you to end the pain, to end the bloodshed, to end all suffering.

On the holiest day of the year, in midst of the prayer of transcendence (*Chaya*), immediately following the account of the pinnacle of all life experience - entering the Holy of Holies - we do not forget that we live in a world of pain. And we demand a response.

No denial. No escape. Even at the height of our spiritual elevation, we remember our losses, and we implore of G-d to amend for them.

This is ultimate transcendence.

~ Conclusion

Musaf concludes with the special Penitential Prayers (as in the morning service), *Vidui*, and the Priestly Blessing which takes on new meaning after the recounting of the Temple service on Yom Kippur and the High Priest's blessing on that day.

AFTERNOON SERVICE (MINCHA)

The afternoon service (Mincha) corresponds to the third level of soul—Neshama ("soul")—which relates to our intellectual life. **Following the transcendental dimension of the soul in Musaf, we now integrate it with our minds in Mincha. This prepares us to then be able to enter the ultimate prayer - Neilah, the highest level of the soul, yechidah.**

Following the brief preliminary prayers, comes the Torah reading from Leviticus (18:1-30). It deals with forbidden sexual relationships, because it is such a great and common temptation. This teaches us that even at the loftiest place of Yom Kippur, we must always be vigilant on the most basic levels. The cornerstone of morality is self-control over animal sensuality.

Another message we learn from this is, that no matter what level you stand on, even if you have reached a deep spiritual transcendence, you have to always continue your soul searching. "Sin"(*chet*) comes from the root "*chesaron*" deficiency. A sin is not always literal; it can refer to an inadequacy on your part, that relative to your particular lofty level is considered deficient. When we reach great heights, then suddenly new, subtle deficiencies can emerge that we were unaware of earlier.

Then the Haftorah is read, consisting of the entire Book of Jonah. We conclude the Haftorah with the Thirteen Attributes of Compassion; this is taken from the Book of Micah (7:18-20), rather than from the Book of Exodus (34:6-7), indicating that today we relate to these Thirteen Attributes from the higher soul levels, which gives us a deeper perspective than that which was revealed to Moses.[7]

The Book of Jonah is read on Yom Kippur because it discusses the power of *teshuvah* and how one cannot escape from G-d (as Jonah tried to do).[8] The repentance of the people of Ninveh serves as an inspiration to us to repent, and shows us that repentance can overturn a Divine decree.[9]

The story of Jonah is the story of the soul's descent into this universe. Water symbolizes the dimension of

Chayah and *Yechidah*—the unconscious dimension of the soul (water) descends into the conscious world (land) of *Nefesh Ruach Neshamah*. It tries to deny its mission until the universe itself forces it to embrace its calling. Thrown into water—its unconscious source and into the belly of the whale (fish connected to its source)—it reconnects and regains its sense of purpose. It then goes and calls the world to *teshuvah*, and reveals the highest levels of the Thirteen Attributes of Compassion.

~ The Amidah — with Vidui

~ The repetition of the Amidah — with Penitential Prayers, Vidui, and Avinu Malkeinu .

~ Conclusion

☙

SUNDOWN PRAYER (*NEILAH*)

The last service of Yom Kippur (Neilah) corresponds to the fifth and highest level of soul— yechidah ("oneness")—which relates to our essence and our union with G-d. This is the highest point of the year—and of Yom Kippur—when the soul comes in touch with its source in G-d.

The service begins as the sun begins to set over the hills. This is the last chance, so to speak. The Ark remains open during the entire service, signifying that now all the doors are open.

Neilah (meaning literally "locking") refers to the closing of the gates of the Holy Temple at the end of the day and the closing of the gates of prayer as Yom Kippur is ending. In *Neilah*, the word *ketiva* (inscribed) is replaced with *chatima* (sealed), because in the *Neilah* prayer G-d seals our fate for the coming year.

The *Neilah* service contains stirring pleas that our prayers be accepted by G-d before Yom Kippur ends. The heavenly judgment inscribed on Rosh Hashana is now sealed during *Neilah*. The cantor chants the service in a special melody designed to stir the emotions and bring the congregation to greater devotion.

Following the preliminary prayers (as in *Mincha*), we recite the silent *Amidah*—with *Vidui* (short *Ashamnu* confession only).

This is followed by the repetition of the *Amidah*—with Penitential Prayers, *Vidui* (short *Ashamnu* confession only), and *Avinu Malkeinu*.

CONCLUSION

The highest point of *Neilah* is its conclusion.

We declare our absolute faith in G-d and our absolute commitment to everything G-d stands for. As the Shaloh, the great medieval 16th century sage writes: "When the *Shema* is recited aloud and with heartfelt intention, every Jew should have in mind giving up his soul for the sanctification of G-d's name. This intention will be considered as if he had indeed actually withstood the test to sanctify G-d's name."

We recite the *Shema* —"Hear O' Israel, the Lord is Our G-d, the Lord is One" and then three times repeat aloud the *Baruch Shem* ("Blessed be the Name").

Finally we shout out seven times *Hashem Hu HaElokim* —"The Lord He is G-d."

Kaddish is recited, and in middle of **kaddish**, before *titkabel*, comes the finale: Sounding the shofar, and exclaiming in a loud voice "Next Year in Jerusalem!"

Some have the custom to first sing a victory march. *Neilah* ends and the Ark is closed.

The significance of this sequence:

Shema is said once, declaring G-d's absolute Unity - *Yechidah* (*Atzilut*). *Boruch Shem* three times signifies our effort to infuse the unity of *yechidah* into the three dimensions of existence, *nefesh, ruach, neshamah* (the three worlds of *Beriyah, Yetzirah, Asiyah*). Seven times *Hashem Hu HaElokim* is a further infusion of the unity into the seven (emotional) faculties of each level of soul (the seven levels in each world). These seven also elevate us through the seven heavens as the Divine presence on Yom Kippur returns upward with the conclusion of the day.

We then integrate and conclude this yechidah experience of unity with the saying of Kaddish, in which we sing a victory march, demonstrating our triumph against all adversary, followed by the blast of the Shofar, which is the level of the Shofar Godol (the Great Shofar) that will be heard with the coming of *Moshiach*, as we declare: Next Year in Jerusalem!

May it happen now, and then we will inevitably be in Jerusalem by next year...

AFTER NEILAH

Neilah is followed by the standard evening service (*Maariv*), the prayer separating the holy from the mundane (*Havdalah*) and the blessing of the moon, which is coming close to full at this time (*Kiddush Levana*).

"HEAR O' ISRAEL, the Lord IS our G-d THE LORD IS one..."

Gut Yom Tov!
Go home and celebrate with a festive meal!

SUKKOT PRAYERS

EVENING SERVICE (MAARIV)

The Sukkot evening prayer is the same as on the other holidays (Passover and Shavuot), and similar to Rosh Hashana (without, of course, the special Rosh Hashana references).

The *Amidah* consists of seven blessings like on Shabbat, with the middle seventh one dedicated to the special holiness of the holiday:

You have chosen us from every people, exalted us above every tongue, and sanctified us with His commandments. And You gave us, Hashem, our God, with love, appointed festivals for gladness, festivals and times for joy, this day of the festival of Sukkot, and this festival of holy assembly, the season of our rejoicing, a holy convocation, a memorial of the Exodus from Egypt. For you have chosen us and You have sanctified us above all the peoples, and your holy festivals in gladness and in joy have You granted us as a heritage. Blessed are You, Hashem, who sanctifies Israel and the festive seasons.

(On Shabbat, special Shabbat references are added.)

Each day of Sukkot the service concludes with the *Hallel* service, in which we offer special praise for G-d's blessings and miracles in our lives. *Hallel* is recited on holidays, when a unique Divine energy is apparent in our lives.

MORNING SERVICE (SHACHARIT)

THE "FOUR KINDS"

Each morning of Sukkot (except on Shabbat) we take up the "four kinds" make a blessing on them, preferably in the sukkah in the morning before prayers:

Blessed Are You, O G-d, King of the Universe, who sanctified us with Your commandments and commanded us to raise the *lulav*.

On the first day a second blessing, *Shehecheyanu*, is also recited:

Blessed are You, O G-d, King of the Universe, Who has kept us alive and sustained us and brought us to this season.

After morning (*Shacharit*) prayers, *Hallel* (the special hymn of praise to G-d) is recited during which we perform the *mitzvah* of *naanuim* ("movements")—waving of the "four kinds." This is done on each day of Sukkot (except Shabbat).

The **"four kinds"** are grasped together, with the *lulav* held vertically throughout, and moved in six different directions of space (south, north, east, up, down, west) for a total of eighteen movements—three times to and fro in each of the six directions. The movements are made forward almost to arm's length and back each time bringing "the four kinds" to touch the chest. Throughout the *naanuim* one faces east, so that south and north are on the right and left respectively.

Four series of movements—eighteen movements each time-are made during *Hallel* (once at *Hodu L'Hashem*, once at *Ana Hashem*, once when this verse is repeated, and once at *Hodu L'Hashem* at the end of *Hallel*).

The exact six directions are:

    south-east

    north-east

    due east

    upwards

earthwards

westward, except that in this case the first two dual movements are directed to the south-west, and only the third dual movement is directed due west.

The first seventeen movements back and forth represent *keilim* ("vessels"); the last dual movement represents or ("light")—the unity of the *Shechinah* (G-d's Presence) in the west.

Throughout the *naanuim* the *etrog* is held enclosed in the hand, except for the last time, when it is uncovered somewhat.

Each time the *lulav* is brought back towards oneself, it should touch the chest "at the place one beats during confession."

Hoshanot

Following *Hallel*, on each day of Sukkot, we recite *Hoshanot*, prayers in which the word *hosha-na* ("save us please") is repeated over and over. A Torah scroll is removed from the ark and brought to the *bimah* (where the Torah is read). The cantor and congregation say the first four *Hoshanot* responsively. They then circle the *bimah* holding the *lulav* and *etrog* and recite the *Hoshana* prayer for the respective day of the festival, as they circled the altar in the time of the Temple.

On the first six days of the Sukkot festival, the *bimah* is circled once. On Hoshana Rabba, the last day of the festival, seven circles are made. This custom commemorates the service in the Temple during which the priests would circle the altar once daily and seven times on Hoshana Rabba.

(On Shabbat, some don't say any *Hoshanot* and don't circle the *bimah*. On the next day, Sunday, they say two sections, the daily *Hoshana* and the one for the previous day, while circling only once. Others have the custom to say a special *Hoshana* for Shabbat—*Om Netzurah*, "Nation Protected"—without circling the *bimah*).

Each of the first six days of Sukkot we recite one section of *Hoshanot* (each one consisting of twenty-two statements in alphabetical order), corresponding to the six emotions (love, discipline, harmony, humility, endurance, bonding). On Hoshana Rabba we recite all the six sections and add a seventh one, corresponding to nobility, plus additional prayers.

Torah Reading

On the first two days of Sukkot, two Torah scrolls are taken out. In the first we read the portion about holidays in Leviticus (11:26-23:44). In the second scroll we read (the *Maftir*), the portion about Sukkot in Numbers (29:12-16).

(For Torah readings during Chol HaMoed, see below.)

The Haftorah for the first day is the last chapter of the Book of Zechariah. It discusses the transformation of the world and its nations in the End of Days. The nations of the world will then undergo a day of reckoning, following the war of "Gog and Magog." Finally, G-d will reveal Himself in all His majesty, for "on that day G-d will be One and His Name will be One."

This Haftorah identifies Sukkot as the time when the ultimate redemption of the world will take place. An essential part of this redemption will be the gathering of all of the nations of the world in Jerusalem where all of the nations will announce their acknowledgment of G-d.

The Haftorah on the second day of Sukkot (Kings I 8:2-21) is about the Temple dedication that took place in these days during the reign of King Solomon. Four years after Solomon succeeded his father David to the throne at the age of twelve years, he undertook the construction of the Temple, which was completed after seven years. In the month of *Tishrei*, the Temple was dedicated amid spectacular festivities, which lasted for fourteen days, including Sukkot.

The priests carried the Holy Ark from the City of David to the Temple. When they approached the Holy of Holies, the doors locked so that no one could enter. Solomon prayed to G-d, but it was only when he invoked the great virtues of his father David, that the doors opened and the Ark could be brought into the inner sanctuary. The young king then gratefully offered a moving prayer, the first part of his could king of which is included in the Haftorah.

ADDITIONAL SERVICE (MUSAF)

The additional (*Musaf*) prayer is the same as on every Shabbat and holiday. This service comes in place of the additional offerings made in the Temple on Shabbat and holidays. In it we recite verses and prayers that commemorate these offerings. Unique to Sukkot were the seventy bullocks that were offered during the course of the entire holiday, corresponding to the seventy original nations of the world who descended from the sons of Noah, and who were the ancestors of all the nations till this day. The children of Israel brought these sacrifices as atonement for the nations of the world and in prayer for their well being as well as for universal peace and harmony between all nations.

Each day of Sukkot a different number of these additional offerings were brought. Thirteen bullocks were offered on the first day of Sukkot. Twelve on day two. Each progressive day the number of bullocks decreased by one, until day seven when seven offerings were brought to a total of seventy. On each day

of Sukkot we say the verse corresponding to each respective day.

Following the prayer service, we go home, recite *Kiddush* and eat another festive meal.
Afternoon (Mincha) service is holiday style.

SIMCHAT BEIT HASHOEVA

On the second night of Sukkot a special celebration began in the Temple, called *Simchat Beit Hashoeva*, the great joyous celebration that took place nightly when they drew water to pour on the altar. It is therefore customary to celebrate every night of Sukkot with dance and song.

Today, until the Temple is restored to us with the coming of *Moshiach*, we are unable to conduct the water drawing celebration in its original form. Nevertheless, the festivities remain. Night-long singing and dancing, reminiscent of the celebrations held in the Temple courtyard, are held throughout the festival in synagogues and streets of Jewish neighborhoods. In fact, there are aspects of these joyous celebrations that are possible only today, precisely because they cannot be held in the prescribed manner.

Due to the prohibition against the use of musical instruments on *Yom Tov* (the opening and closing days of the festival), the water pouring celebrations in the Temple did not begin until the second night of Sukkot. For the same reason, it was not held on Shabbat. Today, however, since our observance is only commemorative, we can celebrate without the music. So a negative situation results in an even greater, and deeper, jubilation.

We hold celebrations on all nights of Sukkot, including Shabbat, calling forth from within ourselves a quintessential joy that does not require any mechanical aids to inspire it. And each night we intensify the great joy, in accordance with the teaching of our sages,[1] that one should constantly elevate in holy and good deeds.[2]

CHOL HAMOED

Chol Hamoed (literally meaning "weekday of the holiday") is a type of intermediary day that bridges the holiday proper with our mundane workday lives.

(In Israel, where the opening, festive day of the holiday lasts only 25 hours and not 49 as in the Diaspora, *Chol Hamoed* begins earlier.)

Chol Hamoed is a quasi-holiday. Work is allowed, yet it is still part of the holiday—we eat in the sukkah, bless and wave the "four kinds" and say special prayers. Some don't put on *tefillin*.

The Torah is read on each of the days of *Chol Hamoed*. Four persons are called up to each reading. (On Shabbat during Sukkot, seven persons are called up, and an eighth for *Maftir*). Each day we read (from Numbers 29:17-34) about the daily Temple offerings of that corresponding day of Sukkot. These are the same verses we recite in the *Musaf* service of the holiday, which include the descending number of bullock offerings on each of the remaining six days of Sukkot, all totaling seventy bullocks.

On Shabbat *Chol Hamoed* we read the well-known portion (Exodus 33:12-34:26) in which Moses asks G-d to shows him a deeper understanding of the Divine. G-d reveals to him the "Thirteen Attributes of Compassion" (see Elul 24). The special connection with Sukkot lies in the verses which refer to the three festivals: Passover, Shavuot and Sukkot.

The Haftorah for Shabbat of *Chol Hamoed* is from the Book of Ezekiel (chapter 38), which contains a prophecy of the war of "Gog and Magog." Following this war will come a new era of peace, when G-d will be recognized by all nations of the world. The prophecy is similar to that of Zechariah (chapter 14), read on the first day of Sukkot.

"There is no GREATER JOY than the RESOLUTION of DOUBT"

Prayers for Hoshana Rabba

HOSHANOT

On Hoshana Rabba, as on Sukkot, we recite special prayers—*Hoshanot,* prayers in which the word *hosha-na* ("save us please") is repeated over and over. As we do so, we circle the platform (*bimah*) where the Torah is read with the "four kinds" in hand. This custom commemorates the service in the Temple during which the priests would circle the altar and say special *Hoshanot* prayers.

On the first six days of Sukkot, following *Hallel,* we circle the *bimah* once while reciting one section of the six *Hoshanot.* On Hoshana Rabba, the last day of Sukkot, seven circles are made, as we clutch the four kinds and recite all the six sections of the previous days, plus a seventh one. (In most Sephardic communities, there is no difference between the text of the prayers on Hoshana Rabba and the other days of *Chol Hamoed.* In Ashkenazic communities, there are some minor variations.) The *Hoshana* service also includes prayers that G-d grant us a year of abundant rain and dew.

At the conclusion of each *Hoshana* section we say *Ani Vo'Hu Hoseah Na,* followed by *Ki'hoshaato eilim b'lud imoch* ("As you delivered the Israelites form Egypt together with Yourself... so deliver us"). *Ani Vo'Hu* is a cryptic expression, referring to G-d's Name comprised of 72 words.[1] It also emphasizes the fact that Hoshana includes G-d—i.e. that G-d too is delivered (so to speak) with us. As it is written: "In all their affliction, He is afflicted" (Isaiah 63:9), and "I [G-d] am with him in distress" (Psalms 91:15).

We conclude the *Hoshanot* with Psalm 28:9 - *Hoshea et amecha,* "Deliver your people."

WATER SYMBOLISM

These special prayers are recited on Hoshana Rabba because this day is the final judgment for water, which is identified with the "willows (*hoshanot*) of the brook" which grow by the water.[2] Water symbolizes love (*chesed*) which is the first emotion and which includes in it all the seven emotions. Because like water, love is the source of all life, everything alive is dependent on nurturing love.

How and when we will receive love (water) during the coming year is determined with finality on Hoshana Rabba. We therefore add special prayers that focus on the theme of deliverance: that we be freed from all our fears and obstacles that inhibit our ability to give and receive love. Moreover, we are empowered by the fact that G-d Himself is with us in our pain, and He too is delivered as we are delivered. And we circle the *bimah* seven times in a "march of conquest"—compared to the circling of the city of Jericho in order to conquer the city—we conquer all the different obstacles to experiencing love.

The seven circles and the seven *Hoshanot* correspond to the seven emotional spheres—*chesed* ("love"), *gevurah* ("discipline"), *tiferet* ("compassion"), *netzach* ("endurance"), *hod* ("humility"), *yesod* ("bonding"), and *malchut* ("kingship/nobility")—which are specifically mentioned at the end of each *Hoshana.* With each prayer and circle, we are freeing ourselves from the impediments and opening ourselves up to the refinement of each of our seven respective emotions. Like the seven circles under the wedding *chupah,* we review and refine each of the seven emotional faculties which allow for love to be wholesome and complete.

194

HOSHANA RABBA PRAYERS

We then take the five willow branches and strike them on the ground to eliminate all severities that are destructive to love, and sweeten any of them that are necessary for a healthy, disciplined love.

[The custom of striking a willow on the ground began in the time of the Prophets Chaggai, Zechariah, and Malachi. Unlike other rabbinic obligations, no blessing is recited on this practice since it was enacted as a custom].

A powerful symbol of the willow is its simplicity. It has neither taste nor smell, but precisely for this reason, its simple innocence connects to essence. As the Baal Shem Tov says, "The simplicity of the simple Jew is rooted in (and is of a piece of) the utterly simple essence of G-d."

G-D is DESCRIBED as "simple oneness"

Prayers for Shemini Atzeret

SPECIAL PRAYERS

Morning service (*Shachrit*) is the same as every holiday, with special reference to the sanctity of Shemini Atzeret.

For the Torah reading two Torah scrolls are taken out. Today's primary Torah reading is the portion of *Asser t'asser* (Deuteronomy 14-16) which discusses the laws of tithes, because Sukkot was the time when the various tithes were given away to the Levites and to the poor.[1]

For *Maftir*, in the second Torah scroll, a short portion is read from Numbers (29:35-39) on the offerings of Shemini Atzeret.

The Haftorah (Kings I 8:54-66) is a continuation of the theme of the Haftorah of the first day of Sukkot. After King Solomon concluded his moving prayer and supplication, pouring out his heart to G-d in the Temple just completed, he rose to his feet and blessed the people of Israel.[2] There was a great rejoicing and inspiration on that eventful Sukkot, when the newly built magnificent Temple was dedicated. The Haftorah concludes:

On the eighth day he (King Solomon) sent the people away, and they blessed the king and went to their tents joyful and glad of heart for all the goodness that G-d had done for David His servant and for Israel His people.

Thus, we read this on the eighth day—the day which retains and carries the joy and unity of Sukkot into our lives for the entire upcoming year.

Yizkor (the memorial prayer for the deceased) is recited following the Torah and Haftorah reading.

The additional *Musaf* prayer, which follows *Shachrit* on Shabbat and holidays is the same as on Sukkot (with reference to Shemini Atzeret, of course). In the can-

tor's repetition of the *Amidah*, the special prayer for rain ('geshem') is recited with an open ark. It describes various water experiences of Abraham, Isaac, Jacob, Moses, Aaron and the Twelve Tribes, concluding each description with the alternating plea: "For his sake, do not hold back water" or "For the sake of his righteousness, favor us with an abundance of water." The traditional melody for this prayer is as beautiful as the words themselves.

WATER CONNECTION

Sukkot (and especially Shemini Atzeret) is intrinsically connected to water:

~During this time we celebrate the vegetable world whose sustenance is entirely dependent on water; the "four kinds" as well as the covering of the sukkah which is of vegetable matter are a big part of the Sukkot observance.

~During this time we also celebrate the water drawing (*Simchat Beit Hashoeva*).

~ On the seventh day of the holiday—Hoshana Rabba-we celebrate with the willow of the brook.

It comes therefore as no surprise that during Sukkot the world is judged for the water that it will receive. But despite this profound connection to water, we don't pray for rain during Sukkot. We only do so on Shemini Atzeret, because we want rain after the holiday; rain during the holiday is considered negative. During the holiday we create the rain in its source; only after we leave our sukkot and enter into the retention stage of Shemini Atzeret, do we say the special prayer for rain,[3] and draw down into the universe the blessings and revelations of the entire holiday season.

All this demonstrates how water symbolizes the cycle of life and all its blessings. Thus, the cycle of the *Tishrei* holidays—which is the central nervous system of the year—is very much connected to water.

HAKAFOT

Shemini Atzeret represents the essence of the entire year—it consummates the relationship developed during the holidays of Rosh Hashana, Yom Kippur and Sukkot, and channels it into the entire year, into all our experiences.

This is primarily achieved through our dancing and celebration of Simchat Torah (which in Israel is observed on the same day as Shemini Atzeret, outside of Israel the day after). The seven *hakafot* (circlings) we make with the Torah infuse divine joy into each of the seven emotions which encompass the spectrum of all human experience.

During the *hakafot* every energy is first drawn down in *makif* (surrounding) form, and then internalized. *Hakofah* in Hebrew also means "on loan." On Simchat Torah we are given on loan all the blessings for the entire year, on condition that we repay the loan with our fulfillment of Torah and *mitzvot* throughout the year.[4]

The seven *hakafot* correspond to the seven times we say *Hashem hu ha'Elokim* at the conclusion of Yom Kippur. On Yom Kippur we are reaching upward to the seven levels, on Simchat Torah we are drawing them down into our lives.[5]

[For more on Hakafot, see Prayers for Simchat Torah].

TWO DAYS OF OBSERVANCE

As noted earlier, outside of Israel Shemini Atzeret is observed for two days (the second being Simchat Torah) in commemoration of the time when the Jewish calendar was set on a monthly basis by the Sanhedrin (high court of Torah law) in Jerusalem, and all Diaspora communities, who received word of the exact date of the festival days or weeks later, observed an additional day of each festival out of doubt. Thus, the seven-day festival of Passover was observed for eight days, the one-day festival of Shavuot for two days, etc.

On Sukkot, the matter was more complicated: the Torah ordains a seven-day festival, followed by the single day of Shemini Atzeret; thus the Diaspora observed a total of nine days—seven days of Sukkot, an eighth day which might have been the last day of Sukkot or, alternatively, the festival of Shemini Atzeret, and a ninth day, in the possibility that this is the "real" Shemini Atzeret.

Today, we follow a fixed calendar, so we are no longer in doubt of the festivals' true dates. Nevertheless, having gained extra days of holiness in our calendar, we are loath to give them up, and so we follow the custom of our ancestors. After the seven days of Sukkot, we observe two days of Shemini Atzeret, the second of which is Simchat Torah, this being the day on which we conclude, and begin anew, the annual Torah-reading cycle.

The spiritual reason given for the two days is that outside of Israel, where we do not have the sanctity of the Holy Land, we need two days to contain and absorb the energy that otherwise is concentrated into one day in Israel.

On the question of whether one should dwell in the sukkah on the first day of Shemini Atzeret, which was initially observed as a day that was possibly the seventh day of Sukkot, the Talmud rules: "One dwells in the sukkah, but one does not recite the blessing." This is done in order to emphasize that the *mitzvah* of sukkah, as commanded by the Torah, extends only for seven days.[6]

The result of all this is that we have a nine-day festival period of which the first seven are days of full-fledged dwelling in the sukkah, followed by one day (the first day of Shemini Atzeret) on which we dwell in it but emphasize that this is not a *mitzvah*, followed, in turn, by a day (the second day of Shemini Atzeret or Simchat Torah) on which we do not dwell in the sukkah at all.

The deeper significance of this is that the unity achieved by the sukkah also has these three phases:

a) the seven days of Sukkot, in which the *mitzvah* of sukkah unites us

b) the first day of Shemini Atzeret, on which dwelling in the sukkah is no longer a *mitzvah*, yet we "retain" and "absorb" the essence of sukkah and express this with our custom of dwelling in the sukkah one more day

c) the second day of Shemini Atzeret, on which we have internalized the unity of sukkah to such an extent that there is no need even for any "symbolic" expression of it—indeed, no symbol or act can possibly embody its depth and scope, for it transcends any and all representation

"MY children, please, STAY with ME ONE MORE DAY Your PARTING is DIFFICULT for me..."

Prayers for Simchat Torah

HAKAFOT

Simchat Torah means the Day of Rejoicing with the Torah. The Simchat Torah celebration is unique not just in its intensity, but also in the exclusive way in which we celebrate with the Torah. This way is called *hakafot*, circlings.

In Israel, Simchat Torah is celebrated on Shemini Atzeret (*Tishrei* 22). Outside of Israel, where Shemini Atzeret is observed for two days (*Tishrei* 22 and 23), we conclude and begin the Torah reading cycle on its second day, and it is this day that we celebrate as Simchat Torah. Yet the celebration permeates both days of Shemini Atzeret, and, in certain communities, it is the custom to hold *hakafot* on the first night of this festival as well, making for a total of three *hakafot* celebrations: Shemini Atzeret eve, Simchat Torah eve, Simchat Torah day.

In the evenings the *hakafot* begin after the evening services, lasting often deep into the night. On Simchat Torah day they are done after the morning service, before the Torah reading.

THE ORDER OF HAKAFOT

As an introduction to the celebration we recite *Atah Horeisa* ("You have been shown..."), an anthology of seventeen verses that describe the preciousness of Torah, and essentially establish the Torah basis for our joy.[1] (The word tov meaning "good" has the numerical value of 17.)

After these verses are repeated three times, all the Torah scrolls are taken out of the ark and are carried in a procession around the reading table in the center of the synagogue on which they have been read throughout the year. The procession soon dissolves into dancing and singing; embracing the Torah scrolls

in our arms, we become the dancing feet of the Torah, as the Torah, too, celebrates at the conclusion and beginning of another year as our bond with G-d.

Each of the seven *hakafot* begins with a special prayer that invokes G-d to "deliver us," "grant us success," and "answer us in the day we call." This is followed by the dance of the first *hakofa*. Upon its conclusion the gabbai announces *ad kan hakofa alef*, "until here is the first *hakofa*."[2] This is then followed by the recitation for the second *hakofa*. As so on, until the end of seven *hakafot*. The number seven signifies the cycle of existence—seven days, seven emotions, seven Divine spheres, from *chesed* to *malchut*.[4]

Some study the seven chapters of Sefer Yetzirah today, in order to fulfill the words of the Zohar that we "adorn the Torah" on Simchat Torah.

PRAYERS

The prayers for Simchat Torah are the same as for Shemini Atzeret, except that the Priestly Blessing is recited during the morning service instead of during *Musaf*.

After the morning service comes the *Hakafot* (circlings with the Torah), followed by the Torah reading of the final chapter of the Torah, *V'Zot HaBeracha* (Deuteronomy 33:1-34:12). This is immediately followed by beginning the Torah anew, from *Bereishit* (Genesis 1:1-2:3).

The Haftorah is the beginning of the Book of Joshua, which is the first book following the Torah (i.e. the Five Books of Moses).

This is followed by singing the prayer: *Sisu V'Simchu b'Simchat Torah*, "Rejoice and exult on Simchat Torah."

The entire Simchat Torah prayer service is unique in its joyous exuberance.

Musaf comes next (same as yesterday). Followed by *Kiddush* and the ultra-festive holiday meal of Simchat Torah, the last and final meal of the entire holiday.

CYCLE OF TORAH READINGS

On Simchat Torah—the Day of Rejoicing with the Torah-we complete the yearly cycle of the weekly Torah readings and begin it anew, fulfilling the dictum "the beginning [of the Torah reading] always immediately follows its completion" (*Chatan Bereishit* prayer).

Three scrolls are taken out on Simchat Torah. In the first one we read the last portion of the Torah, *V'zot ha'Bracha*. The reading is divided up into two parts. The first part is read and re-read as many times as is necessary, in order to give every man and boy, from the age of Bar Mitzvah and up, an opportunity to be called up to the Torah. To save time, several men may be called up together.

The contents of this part are clear from the opening words of *V'zot ha'Bracha*, "And this is the blessing wherewith Moses, the man of G-d, blessed the children of Israel before his death." Moses mentions every tribe by name and blesses each one individually, and all Israel together. The last person is called up "with all the boys," that is, with all the boys under thirteen years of age.

After the reading, a special prayer is recited on behalf of the children: "May the angel who redeemed me from all evil, bless the lads; and let my name be their name, and the name of my fathers Abraham and Isaac; and may they grow into a multitude in the midst of the earth." This blessing was originally bestowed by Jacob on his grandchildren Manasseh and Ephraim (Genesis 48:16). Needless to say, it is an exciting and inspiring moment for the boys of pre-Bar Mitzvah age, since it is generally the only occasion during the year when they are called up to the Torah.

The last part (from Deuteronomy 33:27 to the end) is reserved for the "Bridegroom of the Torah" (*Chatan Torah*), usually a distinguished and learned member of the congregation, since this reading concludes the Torah. Before he is called up, a special blessing is recited for him. This closing section of the Torah tells of the passing of Moses at the age of 120 years, after seeing the Promised Land from a distance, standing on the peak of Mt. Nebo. The Torah tells us that Moses died "by the mouth of G-d" and was buried by G-d in the valley below, in the land of Moab, "and no one knows his burial place to this day." The children of Israel wept for Moses thirty days, but they had not been left without a leader, for "Joshua the son of Nun was full of the spirit of wisdom," and he had been appointed by Moses, at G-d's command, to succeed him. In the concluding verses, the Torah tells us that there was not a prophet like Moses before or after him, "whom G-d knew face to face."

Our Sages tell us that these last verses of the Torah, like every other word of it, were written by Moses himself, by the word of G-d, "G-d dictating, and Moses writing it down with tears in his eyes."

For the very last verse the congregants rise to their feet, and at the conclusion exclaim: "Be strong, be strong, and let us strengthen each other!" This is a determined call to continue reading, studying and following the Torah with ever-growing devotion.

In the second scroll, the Torah is begun from the beginning, from Genesis. This reading is reserved for the "Bridegroom of *Bereishit*"(*Chatan Bereishit*), and the honor is again accorded to a distinguished, pious gentleman. Before being called, a special blessing is recited for him, too, as in the case of the other "bridegroom." During the reading, when the reader reaches the verse: "And it was evening, and it was morning, the first day," the entire congregation recites this verse in unison, which is then repeated by the reader. The same procedure is followed in the case of all the other Days of Creation. The final section, including the entire portion of *Vayechulu* (which forms the first part of the Friday-night *Kiddush*) is likewise recited by the entire congregation and repeated by the reader.

In the third scroll the portion of *Maftir* is read, which is the same as the one read on Shemini Atzeret. The Haftorah is taken from the first chapter of the Book of Joshua. The connection is obvious. Joshua was the successor of Moses, and the Book of Joshua, the first of the collection of the Books of the Prophets, is the continuation of the Torah. Thus the tradition was handed down from Moses to Joshua, and from Joshua to the Elders, and from the Elders to the Prophets, and so on, in an unbroken chain, to this very day.

...the invincibility of OUR inherent CONNECTION with G-D and Torah that transcends ALL our weaknesses

Sources

The sources used in *60 Days* reflect the spectrum of wisdom contained in the rich body of Torah literature passed on to us from generation to generation, beginning from Moses at Mt. Sinai. The basic information in this book comes from the Torah: the many books of the *Tanach* (Bible) and its oral interpretation in the *Talmud* and *Midrash*.

The laws and customs were specifically derived from the legal corpus of the Torah, i.e., the works of *Halacha,* which document the laws and customs of the holidays and all days of the year. These works are organized either in order of the holidays (laws of Rosh Hashana, laws of Yom Kippur, etc.) or in order of the seasons and prayers (Elul customs, Tishrei customs, etc.). The main works used: *Tur* and *Shulchan Aruch* and their glosses; *Shulchan Aruch HaRav,* discourses of various *Poskim* (legal authorities) and chroniclers of Jewish customs, namely: *Avudraham, Maharil, Levush, Rokeach, Mateh Efraim.* Material was also taken from various *Siddurim* (prayerbooks), including: *Siddur AriZal* (two versions: Reb Shabsi and Kol Yaakov), *Siddur Shaloh* (Shaar HaShomoyim), *Siddur Yaavetz* (Beit Yaakov), *Siddur Torah Ohr, Siddur Kamarna, Siddur MaHaRid,* and others.

The significant portion of *60 Days* that focuses on the mystical and psycho/spiritual application of these days is taken from Kabbalistic and Chassidic sources. These include: *The Zohar,* writings of the AriZal, the various Siddurim mentioned above, the teachings of the Baal Shem Tov, Chabad Chassidic literature, *Bnei Yissachar,* works of Reb Tzodok HaCohen, and more.

NOTE ABOUT CUSTOMS AND PRAYERS

Jewish tradition is rich with a multitude of customs. From the time of Moses, many aspects of Torah life were determined by different tribes, groups, and communities.

The infrastructure of Torah—its 613 mitzvot and the many laws—expresses the Divine Will that remains unchangeable and is obligatory to all people equally, many of its details and applications were intended to be interpreted by each respective community. This is not unlike music, which has the same, unchanging musical notes, yet can be composed and played in infinite combinations. As long as the interpretation of Torah follows the axioms and guidelines of Torah interpretation (the thirteen rules according to which the Torah can be expounded), and the Torah absolutes are adhered to, there is room for diversity among qualified Torah authorities.

Throughout history, Jewish communities developed different customs and traditions-all without compromising the essential "musical notes" of the 613 mitzvot. Perhaps the most popular example of this are the different customs of Sephard and Ashkenaz. Life conditions, social challenges, different needs and situations all helped the Torah authorities in their respective time and location to determine their specific interpretation and application.

Specifically when it comes to prayer services, prominent differences exist between communities. These are called nuschaot ("versions"). There is for example, *Nusach Sephard, Nusach Ashkenaz, Nusach Ari*, etc. and each one of these includes variations. Many Torah authorities even composed their own siddurim, reflecting their *nusach* of the prayers and its related customs.

In this book, we included a wide range of customs and traditions from the different sources outlined above. Obviously we could not cover every single custom and version. When having to choose, the author therefore included the more universal ones, the ones that are adhered to by most communities, with the natural inclination to the customs that he grew up with, namely *Nusach Ari, Nusach Chabad.*

60 Days was written to encompass and welcome the widest possible audience—people of all backgrounds, traditions and nationalities.

Elul

Introduction

1. *Tur* and *Shulchan Aruch, Orach Chaim* 581. This is also why we read the Torah on Mondays and Thursdays (all year round), because Moses' ascent and descent in the last 40-day period was on a Monday and a Thursday (*Tosafot, Bava Kamma* 82a).

2. *Avudraham, Seder Rosh Hashana u'pirusho,* ch. 1; *Pri Etz Chaim, Shaar Rosh Hashana,* ch. 1; *Reishit Chochma, Shaar HaTeshuvah,* ch. 4; *Bach* on the *Tur, Orach Chaim,* sec. 581; *Shaloh, Mesechta Rosh Hashana* 213a; *Likkutei Torah, Re'eh* 32a.

3. *Arugas HaBosem* in the name of *Sefer Amrichal.* See *Pri Chadash, Orach Chaim,* end of sec. 581, cited in *Elul* 30.

4. *AriZal, Likkutei Torah* and *Shaar HaPesukim, ad loc. Pri Etz Chaim,* ibid.

5. *Talmud, Makkot* 10a.

6. *Baal HaTurim, ad loc.; Bach,* ibid.

7. *Pri Etz Chaim,* ibid. In *Shulchan Aruch* of the *AriZal* he cites it this way: "*Ashiru l'Hashem veyamru leimor.*" The *Pri Etz Chaim* explains why this acronym is backwards: because in the Final Redemption (referred to in this verse) "all the sparks will be redeemed from exile." And these sparks are returned from below to Above, "backwards" from the way they originally descended, from Above to below.

8. These five also correspond with the five dimensions of the soul: *Nefesh, Ruach, Neshamah* (*Gemilat Chassadim,* Prayer and Torah), *Chaya* (*teshuvah*) and *Yechida* (redemption).

Av 30

1. See *Targum Onkelos* on the verse: Moses sent scouts to spy out the land of Canaan (*Numbers* 13:2). He translates "spy"—*Elul,* a form of search and discovery.

2. *Shaloh,* opening of *Mesechta Rosh Hashana.*

3. Fifty-one days in all, in which we say Psalm 27.

4. This is specifically relevant in *Elul,* the month of "I am for my beloved and my beloved is for me," when we prepare for the rebuilding of the feminine *malchut* ("kingship") on Rosh Hashana.

5. *Likkutei Dibburim,* vol. 1, 116a.

Elul 1

1. *Likkutei Dibburim,* vol. 1, 115b.

2. There are two opinions as to when Moses actually ascended Sinai for the third time: 1) *Av* 30, the 1st day of Rosh Chodesh *Elul;* 2) *Elul* 1, the 2nd day of Rosh Chodesh (see sources in next note). For a discussion on this, see *Magen Avraham* 581:2. For a lengthy discussion on this, see the *kuntres acharon* in the addition to *Shulchan Aruch HaRav* from *Divrei Nechemia,* sec. 581. *Mateh Efraim, Elef l'Mateh* 581. *Devar Yom B'Yomo, Av* 28.

3. *Pirkei d'Rebbe Eliezer,* ch. 46 (see Radal, *ad loc.*). *Tur* and *Shulchan Aruch, Orach Chaim* 581 (see *Beit Yosef* and *Perisha, ad loc.*).

4. See *Shaar Ruach HaKodesh, Yichud* 16; *Pri Etz Chaim,* beginning of *Shaar Rosh Hashana*—where Rabbi Chaim Vital writes that in the year 5331 (1571) his master, the Holy Ari, instructed him to fast for two days after Rosh Chodesh *Elul,* and gave him elaborate guidelines as how to conduct himself during the month of *Elul,* when the doors of compassion are open and we recreate what Moses achieved on Sinai, including his fasting for all the days he was on the mountain.

5. *Bach, Orach Chaim* 581. *Reishit Chochma, Shaar HaTeshuvah,* ch. 4.

6. See note 2 in *Av* 30. *Ohr HaTorah, Netzavim,* p. 1280.

7. In our set calendar (established by Hillel), *Elul* 1 can fall either on Sunday, Monday, Wednesday or Friday. This corresponds to Rosh Hashana (29 days later) which can only fall on Monday, Tuesday, Thursday or Shabbat, never on Sunday, Wednesday or Friday (*lo adu rosh*). The average breakdown of these possibilities: 32% of the time, *Elul* 1 falls on Wednesday (and Rosh Hashana on Thursday); 29% on Friday; 27% on Sunday; 12% on Monday.

8. See *Biurei HaZohar,* pp. 505-6. *Ohr HaTorah, Re'eh,* p. 721.

9. *Mateh Efraim* 581:9. This is alluded to in the verse (*Exodus* 18:7) "*Vi'shaalu ish l'rei'eihu l'shalom,*" an acronym for *Elul* (*Likkutei MaHarich*).

10. *Eliyahu Rabba, Orach Chaim* 581, citing *Sefer Amrachal. Levush, ad loc. Likkutei Torah, Re'eh* 25b.

Elul 2

1. *Likkutei Dibburim,* vol. 1, p. 100.

2. *Birchei Yosef,* cited in *Mateh Efraim, Elef l'Mateh* 581:13.

3. *Mateh Efraim* 581. *Chida, Moreh B'Etzba.*

4. *Midrash Tehillim* 27; *Vayikra Rabba* 21:4.

5. See *Siddur AriZal* (R. Shabsi Rashkover). Tzemach Tzedek (*Yahal Ohr*) on Psalm 27. *Shaar HaColel*, ch. 11, sec. 28. For more reasons why we recite Psalm 27 in this season and for a detailed explanation of the Psalm's connection to *Elul* and the *Tishrei* holidays, see *Panim Yafot, parshat Acharei* 16:21. See also *Tishrei* 21.

6. *Panim Yafot*, ibid.

Elul 3

1. Or left kidney according to other versions of the *Sefer Yetzirah* (see Aryeh Kaplan's translation).

2. The corresponding sphere of this month is *yesod* of the masculine (*chesed*). Organ: nose (*Pri Etz Chaim, Shaar Rosh Hashana*, ch. 4. *Taamei HaMitzvot, parshat Bo*). Letter in G-d's name: *Yud*—symbolizing return to G-d (*Yud*) and renewal. First *Heh* of *Havaya*—*teshuvah* (*Pri Etz Chaim, Shaar Rosh Chodesh*, ch. 3). *Yesod d'duchra, gan no'ul* (*Likkutei Torah Ari, parshat Vayeitzei*). *Betulah* rules over Rome (*Bechayei, Deuteronomy* 31:16).

3. For an explanation of this statement, see *Bnei Yissachar, Elul. Pri Tzaddik, Elul.*

4. *Pri Etz Chaim, Shaar Olam HaAsiyah*, sec. 6. See *Likkutei Torah, Re'eh* 33a.

5. See "Introduction to Elul."

6. *Panim Yafot, parshat Acharei.*

Elul 4

1. Which is either *Elul* 2, 4, 6 or 7, depending on whether *Elul* 1 is on Friday, Wednesday, Monday or Sunday respectively.

Elul 5

1. See *Toward a Meaningful Life* (William Morrow, 2002), chapter on Charity.

2. They were all disciples of the second leader of the Chassidic movement, Rabbi DovBer, the "Maggid of Mezritch" (who had passed away five years earlier).

3. *Mishnat Chassidim, Mesechta Elul*, ch. 1.

Elul 6

1. *Pesikta Rabsi*, sec. 30. Cited in Avudraham.

2. See *Tosafot, Megillah* 31b.

3. See also *Pri Tzaddik* (R. Tzodok HaCohen) on these weeks.

4. In the original mystical language: the Three Weeks manifest the concealment of the three intellectual faculties (*Chochma, Binah, Daat*). The following Seven Weeks express the revelation of the intellect of *Atik Yomin* (lit. "Ancient Days," referring to the higher dimension of *Keter*, the Crown—the highest Divine revelation) in the seven emotions. And the Two Weeks of Return is the elevation of *malchut* achieved through the two levels of *teshuvah* ("higher *teshuvah*" and "lower *teshuvah*") that elevates from BY"A (*Beriah, Yetzirah, Asiyah*). This is followed by Yom Kippur, when the Second Tablets were given, the revela-tion of the intellect of *Atik Yomin* into BY"A. This is followed by Shemini Atzeret and Simchat Torah, when the revelation of Yom Kippur is revealed in great joy.

Elul 7

1. Rabbi Schneur Zalman of Liadi, the 18th-century author of the *Tanya* and *Shulchan Aruch HaRav*, the founder of Chabad Chassidism.

2. *Likkutei Torah, Re'eh* 32a.

3. Some say that this happened on *Elul* 17, but according to the *Beit Yosef* it was *Elul* 7 (See *Tur* and *Shulchan Aruch, Orach Chaim* 580).

4. Note as well that G-d's words to Moses: "I have forgiven as you have said"—the expression used on Yom Kippur to declare the Day of Atonement—was actually said in the episode of the scouts (*Deuteronomy* 14:20. See *Radal* on *Pirkei d'Rebbe Eliezer*, ch. 46, commentaries to *Shemot Rabba* 51:4).

Elul 8

1. The transmutation of the Divine name associated with *Elul* is also in this order: *Heh, Heh, Vav, Yud*. First comes the feminine dimension (the two *heh*'s, *binah* and *malchut*)—the initiative from below, "I am to my beloved," arousing the Divine response from Above (*Vav, Yud, Z"A*, and *Chochma*), "my beloved is to me."

2. *Midrash, Shir HaShirim Rabba* 5:2. *Zohar III*, 95a. *Pesikta Rabsi*, sec. 15. *Pesikta d'Rav Kahana, parshat HaChodesh.*

3. *Birchei Yosef* 581:6.

4. *Talmud, Chagigah* 15a.

5. See *Likkutei Torah, Teitzei* 36d, 71d.

6. *Sefer HaSichot 5750*, vol. 2, pp. 631-633.

Elul 9

1. *Yalkut Shemoni, Exodus* 1:1. *Siddur Yaavetz. Seder HaDorot* 5198.

Elul 10

1. *Genesis* 8:6-7, according to Rashi.

2. This is according to the consensus that rules like Rabbi Eliezer in *Rosh Hashana* 11a that the world was created on *Elul* 25. See *Elul* 25.

Elul 11

1. *Tanya, Iggeret HaTeshuvah,* ch. 4.

2. Psalm 27 (recited during *Elul*) is also related to the building of the Third Temple and the revelation of the *Geulah*—see Rabbeinu Bechayei beginning of *parshat Tetzaveh* (cited by the Tzemach Tzedek in *Yahal Ohr*, p. 98). *Shaarei Teshuvah*, Discourse *Acharei*, ch. 41.

Elul 12

1. Third *Haftorah* of the Seven Weeks of Consolation. See *Elul* 6.

2. *Exodus* 22:5.

3. *Pesikta Rabsi*, sec. 30.

4. *Megaleh Amukot Eikev*, par. beginning *Elul* (55a).

5. *Talmud*, end of *Sukkah*.

6. *II*, 78b. See *Likkutei Sichot*, vol. 19, pp. 64-65.

Elul 13

1. Tzemach Tzedek, *Sefer HaMitzvot* 138a.

2. See *Tosafot, Megillah* 31b.

3. Compare with "My head will be raised above my enemies around me" in Psalm 27:6.

Elul 14

1. *Talmud, Pesachim* 6a-b. *Shulchan Aruch, Orach Chaim* 429.

2. *Shach*, end of *parshat Matot*.

Elul 15

1. The Baal Shem Tov ("Master of the Good Name"): the title given to Rabbi Yisrael ben Eliezer (1698-1760), the founder of the Chassidic movement. (It is abbreviated as *Besht*.)

2. See *Elul* 7.

Elul 16

1. Sacred words of Torah particularly offer us refuge, by providing a cognitive oasis that protects us from the forces around us. See *Elul* 3.

2. *Sdei Chemed, Asifat Dinim, Maarechet Chatan v'Kallah*, ch. 21.

Elul 17

1. *HaYom Yom, Tishrei* 3-8.

7. See also *Pesikta* (cited in *Tishrei* 22, note 2) that because of the Golden Calf, G-d did not give holidays in *Tammuz, Av* and *Elul*. And they are compensated with the three holidays in *Tishrei*: Rosh Hashana, Yom Kippur and Sukkot.

Elul 18

1. *Likkutei Dibburim*, vol. 3, p. 946. *Sefer HaSichot 5705*, p. 122.

Elul 19

1. *Deuteronomy* 21:13—read in the third Shabbat of *Elul*.

2. *Likkutei Torah, parshat Teitzei*.

3. *Megaleh Amukot Eikev*, par. beginning *Elul* (55a).

4. See *Olalot Efraim, Drushei Elul*.

Elul 20

1. When Rosh Hashana is on Thursday, this Shabbat is *Elul* 18; *Elul* 16 when Rosh Hashana is on Shabbat; *Elul* 21 when it is on Monday, and *Elul* 20 when it is on Tuesday.

2. *Talmud, Megillah* 31b.

Elul 21

1. "Had I not" in Hebrew is *Lule*—*Elul* backwards.

2. See *Pri Etz Chaim, Shaar HaSelichot*.

3. *Leket Yosher*.

4. During the night, G-d hovers in the higher worlds. In the last three hours of the night G-d hovers in this world (*Talmud, Avodah Zara* 3b). G-d's presence is thus close to us and to all those who call to Him in this time (*Levush*).

Elul 22

1. How did G-d disclose this? R. Yochanan said: [With the verse] "And

G-d passed before him and proclaimed…" (*Exodus* 34:6). This teaches that G-d came down out of His thick cloud like an emissary of the congregation who wraps himself in his *talit* and descends to face the Ark [to read the prayers], and thus disclosed to him the *Seder Selichah* (*Eliyahu Zutta*, ch. 23).

2. *Keter Shem Tov*, additions, ch. 17.

Elul 23

1. *Psalms* 102:1.

2. *Toldot Yaakov Yosef, parshat Va'etchanan*. See *Keter Shem Tov*, sec. 60, 97. *Sefer Baal Shem Tov, amud hatefilah*, ch. 133.

Elul 24

1. The revelation of the Thirteen Divine Attributes of Compassion are revealed to us in *Elul* in our daily mundane lives ("the King in the field") while on Yom Kippur (and in the Ten Days of *Teshuvah*) the attributes are revealed within the "palace." In *Elul* the Thirteen Attributes empower us with the ability to do *teshuvah*. This initiative from below in turn allows us to receive the Thirteen Attributes in the Ten Days of *Teshuvah* and Yom Kippur which bring forgiveness (*Likkutei Torah, Re'eh* 25b, 32a. *Ohr HaTorah, Re'eh*, p. 769ff.; 807-808. *Song of Songs*, p. 558. *Sefer HaMaamarim 5630*, p. 283). Though we say the Thirteen Attributes throughout the year, it then affects primarily our physicality, whereas in *Elul* it awakens also our spirits and enables us to access and return (*teshuvah*) to the deepest recesses of our soul, and experience true renewal (*Likkutei Torah, Re'eh* 32c. *Siddur Shaar HaElul*, 227a ff.).

2. With this, G-d also revealed for us a deeper dimension—and the true nature—of our own being. Created in the image of G-d, our psyches too have these thirteen aspects. This knowledge allows you the opportunity to access your true self and align yourself with your own inner rhythm. See Ramak's *Tomer Devorah* for an elaborate discussion on how we emulate the Thirteen Divine Attributes of Compassion. See also *Siddur Shaloh* for different explanations of the Thirteen Attributes.

3. There are four opinions as to the exact order of the Thirteen Attributes (see *Likkutei Sichot*, vol. 4, p. 1348):

According to the *AriZal* (*Etz Chaim, Shaar Arich Anpin*, ch. 11; *Pri Etz Chaim, Shaar HaSelichot*, ch. 4; *Shaar HaKavanot, Drushei Vayavor*, sec. 3ff.)— the final authority and generally accepted opinion:

Hashem, Hashem (root of all Thirteen Attributes)

1. *E-l*: Almighty
2. *Rachum*: compassionate
3. *V'Chanun*: and gracious
4. *Erech*: slow
5. *Apayim*: to anger
6. *V'Rav Chesed*: and abundant in kindness
7. *V'Emet*: and truth
8. *Notzer Chesed*: keeper of kindness
9. *L'Alafim*: for thousands of generations
10. *Nosei Avon*: endurer of iniquity
11. *V'Pesha*: and transgression
12. *V'Chataah*: and sin
13. *V'Nakeh*: and cleanser

According to *Rabbeinu Tam* in *Tosfot* (*Rosh Hashana* 17b):

1. *Hashem*
2. *Hashem*
3. *E-l*: Almighty
4. *Rachum*: compassionate
5. *V'Chanun*: and gracious
6. *Erech Apayim*: slow to anger
7. *V'Rav Chesed*: and abundant in kindness
8. *V'Emet*: and truth
9. *Notzer Chesed L'Alafim*: keeper of kindness for thousands of generations
10. *Nosei Avon*: endurer of iniquity
11. *V'Pesha*: and transgression
12. *V'Chataah*: and sin
13. *V'Nakeh*: and cleanser

According to Rabbi Nissim Gaon (*Tosafot*, ibid.):

1. *Hashem*
2. *E-l*: Almighty
3. *Rachum*: compassionate
4. *V'Chanun*: and gracious
5. *Erech Apayim*: slow to anger
6. *V'Rav Chesed*: and abundant in kindness
7. *V'Emet*: and truth
8. *Notzer Chesed*: keeper of kindness
9. *L'Alafim*: for thousands of generations
10. *Nosei Avon*: endurer of iniquity
11. *V'Pesha*: and transgression
12. *V'Chataah*: and sin
13. *V'Nakeh*: and cleanser

According to the *Sefer HaChassidim* (sec. 250):

1. *Rachum*: compassionate
2. *V'Chanun*: and gracious
3. *Erech Apayim*: slow to anger
4. *V'Rav Chesed*: and abundant in

kindness

5. *V'Emet*: and truth

6. *Notzer Chesed L'Alafim*: keeper of kindness for thousands of generations

7. *Nosei Avon*: endurer of iniquity

8. *V'Pesha*: and transgression

9. *V'Chataah*: and sin

10. *V'Nakeh*: and cleanser

(the last three are from a later verse, *Exodus* 34:10)

11. *V'Salachto l'avoneinu*: and forgive our sins

12. *U'L'chatoseinu*: and our sins

13. *U'Nichaltanu*: and make us Your own.

4. *Pardes* (Ramak), *shaar* 4, ch. 7. *Torat HaOleh* (Rama), sec. 3, ch. 59. *Chachmuni* (by R. Shabti Dunulu) commentary to *Sefer Yetzirah* 4:4.

Elul 25

1. *Midrash, Vayikra Rabba* 29:1. *Pirkei d'Rebbe Eliezer*, ch. 8. Ran, *Rosh Hashana* 16a. This is according to Rabbi Eliezer—*Rosh Hashana* 10b-11a. See note 1 to "Introduction to *Tishrei*," that the physical creation of the universe was on this day according to all opinions.

2. *Shaloh, Mesechta Rosh Hashana*.

Elul 26

1. *Eliyahu Rabba* 582:8.

2. *Leket Yosher, Orach Chaim*, p. 117d.

Elul 27

1. *Siddur Shaloh. Magen Avraham, Orach Chaim* 581:10.

2. *Zohar III*, 18a.

Elul 28

1. When this Shabbat is either *Elul* 23 or 25 (depending on whether Rosh Hashana is on Shabbat or Thursday respectively), we read *Netzavim-Vayeilech* combined. When it falls on either Elul 27 or 28 (depending on whether Rosh Hashana is Tuesday or Monday respectively) we read only *Netzavim*.

2. *Magen Avraham, Orach Chaim* 428:4.

3. *Keter Shem Tov*, additions, sec. 31.

4. See *Pesikta d'Reb Kahana*, ch. 5.

Elul 29

1. Orphaned from his mother at age three, he was raised by his maternal grandfather, Rabbi Schneur Zalman of Liadi. Rabbi Menachem Mendel assumed the leadership of Chabad in 1827, upon the passing of his father-in-law and uncle, Rabbi DovBer of Lubavitch. Extremely active in communal affairs, he established and funded Jewish farming colonies which provided a livelihood for thousands of families. He also stood at the forefront of the battle against the "Enlightenment Movement" which, with the support of the Czarist regime, sought to destroy traditional Jewish life—a battle which earned him no less than 22 (!) imprisonments and arrests. In the course of his lifetime, Rabbi Menachem Mendel penned more than 48,000 pages of Chassidic teachings and *Halachic* exegeses. He is known as the "Tzemach Tzedek" ("a sprouting

of righteousness") after his work of *Halachic Responsa* by that name.

2. *Levush, Taz, Magen Avraham—Orach Chaim* 581:14. *Magen Avraham* gives another reason: to confuse the *Satan*. For an explanation on this, see *Likkutei Sichot*, vol. 24, p. 222ff.

3. *Talmud, Nedarim* 23b. *Tur, Orach Chaim* 519. See *Tishrei* 9.

4. See *Seder HaYom*, cited in *Siddur Shaloh, Erev Rosh Hashana. Magen Avraham, Orach Chaim* 581:16.

5. *Pri Chadash, Orach Chaim*, end of sec. 581.

Tishrei

Introduction to Tishrei

1. *Talmud, Rosh Hashana* 10b-11a.

2. *Baal HaTurim, Deuteronomy* 11:12. *Ohr HaTorah, Sukkot*, p. 1756.

3. *Ohr HaTorah*, ibid.; *parshat Berachah*, p. 1866ff. *Tzohar Taaseh 5702*, ch. 3. See also *Likkutei Torah, Netzavim* 47a-b; *Rosh Hashana* 58a-b. The beginning of *Ateret Rosh*.

4. *Beit Yosef* to *Tur, Orach Chaim* 492. *Shulchan Aruch HaRav, Orach Chaim* 492:2.

5. In the Bible, *Tishrei* is called the "seventh month" (after the first month of *Nissan*). "Seven" in Hebrew is the word "*shevi'i*," which also means "sated." *Tishrei* is "satiated with everything" (*Midrash, Vayikra Rabba* 29:8).

Introduction to Rosh Hashana

1. The *Talmud* (*Rosh Hashana* 10b-11a) documents a debate between two sages: "Rabbi Eliezer says: 'The world was created in *Tishrei*....' Rabbi Yehoshuah says: 'The world was created in *Nissan*.'" *Tosafot* (*Rosh Hashana* 27a) reconciles between them by saying that the Creation happened in two stages: First it was conceived in G-d's mind, and then it was actualized. The *AriZal* explains that Rabbi Eliezer and Rabbi Yehoshuah are not debating the date of G-d's actual creation of the universe, which, after all, is a matter of historical fact. Rather, Rabbi Eliezer is discussing the physical ("outer") world which was created in *Tishrei*, and Rabbi Yehoshuah is addressing the "inner" (spiritual) dimension of Creation which was created in the month of *Nissan*. They differ on the question of priority and emphasis: Is the primary anniversary of Creation the day when the universe was physically created, or is the world's true date of birth the day when it was spiritually created?

Note as well, that *Nissan* is known to be the new year of the miraculous order, while *Tishrei* is the new year of the natural order. See *Akeidat Yitzchak, Shaar* 38. *Ohr HaTorah, Bereishit* 18bff.

2. The human being, the central force in the universe, has the power to tap the deepest potential in the universe and cause it to realize its purpose by transforming it into a home for G-d.

3. *Talmud, Rosh Hashana* 8a, 16a-b. See *Zohar III*, 100b. *Zohar Chadash* 14c.

4. When someone does *teshuvah* on Rosh Hashana, G-d considers it as if he was just created anew, because through *teshuvah* a person is considered a new creation and G-d calls him with a new name (*Midrash*, cited in *Avudraham, Rosh Hashana*).

Erev Rosh Hashana

1. On the eve of Rosh Hashana, all things revert to their primordial state. The Inner Will ascends and is retracted into the Divine essence; the worlds are in a state of sleep and are sustained only by the Outer Will. The service of man on Rosh Hashana is to rebuild the Divine attribute of sovereignty (*malchut*) and reawaken the Divine desire "I shall reign" with the sounding of the shofar (*Pri Etz Chaim, Shaar Rosh Hashana*, ch. 1. *Shaar HaKavanot, Drushei Rosh Hashana. Siddur AriZal*. See *Likkutei Torah, Netzavim* 51b).

2. *Tur, Orach Chaim, Laws of Rosh Hashana*, sec. 581. From *Talmud Yerushalmi, Rosh Hashana* 1:3. *Yalkut Shemoni, Deuteronomy, remez* 825. See *Zohar II*, 142a: On Rosh Hashana, when the world is judged, every soul hovers and pleads compassion for the living.

3. Before Grace After the Meal, it's appropriate to read the *Talmudic* tractate *Rosh Hashana*, which consists of four chapters, corresponding to the four letters of G-d's Holy Name (*AriZal, Shaar HaKavanot*, opening of *Drushei Rosh Hashana*).

4. See *Talmud, Hoiriyot* 12a; *Kerisot* 6a.

5. *Maharil*, cited in *Darkei Moshe, Orach Chaim* 581. See *Likkutei Sichot*, vol. 9, p. 374.

6. Tzemech Tzedek, *Pelach HaRimon, Bereishit* 61d.

First Day of Rosh Hashana

1. The Ramak begins this count from the last *sefirah*, *malchut* (See *Siddur Shaloh*); the Ari begins this count from the first *sefirah*, *keter* (*Siddur AriZal*).

2. The Tzemach Tzedek however rejects this, arguing that we cannot say that Rosh Hashana and Yom Kippur are lower levels than the other days of *teshuvah* (*Ohr HaTorah, Shabbat Shuva*, p. 1461). Instead, he orders the days as follows: The two days of Rosh Hashana are *chochmah* and *binah*, the next seven days of *teshuvah* are the seven emotions (*chesed* through *malchut*), and Yom Kippur is *keter*.

3. The *Talmud* delineates what took place on each of the first twelve daytime hours of the day: The first hour, the human's dust was gathered; the second hour, he was made into a form; the third hour, his limbs were formed;

the fourth hour, a soul was put into him; the fifth hour, he stood on his feet; the sixth hour, he named the animals; the seventh hour, [man and woman were separated and] Eve was created; the eighth hour, they had relations and two children; the ninth hour, he was commanded not to eat from the Tree of Knowledge; the tenth hour, he transgressed; the eleventh hour, he was judged; the twelfth hour, he was expelled (*Sanhedrin* 38b).

4. Because the two days of Rosh Hashana are regarded as "one long day," the *Shehecheyanu* blessing, recited on the festivals by the women when lighting the candles and by the men in *Kiddush*, requires an additional source of rejoicing.

5. The order of the *Kiddush* is then called *YaKNaHaZ*, an acronym of the Hebrew words for "Wine, Sanctification, Candle, Separation (*Havdalah*), Season": blessing on the wine, blessing on the sanctity of the day, blessing on fire, the "separation" blessing marking the close of Shabbat, and the *Shehecheyanu* blessing.

Second Day of Rosh Hashana

1. For this reason, we don't say penitence on Rosh Hashana, because the work on this day is to accept and coronate G-d, which overshadows any painful feelings. Rather, *teshuvah* on Rosh Hashana is in order to connect to G-d and coronate Him as King; the tears on Rosh Hashana are out of yearning. In the days of *teshuvah* following Rosh Hashana, we begin the work of penitence and repairing our deficiencies (see *Likkutei Torah, Tovo* 49d, 55d; *Maamar Rosh Hashana 5695*, chs. 10, 24; *Sefer HaMaamarim 5703*, pp.

19, 43; *Likkutei Sichot*, vol. 9, p. 435).

2. On Rosh Hashana Adam was created and brought to trial before his Master. He repented and was pardoned by the Almighty. He said to him: "Adam, you will be a sign to your descendants for all generations. On this day they are brought to trial, and if they repent I will pardon them and rise from the Throne of Judgment and sit on the Throne of Mercy and have mercy on them" (*Zohar III*, 100b).

3. *Shulchan Aruch HaRav, Orach Chaim* 600.

4. *Zohar III*, 231a. See *Talmud Yerushalmi, Eruvin* 3:9. *Tosefta Rosh Hashana* 1:10. *Pri Etz Chaim, Shaar Rosh Hashana*, ch.1.

5. *Keter Shem Tov* 1:1.

Tishrei 3

1. *AriZal, Shaar HaKavanot, Drushei Rosh Hashana*, in the preface. *Pri Etz Chaim, Shaar Tefilot, Rosh Hashana*, ch. 7. *Siddur AriZal. Magen Avraham, Orach Chaim* 54:2. *Ateret Zekeinim, Orach Chaim* 582. *Siddur Torah Ohr.* See *Likkutei Torah, Rosh Hashana* 62b.

Tishrei 4

1. Two opinions in *Zohar* (*III*, 69b-70a), Rabbi Yitzchak and Rabbi Abba.

2. *Maamar Shir HaMaalot 5703* (p. 18ff), *5739, 5748*.

3. *Shaar HaKavanot, Pri Etz Chaim, Siddur AriZal* in *Tishrei* 3, note 1. This refers to the ten depths mentioned in *Sefer Yetzirah* (1:5).

Tishrei 5

1. Compare this with the glow of Moses when he descended Mt. Sinai on Yom Kippur (*Exodus* 34:29), successful in obtaining G-d's complete forgiveness.

2. *Pri Etz Chaim, Shaar HaShofar*, ch. 5. *Shaar HaKavanot, Drushei Rosh Hashana*, preface. *Siddur AriZal*, end of the *Seder HaNesirah*. See *Likkutei Sichot*, vol. 9, p. 206ff.

3. See *Zohar II*, 186a; *Likkutei Torah AriZal, parshat Vayeitzei. Kohelet Yaakov, maarechet yud-beit chadoshim*.

Tishrei 6

1. *Rosh Hashana* 18a.

2. *Derech Chaim* 13d, 21b, 91a. *Kuntres HaAvodah*, end of ch. 5 (p. 35).

3. *Ecclesiastes* 12:7.

4. See *Likkutei Torah, Haazinu* 71c ff.; *Rosh Hashana* 60d ff.; *Shabbat Shuvah* 66c; *Drushei Chodesh Tishrei 5698*.

5. *Zohar I*, 106a.

Tishrei 7

1. *Avodah Zara* 17a.

2. *Mishne, Yoma* 85b.

3. *Shulchan Aruch*, and *Shulchan Aruch Harav, Orach Chaim* 606. See there for more details.

Tishrei 8

1. *Siddur AriZal* (Reb Shabsi), *Seder Aseret Yemei Teshuvah.* He concludes there: this is definite, without any doubt. See also *Pri Etz Chaim, Shaar*

Tefilot, Rosh Hashana, end of ch. 6. *Shaar HaKavanot, Drushei Rosh Hashana* (preface to *drush* 1).

Tishrei 9

1. *Pirkei d'Rebbe Eliezer*, ch. 46. *Midrash, Devarim Rabba* 2:26. *Tur, Orach Chaim* 606. *Tur* and *Shulchan Aruch HaRav*, ibid. 619:9. *Rama* and *Shulchan Aruch HaRav*, ibid. 610.

2. *Kings I* 19:12.

3. *Pri Etz Chaim, Shaar Yom HaKippurim*, ch. 1.

4. See *Likkutei Sichot*, vol. 24, p. 564. *Sefer HaSichot 5747*, p. 9.

5. See *Chagigah* 12b.

6. *Siddur AriZal*, *Siddur Torah Ohr*.

Introduction to Yom Kippur

1. *Mishne, Taanit* 26b and Rashi.

2. *Exodus* 30:10. *Leviticus* 16:30. See *Tosafot, Menachot* 18a. For the spiritual meaning, see *Ateret Rosh, Shaar Yom HaKippurim*, ch. 2ff., *Kuntres HaHispaalut*, ch. 4.

3. "*Yechida l'yachdecha*—Clings and cleaves to You...the oneness that affirms Your Oneness" (*Hoshanot* prayer, day 3).

Erev Yom Kippur

1. Though certainly at times in Jewish history it has been seen as a renunciation of wrongful oaths Jews took to save their lives, as in medieval Spain where many pretended to convert to Christianity.

2. See *Mateh Efraim* 608:3. *Keter Shem*

Tov (Gogin), vol. 6, p. 281.

3. See *Midrash Tehillim* 17; *Ritva Bava Batra* 121a; *Mordechai, Yoma* 723. *Orchot Chaim, Yom Kippur* 27. *Rama, Orach Chaim* 610. We wear white because we are like Divine angels (*Mordechai* and *Rama*, ibid.). For more details, see *Talmudic Encyclopedia, Yom HaKippurim* (vol. 22, p. 520) and the sources cited there.

Yom Kippur

1. See *Mikdash Melech* to *Zohar II*, 173a; *Likkutei Sichot*, vol. 9, p. 387.

2. The Rebbe Yosef Yitzchak, *Sefer HaMaamarim 5711*, p. 42.

Tishrei 11

1. The first half of *Tishrei* corresponds to "his left hand is under my head," and the second half, beginning with Sukkot to "his right hand embraces me" (*Song of Songs* 2:6)—*Zohar I*, 64a-b; *III*, 214b. See *Ohr HaTorah*, p. 697. See "Introduction to Hoshana Rabba," etc.

2. *Sefer HaMaamarim 5709*, p. 42. *Igrot Kodesh*, vol. 5, p. 4. *Likkutei Sichot*, vol. 1, p. 13. *Sichat Simchat Beit HaSho'eiva 5764. Haazinu 5782*.

3. Rabbi Yosef Yitzchak, *Sefer HaMaamarim 5698*, p. 67. *Igrot Kodesh*, vol. 1, p. 194; vol. 3, p. 483. *Sefer HaSichot 5688-91*, p. 25; *5696-5700*, p. 161. These four days, corresponding to the four letters of G-d's Name, are higher than the revelation of G-d's Name said seven times at the conclusion of the *Neilah* service (*Sichat Motzo'ei Yom Kippur 5689*, p. 25).

4. *Midrash Tanchuma, Terumah* 8. Rashi on *Tisa* 31:18, 33:11. According to

another opinion, the command to Moses came before the sin, but the Jews received the command and began bringing their donations after Yom Kippur (*Zohar II*, 195a. Ramban, beginning of *Vayakhel*).

5. *Sichat Motzo'ei YomKippur 5710 (Sefer HaMaamarim 5711*, p. 42).

Tishrei 12

1. *Midrash, Vayikra Rabbah* 30:7.

Tishrei 13

1. The quality of the willow, see *Tishrei 21*.

2. Thus we are taught that the Divine presence rests upon a "community" of ten individuals; that ten ignorant boors make a *minyan*, while nine pious scholars do not.

3. *Midrash, Vayikra Rabbah* 30:14.

4. *Maharil, Magen Avraham, Shulchan Aruch Harav* 626:13.

Tishrei 14

1. *Shaarei Teshuvah, Orach Chaim* 625. *Pri Etz Chaim*, the end of *Shaar Chag HaSukkot. Siddur im Dach* 257c.

2. *Parshat Acharei*.

Introduction to Sukkot

1. *Talmud, Sukkah* 28b; Rambam, *Laws of Sukkah* 6:5; *Shulchan Aruch, Orach Chaim* 639:1. This also defines when a person is not obligated to do something in the sukkah: one is not obligated to eat or sleep in the sukkah when, under similar conditions, one would

not do so in one's own home (*Talmud*, ibid.; *Shulchan Aruch*, ibid., subsecs. 2 and 5).

Erev Sukkot

1. Rambam, *Laws of Yom Tov* 6:18.

2. In Chassidic tradition there are also seven corresponding *"chassidishe ushpizin"*: the Baal Shem Tov, the Maggid (Rabbi DovBer of Mezritch), and the first five Rebbes of Chabad: Rabbi Schneur Zalman of Liadi, Rabbi DovBer of Lubavitch, the Tzemach Tzeddek (Rabbi Menachem Mendel), Rabbi Shmuel, and Rabbi Sholom DovBer (*Sicha* of the first night of Sukkot 5697; 5703; *Sefer HaMaamarim 5711*, p. 47).

3. *Shulchan Aruch, Orach Chaim* 639:1.

First Day of Sukkot

1. See *Sukkah* 37b.

2. The four species are like spiritual "weapons" which we use to conquer and sublimate the world (*Midrash, Vayikra Rabba* 30:2). See "Facts," *Tishrei* 18.

3. *Midrash, Vayikra Rabba* 30:7.

Second Day of Sukkot

1. "For all the days of the water drawing," recalled Rabbi Yehoshua ben Chanania, "our eyes saw no sleep" (*Talmud, Sukkah* 53a).

2. *Sukkah* 51b.

3. The letter *samech* corresponds to the 60 *tekiyot*; *chof* to the 20 *shevarim*; and *chof* to the 20 *teruot*.

4. *Mishnat Chassidim* and *Pri Etz Chaim*, the end of *Shaar HaSukkot*. *Siddur im Dach* 235b. *Ateret Rosh, Shaar Yom HaKippurim* 36a ff. *Ohr HaTorah, Sukkot*, p. 1722. *Hemshech V'Kocho 5637*, ch. 84, 93. *Torat Levi Yitzchak*, p. 303. *Likkutei Sichot*, vol. 2, p. 425. *Maamar BaSukkot Teishvu 5736* (*Sefer HaMaamarim Meluket*, vol. 1, p. 176ff.)

5. *Berachot* 28a.

Third Day of Sukkot

1. See *Sukkah* 55b. *Midrash, Bamidbar Rabba* 21:24.

2. Ibid. 1:3. *Tanchuma, Bechukotai* 2. See *Midrash, Vayikra Rabba* 1:11.

Fourth Day of Sukkot

1. *Talmud, Sukkah* 27b.

2. *Likkutei Torah, Shemini Atzeret* 88d ff.

3. *Panim Yafot, parshat Acharei.*

Fifth Day of Sukkot

1. Seven is the number of building blocks G-d used to create existence, the seven Divine attributes, which in turn evolved into our seven human emotions: love, discipline, compassion, ambition, humility, bonding and sovereignty.

2. *Samei'ach Tesamach*, 5657.

3. Aaron was Moses' mouthpiece, and together they approached Pharaoh. They are considered the two spiritual "escorts" binding G-d and the people. *Netzach* and *hod* (endurance and humility) are also like two twins that join as one.

4. *Avudraham, Maharil, Darkei Moshe; Tur, Orach Chaim* 490, 663. *Magen Avraham, Orach Chaim* 490. *Rama, Orach Chaim* 663.

Sixth Day of Sukkot

1. This is especially appropriate during Sukkot, a holiday that unites us all as one. This unity is the container for all blessings and the highest of revelations.

Introduction to Hoshana Rabba, Shemini Atzeret and Simchat Torah

1. There are many levels of *makif* and *pnimi*, relative to our level of growth. On each level, we first begin with an experience on a *makif* level, and then proceed to internalize it. With each internalization, a new, higher level emerges in a form of *makif*, until we integrate that as well. And so we climb from level to level.

In brief, the *Tishrei* journey goes like this: the revelation of Rosh Hashana and Yom Kippur becomes manifest on Sukkot in a revealed way. But on Sukkot it is still in a form of *makif*. On Shemini Atzeret this revelation is retained in a *pnimiyut*, internalized way. And then higher levels of *makif* are revealed during the *hakafot* of Simchat Torah.

More specifically, the joy of Sukkot begins to internalize the *makif* of the Days of Awe. Yet this too is in stages. First comes the sukkah, which itself is *makif*, surrounding us completely in its embrace. We sit in the Sukkah and internalize it. Then we take the "four kinds," which we draw close to our heart, and further internalize the experience.

We circle the Torah platform each day, seven circles on Hoshana Rabba, and then seven circles of unrestrained dance on Shemini Atzeret and Simchat Torah—circles of *makif* that in turn become internalized in our personal lives.

With our relationship intact—both the hugging "*makif*" and the kissing "*pnimiyut*"—we then are ready to take on the world anew.

2. See *Zohar III*, 214b.

Hoshana Rabba

1. How was the *mitzvah* of *aravah* fulfilled? There was a place below Jerusalem called Motza. They would go down there and pick branches of willows and would then come and place them alongside the altar with the heads (of the willow branches) bent over the altar. They then sounded the shofar: a *tekiah*, a *teruah*, and a *tekiah*. Each day they would circle the altar once and say, "*Ana Hashem Hoshiah Na* (Please, G-d, bring us salvation), *Ana Hashem Hatzlichah Na* (Please, G-d, bring us success)"... On that day (i.e., Hoshana Rabba) they circled the altar seven times. When they had finished they would say, "Beauty is yours, O altar, beauty is yours." As was done during the week was done on Shabbat (i.e., if Hoshana Rabba fell on a Shabbat) except (that if it was Shabbat) they would gather them (the *aravos*) on the eve (of Shabbat) and place them in golden basins so that they would not become wilted (*Talmud, Sukkah* 45a).

2. *Zohar III*, 31b-32a; *II*, 132a. The

Zohar explains that this is alluded to in the verse, "And Isaac returned and redug the wells of water" (*Genesis* 26:18). "Wells" is written with a missing letter. What does it mean that "Isaac returned?" This passage refers to the day of Hoshana Rabba. Isaac (*gevurah*), having sat on the Throne of Judgment, which begins on the first day of the seventh month [Rosh Hashana], now returns to awaken the *gevurot* (severities of judgment) and to conclude them. So he redigs the wells of water to pour gevurot upon Israel to stimulate the waters, because *gevurot* (their power and might) cause water to fall to earth. On this day we awaken the *gevurot* which send the rain, and circle the altar seven times and sate it with the water of Isaac, in order to fill the well of Isaac with this water, and then all the world is blessed with water. [Hoshana Rabba is the day of judgment for the waters, and this day concludes the judgment that began on Rosh Hashana.] This is also why on this day we take "willows of the brook" and strike them on the ground to put an end to the severities that come from the brook, which refer to Isaac's wells.... On Hoshana Rabba the idolatrous nations come to the end of their blessings and enter into judgment, and Israel come to the end of its judgments and enter into blessings. For on the next day [Shemini Atzeret] they rejoice privately with the King and receive blessings from Him for the entire year and obtain any request that they make.

3. *Malchut* is the seventh and final emotion, completing the full emotional spectrum of our relationship with G-d, with ourselves, and with other people. On each of the first six days of Sukkot we refined one of the six corresponding emotions; on Hoshana

Rabba we conclude and elevate all of them (thus, the seven Hoshanot and the seven circles), culminating the building of *malchut*, the coronation of G-d as our King that began on Rosh Hashana 21 days ago.

Malchut also relates to the inherent dignity and majesty within each of us, by virtue of the fact that each of us is created in the Divine image and is a child of the Divine King. (See also *Tishrei* 3.) In his blessing today, King David is essentially saying: "no weapon" can succeed in undermining our inherent and indispensable value resulting from our unwavering relationship and absolute connection with G-d. (See also *Tishrei* 3.)

4. See commentaries to *Shulchan Aruch, Orach Chaim* 668. *Minchat Elozar,* vol. 4, sec. 31.

5. *Siddur Torah Ohr.* See *Shaar HaKolel,* ibid., citing the *Chida* (in *Moreh B'Etzba*). In some places it says to recite the psalm until Simchat Torah (*Siddur AriZal* of Rav Shabsi).

6. With the blessing "Blessed are You, O G-d, King of the Universe, Who has sanctified us with Your commandments and commanded us to light the flame of the holiday." (On Shabbat say, "...to light the flame of Shabbos and the flame of the holiday.") Then say the *Shehecheyanu* blessing: "Blessed are You, O G-d, King of the Universe, Who has kept us alive and sustained us and brought us to this season."

7. This day has several names: seventh day of the willow (*Mishne, Sukkah* 42b); day of the willow (*Siddur Rasag,* the day of the beating of the willow (*Sukkah* 45a). Hoshana (*Vayikra Rabba* 37:2). Hoshana Rabba (*Midrash Tehillim* (Buber) 17:5).

Reasons for the name Hoshana Rabba:

Hoshana Rabba means the "great salvation." This is the final and primary day of judgment (which begins on Sukkot) for the upcoming year's blessing of water, upon which all of life is dependent. We therefore designate this end of the "water" year as an important day, by reciting special prayers beseeching G-d for deliverance (*Rokeach* 221. *Tur* and *Levush* 664).

Hoshana Rabba means the "great Hoshana." Because on this day we recite a large number ("rabba") of *hoshana* prayers.

Today is 26 days from the Day of Creation (Elul 25). 26 is the *gematria* of G-d's holy Name (*Havaya*), which is called a "great" name, "*shem rabba*"; therefore the day is called Hoshana Rabba (*Bechayei, Deuteronomy* 33:21). This is also the reason that on Hoshana Rabba we stop saying Psalm 27, because we have now completed the full cycle of the 26 (days) of compassion related to G-d's great Name, and Hoshana Rabba is "the end of judgments," and we no longer need the Psalm for this purpose (*Shaar HaKolel* 45:6).

Hoshana is another name for the willow twig (*aravah*). Hoshana Rabba is thus "great willow," which is the main focus of this day—"the day of the willow." On this day the priests would circle the Temple Altar with willows in hand. We commemorate this today by circling the *bimah* seven times, and then gather five willow twigs, and at the conclusion of the *hoshanot* prayer, strike them on the ground five times. This *aravah* rite was prescribed for Hoshana Rabba because the *aravah* grows near water, and Hoshana Rabba

is the judgment day for water.

8. G-d says to Abraham, "I am unique and you are unique; I will give your children a unique day to atone for their sins, the day of Hoshana Rabba." Because the name of G-d (*Ehe-ye*) is the *gematria* (numerical equivalent) of 21, and Abraham was unique in the 21st generation after Adam, so is Hoshana Rabba the 21st of *Tishrei*. G-d said to Abraham: "If your children were not redeemed on Rosh Hashana, they can be redeemed on Yom Kippur, and if not then, it will be on Hoshana Rabba" (*Mateh Moshe* 957).

9. "They seek me day [after] day" (Isaiah 58:2)—this is *tekiyah* and *aravah* (*Talmud Yerushalmi, Rosh Hashana* 4:8). Everyone is seeking G-d on Rosh Hashana (*tekiyah*) and Hoshana Rabba (*aravah*), because Rosh Hashana is the beginning of the judgment and Hoshana Rabba is the conclusion (*Yefei Mareh, ad loc.*). See *Zohar III*, 31b-32a; *II*, 132a. The difference between Hoshana Rabba and Shemini Atzeret in this regard is explained in *Zohar I*, 220a, that the decree is sealed on Hoshana Rabba, but delivered to the "messengers" on Shemini Atzeret. See *Pri Etz Chaim, Shaar HaLulav*, ch. 4; *Asareh Maamarot, Maamar Choker Din*, sec. 2, chs. 26-27; *Sheilat Yaavetz*, ch. 33.

10. See Rameh of Pano (*Asarah Maamarot, Choker Din*, sec. 2, ch. 24): On the first Rosh Hashana, when G-d came to judge Adam for the first sin, He spoke to him about the event, and hinted to him the mystery and the days and hour of man's judgment. G-d said to Adam, "*Ayekah*—Where are you?" The four letters of *Ayekah* in Hebrew is an acronym which tells us the mystery of Divine judgment:

Aleph—the 1st of *Tishrei*, Rosh Hashana—the beginning of the judgment;

Yud—the 10th of *Tishrei*, Yom Kippur—the conclusion of the judgment;

Chof—the 20th of *Tishrei*, after which comes Hoshana Rabba, when the judgment is sealed;

Heh—the 5th day of the week (when the first Hoshana Rabba fell), and the 5th hour of the day, when the sealed judgment is given to the messengers for delivery.

There are 243 hours from Rosh Hashana till the end of Yom Kippur (including the additional hours that we add to holy days). *Gemar* ("end of judgment") is 243.

There are 243 more hours between Yom Kippur and Hoshana Rabba for a total of 486—*b'tof u'machol*—after *tof* (486) hours your *machul* (forgiveness) will be complete.

On Hoshana Rabba we have the power to achieve complete forgiveness and healing—it is 21 days after Man was created and 26 (Havaya) days after the Creation.

This is why we add in prayers and forgiveness on Hoshana Rabba.

Shemini Atzeret

1. Rashi on *Leviticus* 23:36; cf. *Midrash, Shir HaShirim Rabba* 7: The Atzeret of the festival of Sukkot ought to have been fifty days later, like the Atzeret of Passover. Why, indeed, does Shemini Atzeret immediately follow Sukkot? Rabbi Yehoshua offers the following parable in explanation:

A king had many daughters. Some of

them were married off nearby, and some of them were married off in faraway places. One day, they all came to visit the king, their father. Said the king: "Those who are married off nearby have the time to go and come, but those who are married off afar do not have the time to go and come. Since they are all here with me, I will make one festival for them all and I shall rejoice with them."

Thus, with the Atzeret of Passover, when we are coming from winter into summer, G-d says: " have the time to go and come." But with the Atzeret of Sukkot, since we are coming from summer into winter, and the dust of the roads is difficult and the byroads are difficult ... G-d says: "They do not have the time to go and come; so, since they are all here, I will make one festival for them all and I shall rejoice with them." See also note 3.

2. This is also emphasized in *Midrash* (*Pesikta d'Rav Kahana*, on Shemini Atzeret): G-d wanted to give Israel a holiday in each of the summer months. In *Nissan*, Passover; *Iyar*, Pesach Sheini; *Sivan*, Shavuot; in *Tammuz* he wanted to give them a great holiday, but because they built the Golden Calf they lost [holidays in] three months, *Tammuz*, *Av* and *Elul*. *Tishrei* compensates for these three months with its three holidays: Rosh Hashana compensates for *Tammuz*, Yom Kippur compensates for *Av* and Sukkot compensates for *Elul*. Then G-d said: "He [*Tishrei*] is able to compensate for others, but not for himself?! [What holiday does *Tishrei* get?] Give him the day of Shemini Atzeret. And this is the meaning Shemini Atzeret "will be to you." Shemini Atzeret is thus the essence of all the holidays of *Tishrei*.

3. This is also related to the fact that the 515 prayers of Moses to enter the Promised Land began on Rosh Hashana and concluded on the morning of Shemini Atzeret—a period of 516 hours (21 days x 24 hours + 12 hours of Shemini Atzeret eve), one hour for each of Moses 515 prayers. In the final (516th) hour, the decree was sealed and delivered and Moses was told he should no longer pray.

4. Shemini Atzeret is the final day of sealing all the judgments. On Rosh Hashana the judgments and edicts are written, on Yom Kippur they are sealed, and on Hoshana Rabba the sealing is finalized. On Shemini Atzeret the sealed edicts are delivered to the "messengers" in order to be implemented (*Zohar I*, 220a. *Pri Etz Chaim, Shaar HaLulav*, ch. 4. The Rameh of Pano (*Asarah Maamarot, Chokur Din* sec. 2, chs. 26-27) explains that the edicts are sealed and sent out on Hoshana Rabba, and on Shemini Atzeret begins a new order). That is when we dance in unbridled joy, with the absolute confidence that we have prevailed. This dance in turn bewilders the "messengers" and helps guarantee that the edicts be only sweet ones.

5. The prayer for rain on Shemini Atzeret brings to conclusion all the blessings and love of the holiday season, symbolized by water. Shemini Azteret absorbs and consummates the relationship developed through the month of *Tishrei*, and ensures that it will be "watered" and nurtured throughout the year. That's why Shemini Atzeret is so vital to the welfare of our lives for the upcoming year.

6. *Talmud, Sukkah* 55b. Cited in Rashi, *Numbers* 29:35-36. See *Midrash, Bamidbar Rabba* 21:24. *Midrash Tehillim* 109.

7. See *Zohar I*, 64a-b; *II*, 187a. See *Zohar III*, 32a: On Shemini Atzeret the joy is reserved for Israel alone; as private guest of the king, Israel can obtain any request he makes. See also *Zohar I*, 208b on the verse "no other person was there when Joseph confessed to his brothers" (*Genesis* 45:1).

8. *Proverbs* 5:17; *Midrash, Shemot Rabba* 15:23.

9. In the continuing analogy of our developing relationship with G-d: After the preparatory days of *Elul* and the renewal of Rosh Hashana comes Yom Kippur, "the day of marriage," with the Giving of the Torah in the Second Tablets. This is followed by the Sukkot celebration with all the guests—the seventy nations—and all receive their blessings and gifts. Shemini Atzeret is the conclusion and consummation of the marriage, when we are alone with the King.

On each of the seven days of Sukkot, we make a complete circle during Hoshanot, each day/circle corresponding to one of the seven emotions, one of the seven Sabbatical cycles of time. On Hoshana Rabba we circle seven times, encompassing and uniting all the seven cycles that affect all of existence (like the seventy offerings corresponding to the seventy nations). We then are ready to enter Shemini Atzeret, the great Jubilee, when we spend time with the King alone (*Tolaat Yaakov*, Shemini Azteret. Cited by *Shaloh*, end of *Mesechta Sukkah*. See also *Asarah Maamorot, Choker Din*, sec. 2, ch. 27). This also corresponds to the four letters of G-d's holy Name: *Yud*—Yom Kippur (10th—*yud*—of *Tishrei*); *Heb*— 5 days after Yom Kippur is Sukkot; *Vav*—six days later is Hoshana Rabba; *Heb*—Shemini Atzeret, the "small meal" (*Shaloh*, ibid).

Simchat Torah

1. Rashi on *Deuteronomy* 34:12. "His heart emboldened him to break the tablets before their eyes, as it is written, '[and I took hold of the two tablets and threw them from my two hands] and I broke them before your eyes' (ibid., 8:15). G-d's opinion then concurred with his opinion, as it is written, '[... the First Tablets,] which you broke' (*Exodus* 34:1) — I affirm your strength for having broken them."

2. "He will tell you secrets of wisdom, doubly powerful" (*Job* 11:6). *Midrash, Shemot Rabba* 46:1: G-d said to Moses: "Do not be distressed over the First Tablets, which contained only the Ten Commandments. In the Second Tablets I am giving you also *Halachah, Midrash* and *Agadah.*"

3. *Sefer HaMaamarim 5711*, p. 79.

4. *Sichat Simchat Torah 5703, 5736.*

5. "It is the custom in these lands on the night and day of Simchat Torah to take all the Torah scrolls out of the ark. Psalms and prayers are recited, in each community according to its custom. It is also customary to circle the reading table in the synagogue with the Torah scrolls ... all this to increase the joy" (*Shulchan Aruch, Orach Chaim* 669:1).

6. Which is what makes this such a powerful celebration, being that it is initiated from "below," out of our love for G-d (see "Introduction to Hoshana Rabba"). Yet every authentic Jewish custom is based in Torah. Indeed, we find reference to Simchat Torah in the *Zohar* (III, 256b): Jews have the custom to celebrate on Shemini Atzeret, and it

is called by the name "Simchat Torah." They adorn the Torah scroll with its crown.... See also *Zohar III*, 214b.

We also have a source in *Midrash* for celebrating at the conclusion of the Torah. The *Midrash* derives this from King Solomon's celebration upon hearing that G-d is granting him more wisdom than anyone who ever lived or will ever live (*Midrash, Shir HaShirim Rabba* 1). Early sages write that this is why we celebrate on Simchat Torah to honor the conclusion of the Torah (*HaEshkol*, p. 105. See *Tikkunei Zohar, Tikkun* 21 (56a). *Nitzutzei Zohar*, ibid. Rabbi Zevin in *HaMoadim b'Halacha*, ch. 6).

One can say that Moses was actually the first one who celebrated Simchat Torah, when he concluded the Torah (*Torat Sholom*, p. 2).

7. "There are 13 days between Yom Kippur and Simchat Torah, in which the Thirteen Attributes of Compassion (of Yom Kippur) manifest and are revealed below... all the forty days from Rosh Chodesh *Elul* to Yom Kippur) are a preparation for Simchat Torah." (*Siddur Shaar HaElul* 227d, 231a).

8. After all the revelations of the holiday season, in the form of *makif* and *pnimi* (see "Introduction to Hoshana Rabba"), we are now ready to receive the greatest *makifim*, and then internalize them. The revelation of Rosh Hashana and Yom Kippur becomes manifest on Sukkot in a revealed way. But on Sukkot it is still in a form of *makif*. On Shemini Atzeret this revelation is retained in a *pnimiyut*, internalized. And then a higher level of *makif* is revealed during the *hakafot* of Simchat Torah (*Ohr HaTorah, V'Zot*

HaBeracha, p. 1867). Shemini Atzeret is retention and consummation. Simchat Torah is the beginning of the revelation and drawing down, which empowers us to integrate the energy of *Tishrei* into the entire year (*Sichat Shemini Atzeret*, 5703. *Likkutei Sichot*, vol. 9, p. 394). On Shemini Atzeret G-d gives us the ability to become true containers to contain all the energy. Shemini Atzeret is the revelation of an Essential light, but the light is sealed and locked from every side. We open these containers with our dancing on Simchat Torah (*Likkutei Dibburim*, vol. 1, p. 259).

Tishrei 24

1. Conclusion of *Pri Etz Chaim*, the end of Shaar HaLulav.

Tishrei 25

1. *Sichat Shemini Atzeret*, 5696 (*Likkutei Dibburim*, vol. 2, p. 409).

Tishrei 26

1. *Sichat Shemini Atzeret*, 5707.

Tishrei 27

1. *Likkutei Dibburim*, vol. 4, p. 1421.

2. Shabbat *Bereishit* can be either on *Tishrei* 24, 26, 27 or 29, depending whether Simchat Torah (*Tishrei* 23) is on Friday, Wednesday, Tuesday or Sunday respectively.

Tishrei 28

1. *Genesis* 32:2.

2. *Sichat Simchat Torah*, 5686, 5697. *Sefer HaMaamarim 5711*, p. 78.

Tishrei 29

1. See *Siddur Yaavetz, Levush, Orach Chaim* 669.

Tishrei 30

1. Rashi's interpretation.

2. *Midrash, Yalkut Shemoni, Kings I* 184. See the explanation there for the missing "*mem*" ("*bul*" without the *mem* of "mabul"): Even after the flood, the forty (*mem*) days of the flood had an effect on the world (i.e., that more rain would fall), until King Solomon built the Temple in this month, which terminated this effect of the *mem*. Hence "*bul*" without the "*mem*."

3. Hence, there are no holidays in *Cheshvan*, in direct contrast to *Tishrei*, which is filled with them. *Mar Cheshvan* represents the hard work of building our lives when there is no revelation, in order to demonstrate what we are truly capable of through our own initiative and efforts, once armed with the tools and resources we gathered in *Tishrei*.

This is also the symbolism of this month's *mazal* ("sign"): Scorpio. The venomous scorpion represents the challenges of material life which begins in *Cheshvan*. Materialism can be toxic if it is not tamed and channeled. (More practically: throughout history, many of the worst persecutions of Jews began in this month of the scorpion.)

Because *Cheshvan* is "empty" of holidays and Divine revelation, it is a month fraught with tension, as we worry about too little or too much rain. This is the season in Israel when we are anxious for the rain to come, to refresh the earth and allow the crops to grow; yet, at the same time, an excess of rain would endanger us through flooding. *Cheshvan* reflects this tension.

In the northern hemisphere, *Cheshvan* begins to bring the winter's cold. The biting cold, dark months of winter represent a type of spiritual distance, when we are less aware of the Divine presence in our lives. This comes in direct contrast to the month of *Tishrei* when "the source nears the spark" and its warmth is felt. Yet the warmth of the holidays, concluding with the special meal with the King on Shemini Atzeret, empowers us to illuminate the dark, and to warm the cold bite of winter (the scorpion) as we enter *Cheshvan*, which begins the six months until we will return on Passover.

When we do succeed in transforming *Cheshvan* and the months that follow, we tap into something greater than *Tishrei* itself—the power of transforming darkness to light, cold to warmth, the scorpion into a vehicle for G-dliness, as will be revealed in the times of Moshiach, with the Third Temple rebuilt and dedicated in *Cheshvan*.

This is also connected to the fact that the 11th of *Cheshvan* is the *yahrzeit* of our Matriarch Rachel, as well as her younger son Benjamin, in whose part of the land the Temple was built. Rachel is buried on the road to Bethlehem, where she died during childbirth, and not in the Cave of Machpelah with the other Matriarchs and Patriarchs. Jacob buried her there because he prophesied that the exiled Jewish people would pass by there as they were expelled from Jerusalem and Rachel would seek mercy for them: "Rachel cries for her children" (*Jeremiah* 31:14. See Rashi, on *Genesis* 48:7).

Cheshvan teaches us that though we may find ourselves destitute and empty, we have the power of Rachel to overcome every challenge, and ultimately transform even the darker moments of our lives into intense spiritual light.

Prayers

Prayers for Rosh Hashana

1. The *AriZal* explains the additions and their variations: In the first addition we mention remembrance and inscription; in the second one, only remembrance; in the fourth, only inscription; and in the fifth again both remembrance and inscription (*Shaar HaKavanot, Rosh Hashana* in the beginning).

2. These four paragraphs correspond to the four worlds; the four legs of the Divine chariot; Abraham, Isaac, Jacob, and David; to the four sounds of shofar. *Zohar II*, 52a, and in *Ohr HaChama* and *Mikdash Melech, ad loc. Pri Etz Chaim, Shaar Rosh Hashana*, ch 7. *Shaar HaKavanot, drush* 6. *Biurei HaZohar, Emor*, p. 396ff. *Ohr HaTorah, Siddur*, p. 372. *Sefer HaMaamarim 5634*, p. 313ff. The first and third *U'vechein*, corresponding to the love (*chesed*) of Abraham and the compassion (*tiferet*) of Jacob, sweeten the *gevurah* of Yitzchak (*U'vechein tein pachdecha*). Through our awe of G-d we free ourselves of all our negative fears (*Ohr*

Hachama and *Ohr HaTorah, Siddur,* ibid.).

3. Once, when the Holy Reb Aaron of Karlin (one of the eminent disciples of the Magid of Mezritch) began to recite *HaMelech*, he fell into a deep faint. When later asked the cause for this, he replied that he reflected upon the statement in the *Talmud* (*Gittin* 56a): "If I am a king, why did you not come before?" If the Holy Reb Aaron felt so, how should we feel....

4. *Talmud, Megillah* 31a.

5. *Genesis* 21.

6. *Talmud, Megillah, loc.cit.*

7. *Talmud, Rosh Hashana* 10b-11a. Rashi, on *Megillah, loc.cit.* The *Shaloh* writes that Chana's prayer was also on Rosh Hashana (*Mesechta Rosh Hashana* 214a).

8. See *Ohr HaTorah, Shabbat Shuva,* p. 1530.

9. *Talmud, Megillah, loc. cit.*

10. *Rosh Hashana* 16a. Rashi on *Megillah, loc.cit.*

11. *Midrash, Pesikta Rabsi,* sec. 40. *Zohar III,* 18a.

12. *Genesis* 22:17-18.

13. See *Ateret Rosh,* ch. 16.

14. The birth of Efraim (son of Joseph) also resulted from G-d remembering Rachel and opening her womb with the birth of Joseph, which happened on Rosh Hashana (*Rosh Hashana* 10b); the Haftorah also mentions "Rachel weeping for her children," *Ohr HaTorah, Rosh Hashana,* p. 1304.

15. Rashi on *Megillah, loc. cit. Avudraham.*

16. *Siddur AriZal* of R. Shabsi and R.

Yaakov Kopel (Kol Yaakov).

17. *Avudraham* citing R. Saadiah Gaon.

18. Rambam, *Hilchot Teshuvah,* ch. 3:4.

19. *Rosh Hashana* 33b. See Rashi there.

20. *Midrash Tehillim* 47. *Vayikra Rabba* 29:3. *Rokeach,* ch. 200, citing the *Pesikta.*

21. *Psalms* 118:5.

22. *Likkutei Torah, Rosh Hashana* 58d-59a, 55d. See there, 56d, for another explanation. See also *Biurei HaZohar,* p. 405. *Maamar Min HaMeitzar 5671.* The *Shaloh* (*Mesechta Rosh Hashana*) writes that the first *tekiah* is the pure, unadulterated call of the one who walks the straight path. The *shevarim* are the gasps of spiritual illness. The *teruah* are the sobs of the "dying" soul suffering from the worst sins. The final *tekiah* is the call of *teshuvah* that returns the soul to it pure roots.

23. *Zohar III,* 99b; *Tikkunei Zohar* 18; *Biurei HaZohar,* p. 396ff.; *Sefer HaMaamarim 5634,* p. 313ff.

24. *Zohar III,* 231b. In the *Siddur Shaloh* he reconciles by explaining that *teruah* is essentially *tiferet* (Jacob). *Tiferet* has within it both *gevurah* and *chesed.* The *gevurah* side of *tiferet* is connected to *malchut* (David). However, the other side of *tiferet* leans toward *chesed.*

25. The *AriZal* explains that the thirty sounds correspond to the three levels of *malchiyot, zichronot* and *shofarot* (see later text). *Malchiyot* correspond to the recipient, *zichronot* to the entity itself, and *shofarot* to the transmitter. The first set of 30 sounds correspond to the Patriarchs as they are in the world of *Asiyah*; the next 30 (in the silent *Amidah*) as they are in the world of *Yetzirah*; the third set (in the cantor's repetition) in the world of *Beriyah*; and the final set (said in the final *Kaddish*)

in the world of *Atzilut* (see *Siddur Shaloh*).

26. *Hemshech 5666,* in the beginning.

27. *Biurei HaZohar,* ibid. pp. 404-405. For more on this, see *Ateret Rosh,* ch. 19. *Maamar Rosh Hashana 5705, 5710.*

28. *Berachot* 29a; *Rosh Hashana* 32a; *Yerushalmi Berachot* 4:3; *Tikkunei Zohar* 55; *Zohar III,* 179b.

29. *Rosh Hashana* 16a.

30. *Ikrim.*

31. See the conclusion of *Hemshech 5666.*

32. *Ethics of the Fathers* 5:1.

33. *Siddur im Dach* 138b ff. *Biurei HaZohar Tzemach Tzedek* p. 402 ff. 960.

34. *Rosh Hashana* 16a.

35. See *Talmud Yerushalmi, Taanit* 2:1.

36. The primary judgment on Rosh Hashana is on material matters—*Hagahot Maimoniyut,* Laws of Teshuvah 3:1 citing the Ramban. See *Likkutei Torah, Rosh Hashana* 59b.

37. *Sanhedrin* 106b.

38. *Idra Rabba, Zohar III,* 138a. See *Likkutei Torah, Re'eh* 34b. These (higher) attributes mentioned by *Micha* are also added at the end of *Maftir Yonah* in the Yom Kippur *Mincha* service.

Prayers for Yom Kippur

1. *Pri Etz Chaim, Shaar Rosh Hashana,* ch. 1. *Likkutei Torah, Rosh Hashana* 58a.63c.

2. Reb Hillel of Paritch explains that the five prayers correspond to the five *chasadim* of *atik*: 1st prayer, *chesed* of *hod* of *atik*; 2nd, *chesed* of *netzach* of *atik*; 3rd, *chesed* of *tiferet* of *atik*; 4th, *chesed* of

gevurah of atik; 5th, chesed of chesed of atik. Second interpretation: Musaf, chesed of chesed of atik; Neilah, chesed of tiferet of atik (Pelach HaRimon, parhsat Acharei).

3. Tur, Shulchan Aruch and Shulchan Aruch HaRav 619:9 in the name of the Midrash (Devorim Rabbah 2:36).

4. Tanchuma, Haazinu 1. Maharil, Rama and Shulchan Aruch HaRav Orach, Chaim 621:14. See Maaver Yovok, Sifsei Rannanot, ch. 23. Yoreh Deah 249, citing the Rokeach.

5. See Sefer HaSichot 5749, p. 233.

6. The primary service in the Holy of Holies was the incense offering. "And he shall take a censerful of burning coals from the altar, and the fill of his hands of finely-ground incense (ketoret); and he shall bring [these] inside the curtain. And he shall place the ketoret upon the fire before G-d; and the cloud of the incense shall envelop the covering of the [Ark of] Testimony" (Leviticus 16:12-13). The ketoret reflects the most sublime service of yechidah—one that affects the fragrance of the entire environment.

7. See note 36 in Rosh Hashana prayers.

8. Shulchan Aruch HaRav 622:4.

9. Siddur Shaloh.

Prayers for Sukkot

1. Explained in a Sicha of Simchat Torah, 5669, sec. 21 (Torat Sholom, p. 143). [Summarized in HaYom Yom, entry for Tishrei 20.]

2. Berachot 28a.

Prayers for Hoshana Rabba

1. Rashi on Sukkah 45a. See Shaarei Zohar, ad loc. Shaar HaKolel, ch. 45:5.

2. Rokeach 221. Tur and Levush 664.

Prayers for Shemini Atzeret

1. There were two tithes each year. The First Tithe had to be given to the Levites, and the Second Tithe had to be taken to Jerusalem and enjoyed there. Every third and sixth year there was a Poor Man's Tithe instead of the Second Tithe. (No tithes were due from anything that grew on the seventh "sabbatical" year, which anyway did not belong to the owner, but was free to all.) The portion also speaks of the Sabbatical Year (shemitah) and the remission (forgiveness) of debts, as well as the liberation of slaves on that year.

2. "Blessed be G-d Who hath given rest unto His people Israel, according to all that He promised; there hath not failed one word of all His good promise which He promised by the hand of Moses His servant. May G-d be with us, as He was with our fathers. Let Him not leave us, nor forsake us; that He may incline our hearts unto Him, to walk in all His ways, and to keep His commandments, and His statutes, and His judgments, which He commanded our fathers.

"And let these my words, wherewith I have made supplication before G-d, be nigh unto G-d our G-d day and night; that He maintain the cause of His servant, and the cause of His people Israel at all times; that all the people of the earth may know that G-d is G-d, and that there is none else.

"Let your heart therefore be perfect with G-d our G-d, to walk in His statutes, and to keep His commandments as on this day."

3. On Rosh Hashana G-d decrees all events of the year, including how much rain should fall. But the rain can fall in the wrong place and at the wrong time. On Shemini Atzeret it is decreed when and where the rain should fall (Mateh Moshe).

4. Maamar, Shemini Atzeret 5695, ch. 26. Likkutei Dibburim, vol. 1, p. 391. Sichat Simchat Torah 5702, 5705.

5. Siddur MaHaRid.

6. Talmud, Sukkah 46b-47a; see Shulchan Aruch and commentaries, Orach Chaim 668:1.

Prayers for Simchat Torah

1. Similar to the verses of malchiyot, zichronot and shofarot which we say on Rosh Hashana to establish the Torah sources for coronating G-d as King through the sounding of the shofar (Sefer HaMaamarim 5704, p. 54).

2. "Ad kan—only to here and not further"—signifies a boundary created by Shemini Atzeret and Simchat Torah that does not allow the negative energy to enter (Shaar HaKolel, ch. 45:6).

3. In some Siddurim a special "yehi ratzon" prayer follows each of the seven hakafot, each one specifying the respective sphere of that hakafah (hakafah one, chesed; hakafah two, gevurah; etc.). See Siddur MaHaRid. Maamar Shemini Atzeret 5695. Sichat Simchat Torah 5704.

4. Seder HaYom, seder HaLimudim, b'moadei Hashem. Cited in Shaloh, Mesechta Sukkah.

Acknowledgements

No book like this is possible without the collaboration of a team.

We thank in alphabetical order:

Batsheva Buchman

Neria Cohen

Shiraz Delerins

Richard Gayzur

Rashi Jacobson

Shaindy Jacobson

Esther Malka King

Sara Lieberman

Yael Mor

Phillip Namanworth

Uriela Sagiv

Rochel Chana Schilder

Above all, the Rebbe, my Rebbe, without whose direction and inspiration I would not be capable of writing these words.